MADE FROM THIS EARTH

Also by Susan Griffin
Pornography and Silence: Culture's Revenge Against Nature
Rape: The Power of Consciousness
Woman and Nature: The Roaring Inside Her
Like the Iris of an Eye *(poetry)*
Voices *(play)*

MADE FROM THIS EARTH

AN ANTHOLOGY OF WRITINGS

SUSAN GRIFFIN

HARPER & ROW, PUBLISHERS, New York

Cambridge, Philadelphia, San Francisco,

London, Mexico City, São Paulo, Sydney

1817

This book was originally published in Britain by The Women's Press Limited in 1982. It is here reprinted by arrangement.

Portions of this anthology originally appeared in various magazines and books. Previous publication information is included in the introductions preceding each selection.

FIRST U.S. EDITION

Library of Congress Cataloging in Publication Data

Griffin, Susan.
    Made from this earth.

    I. Title.
PS3557.R48913A6 1983   818.5409   82-48229
ISBN 0-06-015118-8   83 84 85 86 10 9 8 7 6 5 4 3 2 1
ISBN 0-06-090995-1 (pbk.)   83 84 85 86 10 9 8 7 6 5 4 3 2 1

Contents

Foreword

This book is an anthology of my writing over the past fifteen years, from 1967 until 1982. One unique vision of the world emerges here from my own particular confrontation with my life as a woman in this twentieth century. In the book, I trace how one thought or one book led to another. Though the book can be read piecemeal, it is meant to be read straight through, from beginning to end.

The book is divided into three parts. I have assembled selections from all of my essays into the first part, and this can be read as one cohesive theoretical work. In introducing this part, I follow the genesis of my own ideas through a private and personal context, and I record the social history I have witnessed. I grew up as a woman and as a writer into a time of change. My thought has been shaped by these times.

The second part of the book is about literature and the process of writing. In the introduction to this part, I speak of the dilemma of the female writer, our shared history of silence, and how in these recent decades we have found ways to help each other to speech.

The last part of this book contains poetry, plays and stories. That I am a poet has had a profound effect on the way I think. In the essay that provides the introduction for the last part of this book, I describe poetry as a way of knowledge, a different consciousness which brings one to see differently, free of orthodoxy, curious, wanting to tell, to set it down, word by word, and sing.

If I were to thank all those who gave to me and contributed to my work over this time, the list would be too long. Kim Chernin read this manuscript with great care and perception and gave me much support for the project; Kirsten Grimstad read the manuscript and encouraged me. Leslie Gardner and Stephanie Dowrick suggested the idea for this collection to me. Ros de Lanerolle has been a sensitive editor. Hugh Van Dusen and Diane Cleaver helped the book into realization. Tracy Gary lent me kind support. Let me also thank the feminist presses and bookstores who have made so much of our literature possible.

For Tillie Olsen,
that voice of hers,
her faith in us,
her patient telling and showing and wide-ranging memory

Part I
Made from this Earth

Introduction

All my life my writing has led me beyond what I thought I knew. Goethe has said that, 'of the truly creative no one is ever master; it must be left to its own way.' Whenever I have attempted to make my words fit preconceptions, I fail to write anything that interests me. And in this way I have come to understand that what Goethe calls the creative is an impersonal force, larger than myself, which will have its way despite my smaller, private concerns. As a writer, I have always felt myself to be a kind of crucible, my mind a medium in which the many voices, spoken and unspoken, belonging to our age, are melted, mixed and transformed.

Yet, I have always written out of the experience of my own life, beginning with acutely personal feelings. For this I believe is the paradox of art. In the very specific, one discovers a universal design; in the familiar terrain of one's own soul, one finds the answers to mysteries.

I was born in 1943, near the end of the Second World War. I came of age in California, and lived near Hollywood during the period in America known as the Red Scare, a time when Senator McCarthy was hunting down and persecuting radical writers and screenwriters in order to silence them. Luminous figures such as Bertolt Brecht, Lillian Hellman and Dalton Trumbo, to name a few, were called before this committee in an effort to expose them to public ignominy. Yet, even though I was raised in a Conservative Republican family, and was used to hearing my grandfather complain about the 'Commies', anyone who had appeared before this committee as an unfriendly witness immediately became my hero.

In my passionate belief in liberty and social justice, I was typical of my generation. We were the ones who peopled the student movement, protesting and seeing an end to McCarthyism, joining the newly risen Civil Rights movement, crying out against our country's part in the Vietnam War.

Though we were the originators of this movement we were also shaped and educated by it. I began to understand the need for economic as well as political equality. I witnessed and then studied the growth of a new movement for Black Power which spoke of the anger of the oppressed, and of the many ways in which a racist culture can subtly destroy one's sense of natural authority. And, most important, I learned that it is necessary to have a pride in one's own identity in order to restore that natural authority.

It was against the backdrop of this movement that I became a feminist. Were I to draw a portrait of myself as I would wish myself to be, I would not draw a picture of a 'political writer'. I have always wanted to touch more deeply the intricacy of human emotion than a political viewpoint allows. Before I found myself a feminist, my political writing, for the most part, had a hollow sound, as if the mind had dictated its shape without the body and the heart participating. But when I became a feminist this was no longer true. I could no longer separate any part of myself from my political consciousness.

The year when my knowledge of myself as a woman in society became conscious was a kind of watershed in my life. I had been married the year before. The next year I was to give birth to my daughter. I had been on the staff of an American radical magazine. There I was disturbed at a clearly prejudicial attitude which the radical employers had towards their female staff. But it was when I stopped working at that magazine to spend a year in solitary writing, working at home alone, at times very lonely, despairing of ever being heard, that I was deeply changed.

I cannot say which came first. At one and the same time I began to write more simply and honestly about what I felt and lived – remembering again whole moments from childhood, discovering a direct and intense language of emotion – and I began to write and think through my growing anger at the oppression I suffered as a woman.

To write one must have a sense of self. It is not that one must feel one knows for certain what the truth is. Rather, as Goethe implies, truth comes to one. But, one must begin with the sense that one's own life is worthy of scrutiny.

I know that all human beings who grow up in this culture suffer, to one degree or another, from a sense of unworthiness. But society systematically teaches and intensifies this feeling in women. Directly, through the words, for instance, of a literary critic who can praise twenty novels about adolescent boys, but who is impatient of more than one novel about a woman divorcing; and indirectly, through a multitude of gestures, words and a literature which commonly treats female characters as trivial or auxiliary beings. In this way, the young woman who writes learns that she is not a fit subject for literature. When I was eight years old and I decided to write a novel, I chose to centre my narrative around the life of a war hero. Later, at fifteen, I made the hero of my short story a teenage boy.

I cannot say whether it was feminism that gave me the right to speak about my own life in my writing, or whether it was speaking about my own experience that transformed me into one who would demand her own rights. It is one of the errors of our civilization's habit of mind to look for single causes. In nature, most things are both cause and effect. In my life, probably each change ignited the other.

But I do know that even though I came to my own consciousness in a solitary way, I was not alone. Countless women of my generation and older, many also isolated from each other, suffered a similar change.

To speak, write and act out of one's own experience is a radical idea, but not new. And yet, whenever in this society a woman speaks from her own experience, something new is revealed. For in this culture, female experience has been silenced and it is, therefore, unknown.

I had turned inward, to question myself and to reform the notion of who I was, and what I wanted. I discovered secrets. Women began to confess to one another. We met formally and informally, socially and in small 'consciousness-raising' groups. We confessed we were afraid we were ugly. We did not like housework. In our sex, we were afraid we wanted too much, or too little, or were not pleased enough. We spoke of large things and small. Anger that a husband never did the dishes. Shame, fear and anger over rape, over abortion. We were, as Marge Piercy has written, ' unlearning not to speak.'

I had had an abortion before I was married. I decided to write about it. I wanted to reveal how common the experience was, and how frequently abortion was kept secret, and thus I interviewed women who had had abortions. I interviewed women about abortion. In these interviews, I did not pretend to be objective. I questioned the notion of an 'objectivity' which claims that one can arrive at truth without feeling. I spoke about my abortion, and revealed my own feelings. Hence my interviews resembled conversations between women.

It was from such conversations that the feminist movement was being born. Women's talk had been considered insignificant in the

social sphere. In 1968, at the very beginning of this feminist movement, much of a woman's experience was invisible to intellectual
scrutiny. The events of our lives – childbirth, domestic labour, child-
raising, abortion, our sexual lives, rape, our work as secretaries, or
nurses – faded into the background, as if these events had nothing to
do with the social structure or politics or culture but rather were part
of the landscape, the given of existence. When I came to write about
rape I said, 'I, like most women, have thought of rape as part of my
natural environment – something to be feared and prayed against like
fire or lightning.' And because these events remained unquestioned,
our oppression, too, was invisible.

But now, our ears were tuned to hear the political significance of
our conversations. We said, 'The personal is political.' This was a
rallying cry. By saying these words, we asserted that our lives, as well
as men's lives, were worthy of contemplation; that what we suffered
in our lives was not always natural, but was instead the consequences
of a political distribution of power. And finally, by these words, we
said that the feelings we had of discomfort, dissatisfaction, grief,
anger and rage were not madness, but sanity.

The feminist movement itself, in the first years of its formation,
became a vessel of anger. We had entered upon an argument with
society. Society had told us that housewives do nothing, were lazy.
We answered with a statistic from the Chase-Manhattan Bank:
housewives work an average of 99.6 hours each week. It was said that
women were no longer oppressed. We pointed to statistics showing
that women earned consistently lower salaries (sometimes for the
same work men did), worked more often at menial jobs, and suffered
a higher rate of unemployment. We uncovered and protested a
multitude of injustices, large and small: that fewer women were
lawyers or doctors, that we lost our names in marriage, that we were
denied the right of abortion, were terrorized by rape. And we were
not tenuous nor apologetic in our protests. What we said was said
in anger.

As I became more conscious of my oppression as a woman, I found
myself entering a state of rage. Everywhere I turned I found more
evidence of male domination, of a social hatred of, and derogation of
women, of increasingly insufferable limitations imposed upon my
life. Social blindness is lived out in each separate life. Like many
women, I had been used to lying to myself. To tell myself that I
wanted what I did not want, or felt what I did not feel, was a habit so
deeply ingrained in me, I was never aware of having lied. I had shaped

my life to fit the traditional idea of a woman, and thus, through countless decisions large and small, had sacrificed myself. Each sacrifice had made me angry. But I could not allow myself this anger. For my anger would have told me that I was lying. Now, when I ceased to lie, the anger I had accumulated for years was revealed to me.

A self more whole than I had allowed to live before was being born in me. 'There is a meaning for us in birth,' the midwife Arisika Razak writes, 'there is a seed, and a strength, and a place of knowledge and power.' And there is some pain in labour. All change is accompanied by pain.

I left my marriage. Poetry often comes before conscious knowledge for me. A year before, in 1969, I had written in a poem,

> *I would not have gotten in this boat with you.*
> *I would not*
> *except*
> *where else was there*
> *at the dock's end*
> *to go?*
> *The water*
> *was cold.*

Marriage had been seclusion and protection for me. I did not want to be a single woman. I did not want to be a woman alone raising a child. I was afraid I could not earn a living, and be a mother at the same time. And there was more.

I knew that I was a woman who loved other women more than I loved men. But I did not want to use the word 'lesbian' about myself. It was a word whose implications I knew well. My sister had been a lesbian for years. In my hidden self I suffered from all the many forms of social disapproval directed at her. To be a lesbian, I knew, was to become in the eyes of convention ridiculous. Unnatural. Untenable. (In those years, all women who were feminists were accused of being lesbians, as if the presence of homosexuality immediately corrupted an authentic argument for justice.) To become a lesbian was to become a social outcast.

Yet, as the depth and dimension of the oppression of women became more real to me, I became more real to myself. And this gave me the courage. Feminist insight had allowed me to reach a deeper self, a self untouched by convention, a self not moulded to society's idea of who a woman should be. This was an earlier, pre-social being who had come to life in me. And now, because of this self, I was more radical and more demanding of life than I had been before. I felt everything more intensely, including desire, and the wish to love and to be loved. I could no longer pretend that I did not love women.

I had become far more radical than that radical movement which had been a parent to my political thought. I have said that when female experience is revealed, the unknown is revealed. But the unknown is not always welcome. It unsettles old assumptions and old ways of being. Many parents fail to recognize their own principles when their children take these principles to heart. 'Is this my child?' a parent will say, disowning influence.

Men on the left said to us that we were not oppressed. Or that our oppression, in the light of historical change, being outside of the question of production, was not significant. You need to wait, we were told, until after a socialist revolution.

But the feminist movement was also critical of its radical progenitors. I remember the beginnings of my own critical opposition. In the year before the birth of my daughter, Martin Luther King was murdered. The United States was pursuing a merciless campaign of violence in Vietnam. But at the same time, the left was taking a turn toward violence.

There is, in the American left, an old and ardent tradition which believes, as Barbara Deming wrote in 1971, 'If we kill, we kill . . . our ability to bring into full being the new society.' This non-violent tradition continued in this decade with strength and tenacity. Yet many young, white radicals began to fashion an image of revolutionary courage modelled on terrorist acts committed by those suffering from far more urgent circumstances, living under colonial governments, or military dictatorships. In the United States a group of radical men and women split themselves off from the rest of the radical movement and went underground to act as terrorists. While most of the left in America did not take this course of action, violence had taken on a kind of numinosity, as if to risk or to lose a life were the ultimate test of revolutionary passion.

During these years, the late sixties, it was popular to speculate that the true revolutionary should have no strong personal ties, no wife or husband or children. But I began to think differently. After the birth of my daughter, a new capacity to be connected to others had grown in me, and as a mother, I made a new acquaintance with human vulnerability. Now it occurred to me that a revolutionary ought to have a deep commitment, not only to abstract humanity, but to actual flesh and blood beings, that a radical should risk intimacy, and enter the simple world of the child.

One day *Life* magazine arrived at our house. When my daughter was taking her nap, I opened to pages of photographs of women's and children's bodies, wounded, dying. A child lying in the mud, face down, its small ass uncovered, the way I let my daughter walk about, a child's body with the same delightful beauty. I wrote,

> *(Oh God, she said, look at the baby)*
>
> *saying 'hi' 'Ho' 'Ha' hi hi goggydoggymamadada HI*
> *and the light was coming through the window*
> *through the handprints on the glass*
> *making shadow patterns, and the cold day*
> *was orange outside and they were muddling*
> *in their underwear, getting dressed,*
> *putting diapers on the baby,*
> *slipping sandals on her feet.*
>
> *(Oh God, she said, look at the baby*
> *He has blood all over, she cried.)*

These women and children were Vietnamese villagers, shot by American soldiers at Song My. I cursed and wept for a week, and through my tears began to see myself not as an American, nor a radical either, but as a woman with a child.

I was not the only one to perceive that the violence of these times bore a relation to our idea of masculinity. In 1973 Adrienne Rich wrote of the American bombing of Vietnam, '. . . the bombings are so wholly sadistic, gratuitous and demonic that they can finally be seen, if we care to see them for what they are: acts of concrete sexual violence, an expression of the congruence of violence and sex in the masculine psyche . . .'

During the years of this violence, and the more prevalent violent rhetoric, I began to see a disturbing resemblance between the cocky stance of my radical brother and the brutal policeman who aimed his club at our heads. In the ensuing years a series of incidents, including the Manson family murders, the murder of Marcus Foster – the superintendent of Oakland schools – and the kidnapping of Patricia Hearst by the 'Symbionese Liberation Army',* caused the left to

---

*An underground radical group of men and women who practised terrorism.

begin to question this atmosphere of violence. There was no dramatic repudiation. It was just that the sacrifice of the living became less romantic, and instead inglorious, sad, senseless.

Now, with the advantage of hindsight, I see that this violence was an act of despair arising not so much from material suffering, as from a bankruptcy of vision. It was a suicidal course for the left, followed by some at a moment when they could see no other way. The left had reached a kind of impasse and this expressed itself not only in ideas of violence, but also in a general waning of the radical movement itself.

Looking back on this moment in history, one sees that in the decade preceding, the left had had a significant effect on American society. The Vietnam War had been forced to an end. And though racism, and the effects of racism, remained, and the power of a military-industrial complex was still a danger to all our lives, a new generation had learned to think differently about this society.

This new generation wanted equality and peace, had learned to recognize the injustice of racism, had questioned the value of might and thus had precipitated a change in consciousness. But now that shift in consciousness had gone as far as it could. It had come up against an old blindness that the left could not acknowledge: a prejudice against women, and against those qualities in human nature which women have come to symbolize. The aesthetic of the left required hardness, 'guts', rigour. And to argue against violence or for reform had become soft, 'feminine', sentimental. The image of the radical was an image of machismo. We know now that this image placed disastrous limitations on the imagination. It truncated radical consciousness, and affected not only tactical questions, but also theory and analysis.

When the boundaries of consciousness are closed, the mind begins to despair. I found myself despairing. Yet, as the poet Roethke wrote, 'In a dark time/the eye begins to see.' Now it was women who would waken consciousness to new understandings. Out of our lives and our thoughts which had been obscure we formed a new way of seeing.

In its earliest beginnings the feminist movement was imbued with the tone, the style and the thinking of the radical left of the late sixties. We carried on the politics of confrontation, used the tactics of the sit-in, the speak out, the picket, the demonstration. We framed our identity as women within the concept of oppression. But feminist theory moved through and beyond radical ideas. We enlarged those ideas not only by including the female image in the old categories, but by changing the very fabric of radical thinking.

As I became more and more a feminist, my thought became autonomous. And then original. In the United States and internationally, a feminist movement exists which is at the same time a socialist movement, and Marxist. This is a valuable movement, but I am not part of it. This movement asks that the socialist movement include the oppression of women within its understanding of oppression. But I was seeking a more essential change of mind than this.

I wanted to free my thought from the old categories so that I might look at each phenomenon from the perspective of a woman, and from my own experience. I wanted to erase old assumptions, and let theory evolve from the conditions of my life. This I did. That I could even begin to think and write as I did depended on the fact of a social movement for feminism, and on the many other women who also dared to tread over the line of what is accepted as sane thinking. From our transgressions against the acceptable, a new way of seeing became possible.

Among many men and some women we encountered a strong opposition to our thinking. But we had begun to establish our own atmosphere. Yes, it was easier for a critic of feminism to be published in the trade press, than a feminist. But we established our own presses (my first three books of poetry were published by women), our own publishing houses, magazines, newspapers, bookstores. Women musicians formed groups, record companies, and held concerts. We held meetings and formed organizations which excluded the censorious presence of men.

Whether we separated ourselves entirely from men or not, we had succeeded in making a separate movement which had the flavour of a separate place, a nation, a world. And of course, we carried the conflicts and differences of society into our world. Within us there were working-class women, middle-class women, white women, women of colour, Jewish women, Catholic women, heterosexual and lesbian women, women with and without children. We had to learn to speak among ourselves not only about our shared oppression but about the different conditions of our lives, and like any movement, we have at times faltered over these differences, and quarrelled over the definition of who we are. But above all we have created for ourselves a measure of independence, a culture within culture that allows us to question all that we were taught, and to think in new ways about the world.*

*Even though it has been necessary for women to meet separately from men

When I look back on my own theoretical work, I can discover a line of thought which moves from one insight to another. But my progress was not linear. Rather, with each issue that I wrote about I felt as if I were in the centre of a labyrinth, sometimes covered with mirrors, sometimes with mirages, through which I had to make a path to the light.

In one of the interviews that I did on the subject of abortion, a woman said to me, 'I simply did not recognize that I was a woman and capable of conceiving. In some very basic way I did not believe in my own existence.' It is common for the oppressed either to deny the existence of their oppression, or to deny their own existence. To be a woman, for example, is to live almost continually with the possibility and hence fear of rape. It is to live in a state of suspended terror. One cannot go about one's life always feeling afraid. Thus, one says to oneself one is not afraid. Or, in a voice not fully before consciousness, one tells oneself one is not really a woman, and therefore will not be raped. Or one denies that very many rapes take place. Or says to oneself that the woman who has been raped has acted foolishly; she has brought it upon herself. Underneath all this, one knows better; one fears. But in consciousness, one chooses not to believe oneself.

Left secret and unexamined, a fear of rape can cause a timidity which then would lead one to believe that women are naturally reticent creatures who do need the protection of men. But when it is admitted, this fear leads to another line of thought. Suddenly one asks why this circumstance – that before seemed a part of nature – exists. Could it be natural that women live in a state of terror? 'Why does rape take place?' one asks.

to forge our own ideas. I am not a partisan of separatism, in the strict political sense in which that word means to cut off all relations with men. I have come to feel that forging coalitions and understandings with groups that include men is an essential need, not only for our survival, but to the quality of feminist thought. I have observed that the most fruitful and creative political movements have come from those directly affected by the social circumstances they protest: the women's movement, the trade union movement, the Asian-American movement. I used to believe that these movements were viable because they were direct expressions of self-interest. But now my ideas have changed. Now, I feel that the strength of these movements comes from the direct experience and therefore knowledge of oppression that oppressed people have. And, at the same time, I have come to see that the idea of self-interest can be narrow and blind in its vision of the human condition. It is a human need, scarcely recognized but still felt, and often felt as an unmet hunger, to care about the fate of others, of every gender, race or culture.

This is no longer the surprising question it once was. I remember a long argument with a friend, a radical and a man. When I said I was writing about rape, and the fear of rape, he asked me why would a woman be afraid? After all, rape was simply sex, he said. In the back of his mind, no doubt, was the old idea that women want to be raped. I could not convince him that rape was a brutal experience for women, until I reminded him of a suspense film we had seen, in which a man was attacked, and murdered by a stranger. Only then did it come home to him that when a woman is raped her life has nearly always been threatened, and that sometimes her life is taken. When he encountered a woman's subjective experience in himself, his thinking was transformed.

As I thought through the question of rape, I saw that rape is essentially an act of dominance and aggression. I wrote that women in a society dominated by men were the weakest members, and that thus we had become the scapegoats for aggression. Yet, so intimately connected in this culture are our ideas of sex and violence that, when I wrote about rape, I failed to ask why a sexual act should become the vehicle for aggression. I was not to ask or answer this question for myself until almost ten years later, when I wrote *Pornography and Silence*.

In the next decade the feminist movement spoke out against rape and the threat of rape as a daily fact of women's lives. All over America women formed rape crisis centres, places where women could go to talk about what had happened to them. Court procedures which included a woman's private sexual history as evidence were challenged and changed. Women acted as advocates for one another during police investigations. We learned self-defence. And more. In protesting the fact of rape, and a continual threat of extinction, we defined ourselves as essential to ourselves, as subject and not object, as beings who existed in order to exist.

In the next two years I was to write two articles about motherhood. During these years, I raised my daughter, rented rooms in my house, worked at three different part-time jobs, all this time living in that economic hinterland so well known to women raising children alone, a world of food stamps and clinics, and no credit, and many bills. The cost of child care took up much of my salary. I found it difficult to do all I needed to do, to be a mother to my daughter, to earn a living, and to find time to write.

But I did write. In stolen moments. Robbing Peter to pay Paul. In one essay, 'Women and Children Last', I simply unearthed a social picture: women and children together made up the greatest mass of the poor. We had the least social and economic power, the least ability to affect the course of the world. I felt overtired, overworked, unable to make ends meet, worried over my child and my neglect of her. And I was not alone. Too many women and children knew these difficulties. Our condition spoke a grave criticism of the society in which we lived, a society that does not cherish its young.

In 'Feminism and Motherhood' I explored the resonances of this situation. Women held responsible for children. Men ignorant of the child's need, not knowing how to mother, to feed. Forgetting the vulnerable feeling world of the child. Women, with the knowledge of how to help a child grow, with a knowledge of human life's frailties and capacities and imaginings, but without the power to shape the social body to these understandings.

It is an extraordinary feeling to be part of a movement at once social, political, intellectual and cultural. I wrote about motherhood out of the urgencies of my own life. Yet, returning from the solitary act of writing, I found I was not alone in my concern. And neither was I alone in my heterodox view of society. An organization for single mothers, 'Momma', now existed. It formed support groups, lobbied, published a newspaper and then a book. Adrienne Rich was completing her classic study, *Of Woman Born*. And Merlin Stone published a scholarly book, *When God Was a Woman*, which suggested that a social body governed by mothers, and worshipping the image of the mother, had existed before patriarchy. Within the feminist movement, another movement grew up around the idea of matriarchy. Women began to imagine a female cosmos, to retrieve the history of witches; they conceived of a spirituality which worshipped the goddess.

What existed in prehistory is now only a subject for speculation. We cannot know. And yet, what one imagines to have existed in the past, in a Golden Age, stands in the mind for the hope of wholeness we might be able to find in the future. To consider the possibility of matriarchy requires a shift in thinking. To be certain, the idea of female rule is a significant part of that shift. But women entertaining the idea of matriarchy were not seeking exclusive female governance. Instead, they sought a shift in values. Just as I had explored the difference between the world of mothers and children, and a society dominated by men, so the students of matriarchy explored significant differences between socially masculine and feminine values. The roles society had given to men and women had produced different thinking and different ways of being in us. Now, it was being suggested, as it had also been during the nineteenth century, that men, valuing power, produce nations, conflict and wars, and that women, valuing life, produce relationship, continuity and peace.

Even given that each particular man and woman may not actually fit into these categorical descriptions of their gender, this is far too simple a description of men and women in contemporary society. Yet ideas which are too simple often have an emotional accuracy. They describe correctly what is felt, and point therefore to a new and more complex matrix of explanations, which is to come later.

The mother goddess is most often an earth goddess, and, increasingly, women were beginning to investigate the identification of woman with nature. In the middle seventies I was asked to address a class at the University of California on the subject of feminism and ecology. When I complained that I was not an ecologist, the professors in the course agreed to let me approach the subject philosophically, and so I prepared a lecture. Again, I took my own experience and feeling as the place to enter thought.

At that time, the ecology movement had made a dramatic and moral issue out of the way that households disposed of tin cans, bottles and other refuse. Because I was so overworked, I resented this tactic, and my resentment led me to a discovery. Following the reasoning of my own anger, I said that women are always being asked to clean up after men. We do the dishes, wash the toilets, even take away the baby's faeces, and now we are being asked to take care of a mess created by a society run by men. It was from this complaint that I began to understand that our culture identifies matter and nature with women, but culture and spirit with men.

Speaking to a lecture hall of undergraduates, I told them that because of the division of labour between men and women, many men could live their lives with the illusion that either they did not have bodies, or they were the masters of their bodies. For in general the problems that the physical world presents to us through our bodies are handled by women. When a man is hungry, a woman prepares the meal. When he defecates, a woman cleans the toilet. True, he must work for a living. But already, because of social structures and money, more often than not his efforts take place in a different sphere than the material world, in a world of abstraction. Thus, a man can live his whole life with a disdain for the simple needs of the human body, and for the labour needed to sustain that body. And the more power a man has, or the more he is part of the ruling class, the less his work outside the home includes direct material experience.

I traced this dichotomy between the material female and the spiritual male through the history of speculation back to our creation myth – the story of the Garden of Eden. It was Eve who was said to have brought death into the world. And all women, in this mythos, share in this act because we are reputed to be more corporeal and are therefore agents of the devil. Now I understand why woman had become, as de Beauvoir writes, 'other', the scapegoat. In our culture, men had associated woman with nature; woman had become a symbol for the power of nature to alter our lives, cause suffering, loss and death. Thus I began to see that out of a desire to control nature, men dominate women. I decided to write a book about women and nature.

I have always thought of myself as a poet. Poetry is the easiest form for me to write. Thus, when I began to write *Woman and Nature: The Roaring Inside Her,* I wrote in a kind of prose poetry. I started by writing about domesticity, with this sentence, 'We are the mules,' in the voice of a mule who complains. Because I liked this piece so well, I decided to use this form. And later, when I began to do research regarding the history of science from the thirteenth century to the present, or the development of modern agricultural methods, I realised that my strength as a writer on this subject was not an expertise in science or technology but the poetic sensibility which I could bring to these facts and events. Later, I came to realize that poetry is a powerful way of knowledge.

While I was reading various scientific texts, I found that the words of scientists and historians of science had a chilling effect on my own thought. They had such a tone of authority for me, I was afraid to question their judgments. Moreover, I was worried by an aesthetic problem: how was I to convey scientific attitudes in the very personal, emotional language I had used for the voice of the 'mule'? Finally, in that dream state between sleep and waking, the solution to these problems occurred to me. I would write in two voices. One would be a parody of the scientific voice in which I answered my own fear of authority by making fun of the disembodied, seemingly 'objective' voice of authority. The other voice would be the embodied, feeling voice of woman and nature. Now I had two characters and a drama. The voice of authority – a male and patriarchal voice – attempted over and over again to dominate the female voice of the body, of forests, of wind, of mountains, of horses, cows, of the earth.

In one piece, 'Consequences', I juxtaposed the rape of a woman, and the act of strip-mining. I had learned that what motivates rape also motivates the destruction of ecological balance: the desire to dominate nature, to be in control. I also saw that the derogatory way in which men see women was a mirror of culture's derogatory view of matter, and that this derived from the philosophical separation between spirit and matter. Now, speculation about my own feelings and my own experience as a woman had led me to speculations about the nature of Nature, and about epistemology, and I began to see human psychology in a new way.

My interest in psychology was accelerated by my personal life. Since I was an adult, I had had periods of severe depression. I had read of other writers who would sink into a depressed state after finishing a book. Now, having completed *Woman and Nature*, this happened to me.

I had been in psychotherapy for many years. But now I entered a very intense process of healing, in which I relived the events of my childhood. I experienced the truths of psychological understanding of human nature vividly. It was not only my life that had been affected by this process, but my thinking. I did not so much change my mind as see again what I had understood before, but now through a different lens which added a deeper level of understanding to my thoughts.

One of the first pieces that I wrote out of this new level of understanding, 'Thoughts on Writing', is included in this book. In it I say that the two voices in *Woman and Nature*, the voice of patriarchal authority and the voice of woman and nature, also exist inside me. I had recorded an inner dialogue as well as a social dialogue. What I experienced as myself, in the act of writing poetry, was a split. I was both censor and poet.

It seems obvious that a culture which has created dualisms between mind and body, intellect and emotion, and spirit and matter would also produce, in its individual members, a divided self. But this had not been obvious to me, in the fullness of its implications, before this time. When I began writing about pornography in *Pornography and Silence* I encountered the same dualism again, and I found the divided self again.

Freud compared the process of psychology to an archaeological expedition: the human mind, he wrote, had layers similar to those in a building whose foundation covers the traces of earlier buildings. I believe that pornographic fantasies make up a record of our culture's otherwise hidden thoughts and I approached pornography the way an archaeologist approaches a ruin. But in order to reach pornography for these meanings, one must read as a student of literature reads a text, symbolically.

I soon realized that the dualism between nature and culture is expressed throughout pornography. The pornographic heroine is frequently associated, and in a debased manner, with nature. The pornographic hero represents cultural power. And within pornography, the sexual act is an act of dominance. But now, I came also to see that the woman in pornography is not a woman. She is entirely unrealistic and hardly resembles any actual woman. Thus, I understood that the pornographic heroine is a symbol for a denied part of the pornographic hero's psyche.

The dominant mind of our culture is a mind in conflict. And the pornographic hero who represents this mind plays out this conflict in pornography. Afraid of the vulnerability of his own flesh, he tortures the flesh of a woman. Afraid of his feeling, he ridicules the feelings of a woman. Afraid to lose control of his own body, afraid of the power of natural circumstances, he ties and binds a woman, he rapes her, or even murders her. Pornography provides this hero, and the reader who identifies with him, with the illusion that he can control nature. And pornography itself is part of a larger delusion that culture can control nature.

In a culture of delusion, women symbolize a denied self who experiences what it is to be human, to be in and of nature. This self knows that we die, this self feels, suffers pain, knows love without boundary, grieves loss, knows the world through sensation, through the body, accepts that we are sometimes powerless before the powerful circumstances of this earth.

It was from this understanding that I began to see why the sexual act is used to express aggression toward women. A man can avoid confronting nature when he eats, for example, because the male role protects him from 'domestic' work. But he cannot avoid an experience of nature in his own sex. At the heart of the sexual experience, and of sexual longing, is orgasm, and orgasm itself necessitates a loss of control. Moreover, in a sexual embrace we return to the sensual experience of the infant, a pre-cultural being, not yet educated into culture's delusions of power. To be held, to feel skin against skin, to search another's body with mouth and hands is to return to our original knowledge of the body. And from this I saw that the rapist turns the vulnerable act of coitus into an act of aggression in order to avoid the knowledge that comes from this experience of vulnerability.

Here, too, I saw why women are associated with nature. We are the first 'other' the infant encounters, the mother, and for the infant we represent the power of circumstance: we can feed or not feed, comfort or not, come or go away leaving the infant in fear of pain and death.

I subtitled this book 'Culture's Revenge Against Nature' because I felt that pornography humiliates women as an act of revenge against the natural world. I realized that I had encountered this habit of mind before; for the mind of the pornographer was like the mind of the racist. Both minds choose a scapegoat on which to project a part of themselves they deny. Both take revenge against this scapegoat through humiliation and acts of dominance.

Now I understood why it was that a feminist movement had grown out of the movement for the abolition of slavery in the nineteenth century, and why the contemporary feminist movement followed the beginning of the contemporary civil rights movement. It is not so much that women and black people suffer in the same way. Sometimes we do and sometimes we do not. But in this culture we are defined and victimized by the same habit of mind, a habit of delusion.

In seeking to discover the psychological origins of pornographic imagery, I have come to understand the political significance of self-knowledge and denial. Out of denied selfs and denied realities, the mind creates an enemy, and this enemy 'can be a whole nation, race or sex'. In 'The Way of All Ideology: The Need for an Enemy', I extend my thinking about culture as delusion to include the way in which any theory, even a radical or feminist one, can become a means to deny insight and create enemies.

Once more, I find myself part of a larger movement of heart and mind. A new generation of thought by women and men attempts to heal our social and political troubles with a deeper understanding of the human by entering that undefined realm between a political philosophy and psychology where psyche and circumstance shape each other.*

And what of this word 'human'? What I thought was a break with radical thought was really a coming home. I tore myself away from the old modes and began again from my own experience and my own feeling. Is this not to confirm that matter and spirit are forever linked, to know that the best thought originates from the wholeness of our

---

*See Sue Mansfield, *The Gestalt of War*, New York, 1982, and Deena Metzger, *Tree*, Culver City 1981.

own existence? Thinking I was discovering only my own answers and then answers for women, I came upon a new way of seeing the human. The word 'human' has not really included women, nor people of colour, nor any 'other'. But is this not why the human being has suffered so much in these times? For in excluding otherness from ourselves, we have excluded our own vulnerability and our tenderness, our tears, our anger, our wholeness, our *selves*. Now I reclaim the word human, and I know myself as a radical again.

This is a difficult year. Prospects for women and the world look bleak. The old economies decline, and poverty always falls hardest on the forgotten, other self, the darker, older one, the woman, the child. An American president speaks of the possibility of a 'limited' nuclear war. It becomes a part of sanity to fear that soon there will be no human life on earth.

But fearful as I am, there is joy in me. While one eye sees disaster and the causes of destruction more clearly, the other eye awakens to beauty. I am beginning to put the shattered being, myself and the world, back together. We are all connected. I know this. Dark and light. Male and female. We are a tribe whose fate on this earth is shared. I do not know the outcome. I have moments of despair. But I have learned that when I see out of my own experience, and chart it as precisely and clearly as I can, I see what I have not seen before: I am surprised.

This earth holds a vast wisdom and a capacity to heal that we are only beginning to comprehend. We are made from this earth. This is my hope.

Berkeley, Winter 1982

Interviews on Abortion

In 1969 and 1970, I recorded several interviews with women who had had abortions. I did not pretend to be an objective interviewer. I had had an illegal abortion myself, and I conducted these recordings like conversations. Later, I edited out some of my responses. Abortion was made legal in the United States but it has become a controversial subject again. Many women can no longer receive government aid to pay for abortions. And the legal right for an abortion is under attack from the right wing.

K. L. is a professional photographer in her middle twenties. I had been given her name by a mutual friend active in the women's liberation movement and had never spoken with her before this conversation. When she learned that the book I was compiling was being written to encourage women to speak out against the inhumane treatment they have suffered, she agreed to contribute her knowledge.

Q. Were you using contraceptives when you conceived?
A. I had an intrauterine device. I was the one in a thousand.
Q. Apparently accidents with IUDs are not that rare.
A. The doctor told me that most of the people who had accidents had had children before. I was his first patient who hadn't had children who got pregnant with the device. It was in the ninth month after it had been inserted that I got pregnant. I would not believe that I was pregnant, and the symptoms I had I simply denied. I had a very small period. I got pregnant in the middle of August and had a fake period in September, which I didn't know you could have. I was really ignorant.

In October, though, I missed a period. And I got a bit concerned. I thought I was gaining weight. My weight fluctuates anyway but my waist was getting bigger. And finally, I called the doctor. He said, 'I don't think you have anything to worry about.' But at the end of October, I got an infection, and I went to see him about that. He started to treat me for the infection. After the examination I asked him, 'What do you think about my not having a period?' He said, 'Oh, I think it's funny.' I asked him if he thought I was pregnant. He said that my uterus was not enlarged.

Q. This was almost your third month?

A. Yes. Then I went for another checkup and this time he found that I had another infection, and that I was definitely pregnant.

Q. Did he explain why he had been so confident that you weren't pregnant the week before?

A. He said that he had been so concerned with the infection that he overlooked it. So then he asked me what I was going to do about it. And then I said, 'I have to have an abortion. I can't have this child. I'm not ready for it. It would destroy the relationship with Peter I have now. It's completely unwanted.' And then of course he got really cool and he didn't want to help me.

I was seeing a shrink, so I immediately called him, and he said he couldn't counsel me on this, but he did get in touch with another gynaecologist. And that gynaecologist gave my shrink the names of six shrinks who will advise on abortion. My gynaecologist said that I was about two months along because he was judging from September instead of August.

I saw the other gynaecologist on Monday. He talked to my shrink on Tuesday, and I tried madly Wednesday calling two other psychologists for appointments, because by Friday I was supposed to have two letters from psychologists for the hospital board. Well, I just couldn't get it done in time. Couldn't get appointments with them.

Q. They have pre-scheduled dates on which they meet?

A. Yes, and since I missed the Friday meeting, I would have had to wait another two weeks. So then what happened was my mother, who is psychic, called me that night and asked, 'What's wrong,' and I said, 'Well, I'm not going to tell you. You couldn't handle it.' She said to tell her anyway. So I did. And she said she wanted to help me. So she found me the abortionist, and then I found out that she had had two abortions. She tried a couple of gynaecologists in the Bay Area. Then she took me to one gynaecologist in San Jose, and he dragged me through the whole story again and I told him all the reasons and so on, and he made me cry, he was just a bastard, and the whole thing was he had no intention of giving me an abortion. He just wanted to talk me out of it. He was one of those sentimental slobs who think that it's a life and one shouldn't destroy a life. I told him it was destroying *my* life and it would destroy the life of two people together. So finally in despair we called the one in Nevada.

Q. Did you go with your mother?

A. She took me, and she loaned me the money and stayed with me through the whole thing. The experience was really weird. It was almost surreal. It was this old western, creaky, small town. A man's town. The women were only there to serve the men, who walked around the streets strutting in their boots. There was gambling, and all the restaurants were filled with men. So when we got there we called the doctor, who said he would come over and examine me.

Q. He came to your motel?

A. Yes. And he said he would have his nurse come over later in the evening and take me to the clinic. So the nurse came to get me, she was this very motherly middle-aged woman, very, very nice and tender and soft. And she drove me over to the house.

It didn't look like a clinic, it looked like all the houses around it. And there were no street lights. When I got inside they blindfolded me and led me through what felt like a maze of rooms, and I had to go to the bathroom blindfolded and finally they took me into this room. And then they shot me with something that completely relaxed me. I was fully conscious, but I couldn't move. I didn't feel any pain but I could feel other sensations. They stood around, and I couldn't figure out why they were standing there.

Then the doctor came in, and they laid me out on the table with my legs apart in the stirrups. And then he stood between my legs with his stomach against me, and started manipulating me. And then he raped me. And I couldn't move. I had absolutely no will. And of course I was trapped. I had to get rid of this baby. It was the most incredible insult. And an incredible outrage.

Meanwhile somebody had had a wreck outside of town. Apparently he was the only doctor in town. And someone kept calling him and saying, come, we need you, some people are injured. And he would say, 'Yes, yes. I'll be there.' But he stayed at the clinic for about two hours before he went. He finally did perform the abortion before he left.

Q. After he raped you?

A. Yes. It was really nightmarish.

Q. Do you think the nurse knew what happened?

A. I think it must have been his routine because she left and then she came back after a certain amount of time. And then she held my hand during the operation. I started to come out of the anaesthetic, or tranquillizer, while he was still scraping, and I felt some pain, so they shot me up again, and that really knocked me out. It took him a long time to operate because I was so far along, and after the abortion he said, 'You were three or four months along, and it was a dangerous operation.'

Q. Did he give you any antibiotics?

A. He gave me a penicillin shot. I'm pretty sure he was a doctor. He must have been a fugitive. He obviously was a very sick man. He charged me $650.

Q. Did you pay him after the operation?

A. No, he got the money before. Of course. The nurse drove me home, and she gave instructions to my mother about how to take care of me. I was so out of it by that time, I didn't really remember what she said, except, 'Of course, you won't tell anybody.'

Q. Did you have any complications?

A. Well, I got back and I sort of felt okay. I got back on Sunday. And I didn't bleed very much. Then the next Sunday, I had guests and I was fixing breakfast, and I started bleeding really heavily. I went through one pad after another. Changed every 45 minutes or half-hour. I was haemorrhaging. And I haemorrhaged for about nine hours before I got really hip. So I called my mother again. And she said that if it kept up, or I started getting scared, I should call a doctor.

During the week after the abortion, we called around trying to find some doctor to see for post-abortion care. We heard something about that over KSAN radio. But when we called they wouldn't give us any information. They told us to call the Mission Switchboard. We called them about three times before we got somebody. This guy told us the name of a couple of doctors. I called one in the East Bay. This was Sunday night, so I called him, and he told me it sounded dangerous, and he said, 'If I were you, I would go to Herrick Hospital emergency.'

Q. Why didn't he come to your place?

A. He was at a cocktail party. I was very scared. I had been bleeding for nine hours, with lots of big clots. So we went to Herrick, and then I waited there for an hour before a doctor could get around to me. And they found I didn't have insurance. So I went over to Highland.

By this time I was really weak and scared, and I fainted when I got to the emergency desk. So they put me in a wheelchair and I started hyper-ventilating. So they wheeled me into an emergency room, and God, about ten doctors were buzzing around and saying things that were coming through to me in this semi-conscious state. And I was really angry because the doctor said, 'Well, we're going to have to tell the police.' I called them a bunch of motherfuckers and bitched at them the whole time. They didn't give me any sedatives.

Q. No anaesthetic either?

A. Nothing. They might have given me a local. The whole scrape job again. And it was very painful. Then they kept me under observation for six hours, and gave me plasma.

Well, as I was being wheeled down the hall to the observation room, this young blond, crewcut cop comes up and says, 'Hi.' And I wouldn't speak to him. And then the nurse said, 'Cool it until she gets some rest.' So, about half an hour after I had gotten laid up, this fat cherubic little cop comes in and he says, 'Oh, you lost it huh?' And I thought, 'Oh, he thinks I've had a miscarriage.' So I said, 'Oh yes, I lost it.' So he thought I was a housewife. And this was my first baby, and I lost it. And that's the story I gave him. So then it was all cool. At six o'clock in the morning I went home.

Q. Do they make a report to the police every time a woman has a miscarriage?

A. Every time she haemorrhages and has to have a D and C.

Q. Are you okay now?

A. Yeah. Except that because of the fear of infection after abortion, and the infection before, Peter and I weren't able to make love for about two months. That was rough on both of us. And I wasn't on pills yet. And when I was supposed to have my next period it didn't come around.

Q. You were afraid you were pregnant again?

A. Yes. So I went to a doctor in Berkeley who is very sympathetic, very involved with birth control, and he gave me a series of shots to bring on my period.

Q. Some doctors think of it as immoral to give those injections.

A. Doctors are so behind the times. So insensitive to the needs of the people. And their attitude toward sex is so up-tight. They're supposed to be taking care of people and the world is so over-populated; not only are they hung up about birth control, but they're hung up about abortions and unwanted children. This gynaecologist in San Jose told me that abortion was killing a life. I said, 'It isn't human life until it's conscious.' He said, 'Well, I've known lots of girls who went into homes for unwed mothers and came out all right. It's just nine months out of your life!'

Q. Did you make any attempt to press charges against the abortionist?

A. No. Of course, I'm torn. He shouldn't be practising. He's a sick man. And he could get a young sixteen- or seventeen-year-old girl who is really naive and needs to be protected, and it would completely blow her mind. You know the pressures from a pregnancy are so strong anyway. It could ruin her emotional, her sexual life. So I was torn between justice and my whole attitude toward the establishment's attitude toward abortion.

Q. Is your boyfriend going to help to pay your mother back the money she loaned you?

A. Well, he would if we had any money. We're both photographers. Photography costs a lot when you are just beginning. I'm not saving any money to pay her back, and I guess she's cool about it.

Q. You're lucky that she was there to help you.

A. Oh, yeah. I never knew a whole side of her before this happened. I didn't *know* her. I still don't know her really, but I know more about her. A real understanding comes between a mother and a daughter when the daughter becomes a woman too. Then there are all kinds of things to share. I've told her about women's liberation and she really digs it.

When we talked about it, she said that she felt the next great social upheaval is going to come from women. But it's here I think. I don't know where it's going, but it's got to be. With the level of consciousness many of us have achieved, there's no going back. You can't go back into docility and obeisance.

D.S. has for a long time been a close friend and yet, before I began work on my book, we had never spoken of abortion with one another. What is not apparent in this written transcript of our taped conversation is my sense of shock that she had never before spoken to me of her last, legally performed, abortion, though it clearly had been a painful experience. She is an honest, articulate and talented woman in her early thirties, who has spent several years as a community organizer, a dancer and an actress.

Q. You had three abortions?

A. Three. I had the first in 1958 or '59 in Tijuana. I was twenty-two years old then. And after that, only a year later, I was pregnant again.

I flew to Seattle for the second one. I had to go twice. The first time, he said he was unable to dilate the cervix. He said it was too tight. I was very sick the second time I went. I was vomiting a lot, and very uncomfortable. I was furious at having let myself get pregnant again, and also I was alone. I had had a friend with me in Tijuana, but I was doing penitence in a way, by going alone, for having let myself get pregnant again.

Q. Not for making love, but for getting pregnant?

A. No, I was angry at myself because in neither case did I have any intention of being involved with the guy emotionally, and because I was stupid enough not to use contraception.

Q. Do you think you wanted to get pregnant?

A. That's always the suspicion. But I think stating it that way is almost a Freudian simplification. I think it was more pure. I simply did not recognize that I was a woman and capable of conceiving. In some very basic way, I did not believe in my own existence.

Q. Do you feel you wanted to test whether or not you could conceive?

A. It was more passive than that. I was not conscious of my own existence when I didn't take care of myself. I think it's not untypical for young women, or merely emotionally immature people, that the only thing that convinces you that you are real is some sort of somatic reality, some sort of physical reality, and that if you are not convinced of your body's existence, your existence, you are also not convinced of the body's capacity to conceive. I didn't think it could happen to me. I just didn't worry about it at all.

Q. I think such a feeling may be in part a result of a pristine silence our society cultivates on the subject of sex outside marriage, and a general reticence to discuss contraception publicly. When I was sixteen, you had to know the right gynaecologist. You couldn't just walk in and say, 'Give me a diaphragm.'

A. My situation was different because I come from a family that is more open about sex. I had plenty of information about how to get protection if I needed it. But my carelessness was allied more to my personal development as a person, as a woman. I had sort of tacit approval that I could make it with guys. But I was confused about who to make it with; I felt guilty about making it with guys I didn't love. One of the things my parents said to me was that they made an association between sex and love. I can't think of what I would say to my own children that might be different except to explain that people are at times physically attracted to one another without the presence of the kind of love that would be necessary for marriage or a long affair. One of the things young men are brought up to accept is that they will be attracted to women they may not want to marry. This is not clear for a woman.

Q. We are raised with a psychological double standard.

A. It's a very complex double standard. I mean, I do think sex is serious, and that sexuality for women has something unique to them. Sexuality with women tends to be more serious – a woman does not enter into an experience with as much abandon as a man.

Q. Did you feel that to have an abortion was immoral?

A. I had an intense, ambivalent response to it. On the one hand I felt militant about my right to do what I wanted for myself, and my right not to have a baby. When I had the first two abortions, I was not ready to have or care for children. I didn't want them. But I was unhappy about my own life. I felt that the fact that I was pregnant was indicative of my own lack of mental health, that I wasn't taking care of myself.

Q. How did you first find a contact with the abortionists?

A. The first time it was through a family doctor. I was lucky because he was very concerned that I get good medical treatment, and I did, but it was a horrible experience otherwise. I went down to Tijuana with a good friend, and on the trip, the whole feeling of being outside the law, or being a criminal or being bad, got to me. When we got to San Diego, we were two middle-class bohemian-looking girls and we felt that everyone was looking at us, and that they knew why we were going to Tijuana.

In fact, coming back across the border . . . I had gotten off the table – in this case I had had sodium pentothal – and immediately we took a taxi across the border . . . we were stopped by the border police because we were being driven by a young Mexican cab driver who we made friends with. They stopped us, two white girls with a Mexican, and they took us into an office at the border. I had needle marks in my arms from the sodium pentothal, and they thought we were carrying dope. They took us into a room and searched us. We had to strip completely, and they searched us for drugs, and I mean thoroughly, we were asked to bend over and that sort of thing.

Q. Did they give you an internal examination?

A. They gave my friend one, I assume, because they asked her to bend over. I had a menstrual pad on, so I told them I was having my period. It seemed to me at that point they must have known what we were there for. They were about to book us and arrest us but we talked them out of it.

Q. What did you say to them?

A. Well, I was irrational, rather furious, and I accused them of being racists, which they were, and I said they had only stopped us because of the Mexican kid. I think I was slightly out of my mind. I said, 'I bet you hate Jews, too.' And then I really lost my cool altogether. I think I must have been doped up, frankly. The girl who was with me had more wits, and she just pleaded that we had come down shopping. We simply cried our way out of it. The whole thing made me feel very bad, very unhappy. No matter how I tried to think clearly about it, I couldn't separate how society had treated me from how I felt about myself.

When I went to Seattle a year or two later, I had the same feeling again. I spent the night in a horrible little hotel room and got up early in the morning for the abortion, and walked into a cruddy doctor's office in a downtown building. It was all very secretive, and after the abortion, which was extremely painful, I got up and walked back to the hotel room, still in a lot of pain, walking through a strange city all alone; it was terribly melodramatic and made me feel doubly alienated from myself.

Q. Did the doctor you saw have you back for a post-operative examination?

A. No.

Q. Did he give you any antibiotics?

A. I think he gave me penicillin, and he gave me codeine for the pain.

Q. Did you know what method he used to perform the operation?

A. He inserted an instrument and literally scraped the inside of the uterus.

Q. Did he tell you why he didn't give you any anaesthetic?

A. He said that he could tell what he was doing better. What was also clear, but what he didn't say, was that an anaesthetic would involve the extra expense and the risk of an anaesthetist.

Q. Did you actually feel the scraping?

A. Yes. I remember the pain of the scraping and then I remember being in a good deal of pain afterwards, because the uterus was contracting.

Q. I have heard that some doctors who perform abortions say that they don't use anaesthetics in order to convince the patient that she should not get pregnant again, as if women, if abortions were legal and painless, would be having them once a month.

A. That's one of the reasons that morality about abortion is particularly cruel. When a woman finds herself pregnant and doesn't want a baby, that already is enough pain for her. To add salt to the wound – to make it illegal, immoral, sinful – is the final act of cruelty. If I had been in a country where abortion was legal and could have simply walked into a hospital, though it wouldn't have reduced the state of anxiety I felt about my psychological state, I wouldn't have had to contend with fear or embarrassment or danger. I hate society for doing that to me.

Q. Tell me about your third abortion.

A. I had such a traumatic experience with the last abortion – a little over a year ago – because the time for having babies for me is long overdue. I really would like a child now. And secondly, it's inconceivable to me that I would be pregnant from a man now that I didn't dig, and dig seriously. After making the decision that I could not raise a child by myself, I began what I thought was a natural abortion, a miscarriage. I began to bleed a bit, so that presented the possibility of trying to get a legal abortion. With the help of some friendly doctors who asked me, 'Do you want this baby?' and I said, 'No, I don't,' I got a legal abortion.

Before I found a doctor who was sympathetic, I went to my regular gynaecologist who was sort of an up-tight normal dude. I was bleeding, and I went to find out from him whether in fact I was actually miscarrying, and he said to me something that I will never forget. When I indicated that if I was miscarrying could he give me some medication that would make it come on more quickly, he said, 'Absolutely not. You must remember that I have my own conscience to deal with.' It was a very humiliating encounter for me because he was unsympathetic, and I began to get the feeling again that I was immoral because of this behaviour. I didn't tell him what I later said to him a thousand times in my mind, which was that his morality was absolutely inconsequential, that I was a separate human being and that it was my decision, that his conscience had absolutely nothing to do with my predicament.

Q. You were lucky that you finally did find sympathetic doctors. Many doctors refuse to help a woman obtain a legal abortion.

A. I never went back to that doctor again. But then, when I went to the hospital, something terrible happened. My sister-in-law came to visit me just before I went in to get scraped out. She announced that she had come from her doctor's office, and she had found out that she was pregnant. And she was terribly happy and ecstatic. When she left I fainted three times. I was clearly traumatized by the whole thing. I think I really wasn't feeling well. I'm not the fainting type; I don't pass out very easily. It was one of the first signals I had about how difficult this whole thing was.

Q. Was this operation easier than the illegal abortions you had, despite the ambivalence you felt?

A. There was quite a difference in being able to go to a hospital in my own city with family near and not have to go through a melodrama.

Q. And there were no complications?

A. None. The only thing that was a drag was that the interns kept asking me, 'Mrs Black, how many children have you had?'

Q. Wasn't your correct name on your chart?

A. I don't know, but I very righteously corrected them each time, '*Miss* Black.'

Q. Right on.

A. I recently went with my younger sister when she had an abortion in Juarez, and that was a nightmare. It turned out to be the wrong doctor, and while she was having her abortion she was screaming and I thought he was probably killing her.

Q. He didn't give her an anaesthetic?

A. He didn't give her enough of an anaesthetic. I almost burst into the room, and then I made the decision that to go in in the middle of it when he had her only half covered up would be a disaster, that I would wait until he was finished and then rush her to a hospital. If he had gone on any longer I would have gone in. It went on for about ten minutes and it was the most unbearable thing I have ever sat through. She was very late, and if we had come back to the United States to try to find another doctor it would have been another couple of weeks, so we went through it with a doctor we didn't really know much about. As it turned out, she had to be curetted when she got back. He hadn't gotten all of the tissue out.

Q. That's very dangerous. Is she all right now?

A. Yes. But of course, it never would have happened were it not for the law.

Q. People who argue in favour of keeping laws against abortion always speak of their great concern for the life of the foetus, while they say nothing about the 10,000 women who die every year from illegal abortions, nor do they seem to have any concern for the child once it is born. Illegitimate children are still treated with social disdain.

A. To even think of a child as 'illegitimate' is so – I don't even understand what that means – 'illegitimate.' And it is so difficult to exist in a society whose values you don't agree with, when you still feel the pressure of those values. I know a woman who had a child, she wasn't married, and she has raised the child by herself, a fantastic kid, a very happy child. Now the girl is about twelve and this woman recently had to decide whether or not to tell her daughter that she is illegitimate. Whether or not she was married has nothing to do with her real life, or her daughter's, but it is an irrelevant fact that society is forcing them to deal with.

Q. It's like having to tell your child that he is black, and then having to decide what 'black' means.

A. That's right.

Q. Even if one didn't have to contend with the social pressures, the financial burden of trying to raise a child alone is tremendous, especially since the man is assumed to be the breadwinner, and women's salaries are lower.

A. The factor that made me decide against trying to raise a child by myself was not any of those things, though they were considerations, but it was a more emotional decision based on the recognition of the amount of work that is involved in raising a child, and the need for help and companionship in that work. The women who do it alone are extremely strong.

Q. In this society, if one doesn't live according to the statistical mean – that is, mother, father, child – which I'm not even sure is really 'average' any more, but if one doesn't conform to this family pattern, one is out in the cold.

A. And if you make a law against abortion, then you are relieved of the responsibility of dealing with the problem of women who want to have abortions. You don't have to provide any institutions, medical care, emotional care. You are relieved of all kinds of responsibility because you have made a rule that there are not to be any abortions. It seems to me that if abortions were legal a woman could receive help in making a decision, and then reassurance that she had made the right one.

Q. Rather than have a decision, one which may affect the rest of her entire life, forced upon her.

A. At the bottom of the kind of thinking that is behind a law like the one against abortion is a kind of contempt for other people's judgment. It almost is a class snobbery among intellectuals who raise the question of the morality of abortion. And the debate is intensified by the male-female differences so that in addition to contempt for the judgment of others, it is contempt for women's judgment that is operating. It's amazing how quickly people will abandon moralizing about abortion when their own personal lives are being affected.

Q. Such was the case with me. Though I never really condemned abortion, or believed there ought to be a law, I never saw the issue so clearly, I never saw the necessity of personal choice as such an urgent one until I had an abortion myself.

A. Somehow it's assumed that when people are given freedom they will make the wrong choices. I think that is a sign of a deep kind of suspicion that all people are victims of, which comes out of their own lack of trust in their own motivations and their own powers. What are the worst things that people can do? They can screw people of the same sex – that's a no-no. They can abort. They can have promiscuous sex, all of which belong in realm of private decision.

G.P. is also in her late twenties. At the time of this conversation she had just been married and was completing her last quarter's work for her BA degree. She has been, at different times of her life, an actress, a writer and a student in Asian Studies. Her marriage has recently been dissolved.

Q. You were trying to comfort him?

A. I came out to San Francisco because of this guy. I didn't have a job – I was writing, then. But everything turned into a disaster. In the first place, the guy was committed to another girl, and hadn't told me that. He's now married to her. She tried to commit suicide! And then he came over, he was terribly upset, and our relationship was really over, except for this one night. I was trying to comfort him.

Q. And that is the night you conceived?

A. Yes. He just showed up and said something like, 'She's tried to commit suicide. Here I am. Take care of me.'

Q. What did he feel when he learned you were pregnant?

A. We were very close friends. I had known him for so long. He hung in through the whole thing, he went with me to Vancouver. I was quite lucky because it would have been grizzly without him.

Q. How did you find an abortionist in Vancouver?

A. A psychiatrist recommended the man. When I first learned I was pregnant, I had absolutely no idea what to do.

Q. Did you go to anyone else for help?

A. Only to Bill. His brother had taken his girl down to Mexico. We telephoned one clinic in Mexico and had a hilarious conversation – it might have been from a Peter Sellers film – where everything was in double talk. We were told we would have to be on a waiting list for a *month*. I think they were trying to tell us that they were under surveillance at the time. Then we went to Bill's psychiatrist and he gave us a list of names in British Columbia.

Q. When I was searching for an abortionist several years ago, everyone told me that the *clínica* in Tijuana was *the* place to go. That it was perfectly safe. But since then I have heard that many of the clinics in Juarez and Tijuana are not sterile and that some of the doctors are not competent.

A. It's very frightening to have to rely on word-of-mouth advice when you are looking for a doctor to perform an operation on you. I don't know whether I would ever recommend this man I went to or not. It would depend on how desperate the woman was.

Q. Was this man a doctor?

A. No. He told me that he had been through medical school but that he had flunked out.

Q. That must have inspired your confidence.

A. Well, he told me all this, he actually revealed his whole life story to me; while I was stretched out on the table. He told me incredible things – he said that besides doing abortions, he also performed sterilizations for men and did mercy killings of deformed babies.

Q. Did he have an underground kind of setup, one of those empty warehouse scenes, or did he have an office with his name on the door?

A. He had his name on the door. But he acted very covertly. He had no assistance at all, no nurse. And he asked us, when we called for an appointment, to come in through the back door. We couldn't *find* the back door so we came in through the front. He was extremely upset by this. He told us that what he was doing was illegal, and he got very sarcastic, and said things like, 'Who do you think you are? You think you can just walk in here?'

He was very hostile. But obviously he made a good living off these abortions. He told me he had tried to break away from the business, that he had gotten sick of what he was doing, and that his wife had left him. He said he left Vancouver and came to Southern California to buy a liquor store. But apparently he didn't make it selling liquor either. He was really a desperately unhappy person.

Q. It sounds as if he was simply dumping all his troubles on you.

A. Yes, and this is what was so difficult. I was completely at his mercy. In the first place I was ambivalent. Rationally I knew I could not have the child, that it would ruin everyone's life. But I did love Bill, I had this unspoken doubt, you know, I thought, 'Oh God, what am I doing. Have I destroyed something beautiful?'

Q. Part of you wanted to have his child?

A. Yes, yes. Obviously marriage was out of the question, and so having the child was out of the question too. But still, I had very strong dreams. The week before we went to Vancouver was really the hardest week in my life. I felt an immediate reaction to being pregnant – my breasts had started to swell.

Q. Did you feel that you were doing anything wrong by having an abortion?

A. No, only that I might be violating myself. I mean, I knew that I might be doing damage to my body, though I knew that an abortion is a simple operation under the right conditions.

Q. Were you ever afraid?

A. I didn't know what to expect. I had never talked to anyone who had had an abortion. And this man's personality was so warped.

Q. Did it ever cross your mind that he might have been insane, a sadist or something?

A. This crossed my mind. When I first came in, he was very efficient, even though he was rude, and his 'medical manner' put me at ease. I got up on the table in all my clothes – I wasn't given a robe or anything, and I just pulled up my skirt and there I was, lying on the table going wild – shouldn't I take my shoes off at least? Isn't there some problem about germs? These thoughts were racing through my head.

And in the meantime, he had stripped down to a plastic apron, and then, which I thought very odd, he shaved under his arms. He washed up very thoroughly and he wore this turban around his head, and had all this official doctor gear, and there I was in my street clothes with my skirt pulled up around my hips. At that point, I sat up on the side of the table. I was really torn. I was ready to walk right out of his office and call somebody else. I was frightened of him. But he said to me, 'Look, if you don't like what I'm doing you can go back to San Francisco, and that's it. Either lie down now, or get out.'

So I thought, 'Oh, wow! Here I am,' and I just lay down. He said, 'I want you to do everything I tell you,' and I said, 'Are you going to give me anything?' He said, 'I'm going to give you a local anaesthetic and that is *all*,' and then repeated his line about how I could go back to San Francisco. I said go ahead. And then he told me what to do. He told me to keep my hands folded over my stomach and not to move. He said that it might be painful and that it might not, that people react differently, and as it turned out, it was very painful. I have never had cramps before with my period, but these were severe abdominal cramps, nothing like cutting or tearing, but severe cramps, and I was frightened. My legs started to shake and I panicked, I wasn't sure what to do, and then I moved my hands to try to control the shaking, and he shouted, 'Don't move!' with a very authoritarian tone. Finally I became completely passive and decided to pretend everything was all right, and then he started to tell me his life story.

When it was all over he took this little kidney-shaped pan, in which he put the foetus, and he said, 'Would you like to see this?' I said, 'No!' and he said, sarcastically, 'I didn't think so.' And then he went to flush it down the john. That just did it. I burst into tears, and then I just lay there, like a wet noodle. And then he came back into the room, and he picked me up – I was just limp – I had no will, and he said, 'Put your arms around me as if you loved me.' And at that point I just thought, 'Oh, this poor man!'

Q. You could think about his misery, after what *you* had been through?

A. Actually, he completely took my mind off my own condition at that moment. In a way I did feel compassion for him. He wasn't a monster, he didn't look like a monster. Later, he began to talk to me about his feelings about abortion. He did feel, apparently, despite his sarcasm, that he was being a good Samaritan to perform abortions. He became softer and much kinder after it was all over.

Q. After you began to cry?

A. I was really shot. I was crying uncontrollably and he carried me into this recovery room, and I just stared at the wall. He came and sat down next to me and started to pat me. He said, 'Are you Catholic?' and I said no. And then he said, 'Well, do you feel that you have killed?' And then he asked, 'What do you think you were going to give birth to,' or words to that effect, and I said, 'A baby.' And he asked me, 'What kind of baby?' and I said, 'A beautiful baby.' At that instant I was full of remorse. But that was when he started to tell me about the mercy killings. He said to me, 'How do you know it would be beautiful? You should see what I've seen – babies born with holes in the side of their heads.' And he started off on all these atrocity stories about birth defects and I just decided then to check out. There was nothing I could do, so I just listened to it all. He told me, 'I'm one of the few people who is capable of doing this,' as if he were some sort of superman.

Q. How did he treat you afterwards – did he re-examine you later, or give you antibiotics?

A. He had given me these huge pills, horse pills, before. They were antibiotics, I think. But he didn't see me again, in fact he said when I left, 'Don't get in touch with me again '

Q. When you got back to San Francisco, did you see a doctor?

A. I went to the same gynaecologist who had diagnosed the pregnancy. Actually, when I first saw him, and he had told me I was pregnant, he asked me if I knew what I wanted to do. I didn't ask him what he had in mind, and I wish I had. But when I went to him after the abortion to be sure everything was all right, he was so ramrod-up-his-ass about the whole thing. It was very uncomfortable and I've never gone back to see him again. But that was the reaction of everybody. I've never felt so desolate as afterwards. Bill split immediately. I mean okay, it was over, I survived, and we're still friends, but he checked out and that was the last I saw of him for quite a while.

Q. Did you talk to anyone about what had happened?

A. No. There was nobody. There was just nobody in my life. The grotesque thing was that I had the abortion only three days before my birthday and while I was still feeling pretty rocky and bleeding a lot', I had to go through this whole birthday performance, the 'Happy Birthday to you' sort of thing.

I remember doing a very strange thing – during the birthday party there were some people there whose car wouldn't start and I deliberately went down in my party clothes and really threw my back into helping them push their car down the street – it was like I was trying to punish myself and I knew I shouldn't do that. And in the middle of pushing this thing, sure enough, I got this feeling that something had come loose inside. It wasn't serious, but I did it deliberately. It was one of those deep hidden things that go on because you are made to feel such guilt.

Q. When did you first feel you could talk about it?

A. Well, finally, a couple of weeks after the abortion I told a very close friend of mine what was wrong, but that was only because first, she told me that she had had two abortions. I had known her for five years and she never mentioned it before. I had a feeling of desperate loneliness, and I felt like an outcast. I know that I turned against myself, really, and kept myself out of touch with people and thought,

'Well, this is a cross I must bear.' That's my distorted Christian brain.

Q. How did you ever resolve this feeling?

A. The abortion affected my life very deeply because I began to have wild dreams, just wild, epic, fantastic dreams every night for three months or so. And many of them had to do with birth and babies. I wrote many of them down because they were really something. And I am still exploring them, and trying to figure out what they were about. But they had a healing power, as if my psyche were trying to make things right, to restore a balance.

Q. I can't help feeling that if abortions were legal and if they were talked about openly, whatever psychological problems a woman had would heal more quickly. Every time I tell anyone about having had an abortion, I feel eased of some of the trauma.

A. A very good friend of mine has had three abortions and she's never told her husband about it. And my stepmother had an abortion in her early thirties. She didn't marry until she was thirty-seven. And she feels, 'Well, I can tell you now.' Women in her generation never admit they have had abortions. But my stepmother did say to my sister, when my sister was only fourteen, that she must never get pregnant unless she was married because 'they go in and they open the mouth of the uterus and it is extremely painful – they *force* it open.' And my sister is very confused about boys.

The Politics of Rape

I wrote 'The Politics of Rape' in 1970. During this time, rape was not generally perceived as a political issue, and to call it one seemed a daring and extreme act. And it was not then common to use the pronoun 'I' in a political essay, or to begin such an essay by describing one's emotions. This stylistic choice was conscious and reflected the feminist thought that the 'personal is political'. During this year a group called 'Women for a Free Future' appeared before the Berkeley City Council demanding that the streets be lighted, and that girls be taught to protect themselves in school. Though many of these ideas seem simple, the essay took me several months to write, so difficult was it to see past all the old assumptions about rape. This essay was first published in Ramparts *magazine in 1971 and became part of my book* Rape: The Power of Consciousness, *published by Harper & Row in 1979.*

I

I have never been free of the fear of rape. From a very early age I, like most women, have thought of rape as part of my natural environment – something to be feared and prayed against like fire or lightning. I never asked why men raped; I simply thought it one of the many mysteries of human nature.

I was, however, curious enough about the violent side of humanity to read every crime magazine I was able to ferret away from my grandfather. Each issue featured at least one 'sex crime', with pictures of a victim, usually in a pearl necklace, and of the ditch or the orchard where her body was found. I was never certain why the victims were always women, nor what the motives of the murderer were, but I did guess that the world was not a safe place for women. I observed that my grandfather was meticulous about locks, and quick to draw the shades before anyone removed so much as a shoe. I sensed that danger lurked outside.

At the age of eight, my suspicions were confirmed. My grandmother took me to the back of the house where the men wouldn't hear, and told me that strange men wanted to do harm to little girls. I learned not to walk on dark streets, not to talk to strangers, or get into strange cars, to lock doors, and to be modest. She never explained why a man would want to harm a little girl, and I never asked.

If I thought for a while that my grandmother's fears were imaginary, the illusion was brief. That year, on the way home from school, a schoolmate a few years older than I tried to rape me. Later, in an obscure aisle of the local library (while I was reading *Freddy the Pig*) I turned to discover a man exposing himself. Then, the friendly man around the corner was arrested for child molesting.

My initiation to sexuality was typical. Every woman has similar stories to tell – the first man who attacked her may have been a neighbour, a family friend, an uncle, her doctor, or perhaps her own father. And women who grow up in New York City always have tales about the subway.

But though rape and the fear of rape are a daily part of every woman's consciousness, the subject is so rarely discussed by that unofficial staff of male intellectuals (who write the books which study seemingly every other form of male activity) that one begins to suspect a conspiracy of silence. And indeed, the obscurity of rape in print exists in marked contrast to the frequency of rape in reality, for *forcible rape is the most frequently committed violent crime in America today*. The Federal Bureau of Investigation classes three crimes as violent: murder, aggravated assault and forcible rape. In 1968, 31,060 rapes were *reported*. According to the FBI and independent criminologists, however, to approach accuracy this figure must be multiplied by at least a factor of ten to compensate for the fact that most rapes are not reported; when these compensatory mathematics are used, there are more rapes committed than aggravated assaults and homicides.

When I asked Berkeley California's Police Inspector in charge of rape investigation if he knew why men rape women, he replied that he had not spoken with 'these people and delved into what really makes them tick, because that really isn't my job . . .' However, when I asked him how a woman might prevent being raped, he was not so reticent: 'I wouldn't advise any female to go walking around alone at night . . . and she should lock her car at all times.' The Inspector

illustrated his warning with a grisly story about a man who lay in wait
for women in the back seats of their cars, while they were shopping in
a local supermarket. This man eventually murdered one of his rape
victims. 'Always lock your car,' the Inspector repeated, and then
added, without a hint of irony, 'Of course, you don't have to be
paranoid about this type of thing.'

The Inspector wondered why I wanted to write about rape. Like most
men he did not understand the urgency of the topic, for, after all, men
are not raped. But like most women I had spent considerable time
speculating on the true nature of the rapist. When I was very young,
my image of the 'sexual offender' was a nightmarish amalgamation of
the bogey man and Captain Hook: he wore a black cape, and he
cackled. As I matured, so did my image of the rapist. Born into the
psychoanalytic age, I tried to 'understand' the rapist. Rape, I came to
believe, was only one of many unfortunate evils produced by sexual
repression. Reasoning by tautology, I concluded that any man who
would rape a woman must be out of his mind.

   Yet, though the theory that rapists are insane is a popular one, this
belief has no basis in fact. According to Professor Menachem Amir's
study of 646 rape cases in Philadelphia, *Patterns in Forcible Rape*,
men who rape are not abnormal. Amir writes, 'Studies indicate that
sex offenders do not constitute a unique or psychopathological type;
nor are they as a group invariably more disturbed than the control
groups to which they are compared.' Alan Taylor, a parole officer
who has worked with rapists in the prison facilities at San Luis
Obispo, California, stated the question in plainer language, 'Those
men were the most normal men there. They had a lot of hang-ups, but
they were the same hang-ups as men walking out on the street.'

   Another canon in the apologetics of rape is that, if it were not for
learned social controls, all men would rape. Rape is held to be natural
behaviour, and not to rape must be learned. But in truth rape is not
universal to the human species. Moreover, studies of rape in our
culture reveal that, far from being impulsive behaviour, most rape is
planned. Professor Amir's study reveals that in cases of group rape
(the 'gangbang' of masculine slang) 90 percent of the rapes were
planned; in pair rapes, 83 percent of the rapes were planned; and in
single rapes, 58 percent were planned. These figures should significantly discredit the image of the rapist as a man who is suddenly
overcome by sexual needs society does not allow him to fulfill.

   Far from the social control of rape being learned, comparisons with

other cultures lead one to suspect that, in our society, it is rape itself
that is learned. (The fact that rape is against the law should not be
considered proof that rape is not in fact encouraged as part of our
culture.)

This culture's concept of rape as an illegal, but still understandable,
form of behaviour is not a universal one. In her study *Sex and
Temperament*, Margaret Mead describes a society that does not share
our views. The Arapesh do not '. . . have any conception of the male
nature that might make rape understandable to them.' Indeed our
interpretation of rape is a product of our conception of the nature of
male sexuality. A common retort to the question, why don't women
rape men, is the myth that men have greater sexual needs, that their
sexuality is more urgent than women's. And it is the nature of human
beings to want to live up to what is expected of them.

And this same culture which expects aggression from the male
expects passivity from the female. Conveniently, the companion
myth about the nature of female sexuality is that all women secretly
want to be raped. Lurking beneath her modest female exterior is a
subconscious desire to be ravished. The following description of a
stag movie, written by Brenda Starr in Los Angeles' underground
paper *Everywoman*, typifies this male fantasy. The movie 'showed a
woman in her underclothes reading on her bed. She is interrupted by
a rapist with a knife. He immediately wins her over with his charm and
they get busy sucking and fucking.' An advertisement in the *Berkeley
Barb* reads, 'Now as all women know from their daydreams, rape has
a lot of advantages. Best of all it's so simple. No preparation
necessary, no planning ahead of time, no wondering if you should or
shouldn't; just whang! bang!' Thanks to Masters and Johnson even
the scientific canon recognizes that for the female, 'whang! bang!' can
scarcely be described as pleasurable.

Still, the male psyche persists in believing that, protestations and
struggles to the contrary, deep inside her mysterious feminine soul,
the female victim has wished for her own fate. A young woman who
was raped by the husband of a friend said that days after the incident
the man returned to her home, pounded on the door and screamed to
her, 'Jane, Jane. You loved it. You know you loved it.'

The theory that women like being raped extends itself by deduction
into the proposition that most or much of rape is provoked by the
victim. But this too is only myth. Though provocation, considered a
mitigating factor in a court of law, may consist of only 'a gesture',
according to the Federal Commission on Crimes of Violence, only 4

percent of reported rapes involved any precipitative behaviour by the woman.

The notion that rape is enjoyed by the victim is also convenient for the man who, though he would not commit forcible rape, enjoys the idea of its existence, as if rape confirms that enormous sexual potency which he secretly knows to be his own. It is for the pleasure of the armchair rapist that detailed accounts of violent rapes exist in the media. Indeed, many men appear to take sexual pleasure from nearly all forms of violence. Whatever the motivation, male sexuality and violence in our culture seem to be inseparable. James Bond alternately whips out his revolver and his cock, and though there is no known connection between the skills of gunfighting and lovemaking, pacifism seems suspiciously effeminate.

In a recent fictional treatment of the Manson case, Frank Conroy writes of his vicarious titillation when describing the murders to his wife:

> 'Every single person there was killed.' She didn't move.
> 'It sounds like there was torture,' I said. As the words left my mouth I knew there was no need to say them to frighten her into believing that she needed me for protection.

The pleasure he feels as his wife's protector is inextricably mixed with pleasure in the violence itself. Conroy writes, 'I was excited by the killings, as one excited by catastrophe on a grand scale, as one is alert to pre-echoes of unknown changes, hints of unrevealed secrets, rumblings of chaos . . .'(Frank Conroy, *Manson Wins*, Harper & Row, 1970).

The attraction of the male in our culture to violence and death is a tradition Manson and his admirers are carrying on with tireless avidity (even presuming Manson's innocence, he dreams of the purification of fire and destruction). It was Malraux in his *Anti-Memoirs* who said that, for the male, facing death was the illuminating experience analogous to childbirth for the female. Certainly, our culture does glorify war and shroud the agonies of the gunfighter in veils of mystery.

And in the spectrum of male behaviour, rape, the perfect combination of sex and violence, is the penultimate act. Erotic pleasure cannot be separated from culture, and in our culture male eroticism is wedded to power. Not only should a man be taller and stronger than a female in the perfect love-match, but he must also demonstrate his superior strength in gestures of dominance which are perceived as amorous. Though the law attempts to make a clear division between rape and sexual intercourse, in fact the courts find it difficult to distinguish between a case where the decision to copulate was mutual and one where a man forced himself upon his partner.

The scenario is even further complicated by the expectation that not only does a woman mean 'yes' when she says 'no', but that a really decent woman ought to begin by saying 'no', and then be led down the primrose path to acquiescence. Ovid, the author of Western Civilization's most celebrated sex manual, makes this expectation perfectly clear.

> . . . and when I beg you to say 'yes', say 'no'. Then let me lie outside your bolted door . . . So Love grows strong . . .

That the basic elements of rape are involved in all heterosexual relationships may explain why men often identify with the offender in this crime. But to regard the rapist as the victim, a man driven by his inherent sexual needs to take what will not be given him, reveals a basic ignorance of sexual politics. For in our culture heterosexual love finds an erotic expression through male dominance and female submission. A man who derives pleasure from raping a woman clearly must enjoy force and dominance as much or more than the simple pleasures of the flesh. Coitus cannot be experienced in isolation. The weather, the state of the nation, the level of sugar in the blood – all will affect a man's ability to achieve orgasm. If a man can achieve sexual pleasure after terrorizing and humiliating the object of his passion, and in fact while inflicting pain upon her, one must assume he derives pleasure directly from terrorizing, humiliating and harming a woman. According to Amir's study of forcible rape, on a statistical average the man who has been convicted of rape was found to have a normal sexual personality, tending to be different from the normal, well-adjusted male only in having a greater tendency to express violence and rage.

And if the professional rapist is to be separated from the average dominant heterosexual, it may be mainly a quantitative difference. For the existence of rape as an index to masculinity is not entirely metaphorical. Though this measure of masculinity seems to be more publicly exhibited among 'bad boys' or ageing bikers who practise sexual initiation through group rape, in fact, 'good boys' engage in the same rites to prove their manhood. In Stockton, a small town in California which epitomizes silent-majority America, a bachelor party was given last summer for a young man about to be married. A woman was hired to dance 'topless' for the amusement of the guests. At the high point of the evening the bridegroom-to-be dragged the woman into a bedroom. No move was made by any of his companions to stop what was clearly going to be an attempted rape. Far from it. As the woman described, 'I tried to keep him away – told him of my Herpes genitalis, et cetera, but he couldn't face the guys if he didn't screw me.' After the bridegroom had finished raping the woman and returned with her to the party, far from chastising him, his friends heckled the woman and covered her with wine.

It was fortunate for the dancer that the bridegroom's friends did not follow him into the bedroom for, though one might suppose that in group rape, since the victim is outnumbered, less force would be inflicted on her, in fact, Amir's studies indicate, 'the most excessive degrees of violence occurred in group rape.' Far from discouraging violence, the presence of other men may in fact encourage sadism, and even cause the behaviour. In an unpublished study of group rape by Gilbert Geis and Duncan Chappell, the authors refer to a study by W. H. Blanchard which relates,

> The leader of the male group . . . apparently precipitated and maintained the activity, despite misgivings, because of a need to fulfill the role that the other two men had assigned to him. 'I was scared when it began to happen,' he says. 'I wanted to leave but I didn't want to say it to the other guys – you know – that I was scared.'

Thus it becomes clear that not only does our culture teach men the rudiments of rape, but society, or more specifically other men, encourage the practice of it.

II

> Every man I meet wants to protect me. Can't figure out what from.   Mae West

If a male society rewards aggressive, domineering sexual behaviour, it contains within itself a sexual schizophrenia. For the masculine man is also expected to prove his mettle as a protector of women. To the naive eye, this dichotomy implies that men fall into one of two categories: those who rape and those who protect. In fact, life does not prove so simple. In a study euphemistically entitled 'Sex Aggression by College Men', it was discovered that men who believe in a double standard of morality for men and women, who in fact believe most fervently in the ultimate value of virginity, are more liable to commit 'this aggressive variety of sexual exploitation.'

(At this point in our narrative it should come as no surprise that Sir Thomas Malory, creator of that classic tale of chivalry, the *Morte d'Artur*, was himself arrested and found guilty for repeated incidents of rape.)

In the system of chivalry, men protect women against men. This is not unlike the protection relationship which the mafia established with small businesses in the early part of this century. Indeed, chivalry is an age-old protection racket which depends for its existence on rape.

According to the male mythology which defines and perpetuates rape, it is an animal instinct inherent in the male. The story goes that sometime in our pre-historical past, the male, more hirsute and burly than today's counterparts, roamed about an uncivilized landscape until he found a desirable female. (Oddly enough, this female is *not* pictured as more muscular than the modern woman.) Her mate does not bother with courtship. He simply grabs her by the hair and drags her to the closest cave. Presumably, one of the major advantages of modern civilization for the female has been the civilizing of the male. We call it chivalry.

But women do not get chivalry for free. According to the logic of sexual politics, we too have to civilize our behaviour. (Enter chastity. Enter virginity. Enter monogamy.) For the female, civilized behaviour means chastity before marriage and faithfulness within it. Chivalrous behaviour in the male is supposed to protect that chastity from involuntary defilement. The fly in the ointment of this otherwise peaceful system is the fallen woman. She does not behave. And therefore she does not deserve protection. Or, to use another argument, a major tenet of the same value system: what has once been defiled cannot again be violated. One begins to suspect that it is the behaviour of the fallen woman, and not that of the male, that civilization aims to control.

The assumption that a woman who does not respect the double standard deserves whatever she gets (or at the very least 'asks for it') operates in the courts today. While in some states a man's previous rape convictions are not considered admissible evidence, the sexual reputation of the rape victim is considered a crucial element of the facts upon which the court must decide innocence or guilt.

The court's respect for the double standard manifested itself particularly clearly in the case of the People v. Jerry Plotkin. Mr Plotkin, a 36-year-old jeweller, was tried for rape last spring in a San Francisco Superior Court. According to the woman who brought the charges, Plotkin, along with three other men, forced her at gunpoint to enter a car one night in October 1970. She was taken to Mr Plotkin's fashionable apartment where he and the three other men first raped her and then, in the delicate language of the *S.F. Chronicle*, 'subjected her to perverted sex acts'. She was, she said, set free in the morning with the warning that she would be killed if she spoke to anyone about the event. She did report the incident to the police who then searched Plotkin's apartment and discovered a long list of names of women. Her name was on the list and had been crossed out.

In addition to the woman's account of her abduction and rape, the prosecution submitted four of Plotkin's address books containing the names of hundreds of women. Plotkin claimed he did not know all of the women since some of the names had been given to him by friends and he had not yet called on them. Several women, however, did testify in court that Plotkin had, to cite the *Chronicle*, 'lured them up to his apartment under one pretext or another, and forced his sexual attentions on them.'

Plotkin's defence rested on two premises. First, through his own testimony Plotkin established a reputation for himself as a sexual libertine who frequently picked up girls in bars and took them to his house where sexual relations often took place. He was the Playboy. He claimed that the accusation of rape, therefore, was false – this incident had simply been one of many casual sexual relationships, the victim one of many playmates. The second premise of the defence was that his accuser was also a sexual libertine. However, the picture created of the young woman (fully 13 years younger than Plotkin) was not akin to the light-hearted, gay-bachelor image projected by the defendant. On the contrary, the day after the defence cross-examined the woman, the *Chronicle* printed a story headlined, 'Gruelling Day For Rape Case Victim'. (A leaflet passed out by women in front of the courtroom was more succinct: 'Rape was committed by four men in a private apartment in October; on Thursday, it was done by a judge and a lawyer in a public courtroom.')

Through skilful questioning fraught with innuendo, Plotkin's defence attorney James Martin MacInnis portrayed the young woman as a licentious opportunist and unfit mother. MacInnis began by asking the young woman (then employed as a secretary) whether or not it was true that she was 'familiar with liquor' and had worked as a 'cocktail waitress'. The young woman replied (the *Chronicle* wrote 'admitted') that she had worked once or twice as a cocktail waitress. The attorney then asked if she had worked as a secretary in the financial district but had 'left that employment after it was discovered that you had sexual intercourse on a couch in the office.' The woman replied, 'That is a lie. I left because I didn't like working in a one-girl office. It was too lonely.' Then the defence asked if, while working as an attendant at a health club, 'you were accused of having a sexual affair with a man?' Again the woman denied the story: 'I was never accused of that.'

Plotkin's attorney then sought to establish that his client's accuser was living with a married man. She responded that the man was separated from his wife. Finally he told the court that she had 'spent the night' with another man who lived in the same building.

At this point in the testimony the woman asked Plotkin's defence attorney, 'Am I on trial? . . . It is embarrassing and personal to admit these things to all these people . . . I did not commit a crime. I am a human being.' The lawyer, true to the chivalry of his class, apologized and immediately resumed questioning her, turning his attention to her children. (She is divorced, and the children at the time of the trial were in a foster home.) 'Isn't it true that your two children have a sex game in which one gets on top of another and they–' 'That is a lie!'the young woman interrupted him. She ended her testimony by explaining, 'They are wonderful children. They are not perverted.'

The jury, divided in favour of acquittal ten to two, asked the court stenographer to read the woman's testimony back to them. After this reading, the Superior Court acquitted the defendant of both charges of rape and kidnapping.

According to the double standard a woman who has had sexual intercourse out of wedlock cannot be raped. Rape is not only a crime of aggression against the body; it is a transgression against chastity as defined by men. When a woman is forced into a sexual relationship, she has, according to the male ethos, been violated. But she is also defiled if she does not behave according to the double standard, by maintaining her chastity, or confining her sexual activities to a monogamous relationship.

One should not assume, however, that a woman can avoid the possibility of rape simply by behaving. Though myth would have it that mainly 'bad girls' are raped, this theory has no basis in fact. Available statistics would lead one to believe that a safer course is promiscuity. In a study of rape done in the District of Columbia, it was found that 82 percent of the rape victims had a 'good reputation'. Even the Police Inspector's advice to stay off the streets is rather useless, for almost half of reported rapes occur in the home of the victim and are committed by a man she has never before seen. Like indiscriminate terrorism, rape can happen to any woman, and few women are ever without this knowledge.

But the courts and the police, both dominated by white males, continue to suspect the rape victim, *sui generis*, of provoking or asking for her own assault. According to Amir's study, the police tend to believe that a woman without a good reputation cannot be raped. The rape victim is usually submitted to countless questions about her own sexual mores and behaviour by the police. This preoccupation is partially justified by the legal requirements for prosecution in a rape case. The rape victim must have been penetrated, and she must have made it clear to her assailant that she did not want penetration (unless of course she is unconscious). A refusal to accompany a man to some isolated place to allow him to touch her does not, in the eyes of the court, constitute rape. She must have said 'no' at the crucial genital moment. And the rape victim, to qualify as such, must also have put up a physical struggle – unless she can prove that to do so would have been to endanger her life.

But the zealous interest the police frequently exhibit in the physical details of a rape case is only partially explained by the requirements of the court. A woman who was raped in Berkeley was asked to tell the story of her rape four different times 'right out in the street', while her assailant was escaping. She was then required to submit to a pelvic examination to prove that penetration had taken place. Later, she was taken to the police station where she was asked the same questions again: 'Were you forced?' 'Did he penetrate?' 'Are you sure your life was in danger and you had no other choice?' This woman had been pulled off the street by a man who held a 10-inch knife at her throat and forcibly raped her. She was raped at midnight and was not able to return to her home until five in the morning. Police contacted her twice again in the next week, once by telephone at two in the morning and once at four in the morning. In her words, 'The rape was probably the least traumatic incident of the whole evening. If I'm ever raped again . . . I wouldn't report it to the police because of all the degradation . . .'

If white women are subjected to unnecessary and often hostile questioning after having been raped, third world women are often not believed at all. According to the white male ethos (which is not only sexist but racist), third world women are defined from birth as 'impure'. Thus the white male is provided with a pool of women who are fair game for sexual imperialism. Third world women frequently do not report rape and for good reason. When blues singer Billie Holliday was 10 years old, she was taken off to a local house by a neighbour and raped. Her mother brought the police to rescue her, and she was taken to the local police station crying and bleeding:

> When we got there, instead of treating me and Mom like somebody who called the cops for help, they treated me like I'd killed somebody. . . . I guess they had me figured for having enticed this old goat into the whorehouse. . . . All I know for sure is they threw me into a cell . . . a fat white matron . . . saw I was still bleeding, she felt sorry for me and gave me a couple glasses of milk. But nobody else did anything for me except give me filthy looks and snicker to themselves.
>
> After a couple of days in a cell they dragged me into a court. Mr Dick got sentenced to five years. They sentenced me to a Catholic institution.

Clearly the white man's chivalry is aimed only to protect the chastity of 'his' women.

As a final irony, that same system of sexual values from which chivalry is derived has also provided womankind with an unwritten code of behaviour, called femininity, which makes a feminine woman the perfect victim of sexual aggression. If being chaste does not ward off the possibility of assault, being feminine certainly increases the chances that it will succeed. To be submissive is to defer to masculine strength; is to lack muscular development or any interest in defending oneself; is to let doors be opened, to have one's arm held when crossing the street. To be feminine is to wear shoes which make it difficult to run; skirts which inhibit one's stride; underclothes which inhibit the circulation. Is it not an intriguing observation that those very clothes which are thought to be flattering to the female and attractive to the male are those which make it impossible for a woman to defend herself against aggression?

Each girl as she grows into womanhood is taught fear. Fear is the form in which the female internalizes both chivalry and the double standard. Since, biologically speaking, women in fact have the same if not greater potential for sexual expression as do men, the woman who is taught that she must behave differently from a man must also learn to distrust her own carnality. She must deny her own feelings and learn not to act from them. She fears herself. This is the essence of passivity and, of course, a woman's passivity is not simply sexual but functions to cripple her from self-expression in every area of her life.

Passivity itself prevents a woman from ever considering her own potential for self-defence and forces her to look to men for protection. The woman is taught fear, but this time fear of the other; and yet her only relief from this fear is to seek out the other. Moreover, the passive woman is taught to regard herself as impotent, unable to act, unable even to perceive, in no way self-sufficient, and finally, as the object and not the subject of human behaviour. It is in this sense that a woman is deprived of the status of a human being. She is not free to be.

III

Since Ibsen's Nora slammed the door on her patriarchical husband, woman's attempt to be free has been more or less fashionable. In this nineteenth-century portrait of a woman leaving her marriage, Nora tells her husband, 'Our home has been nothing but a playroom. I have been your doll-wife just as at home I was papa's doll-child.' And, at least on the stage, 'The Doll's House' crumbled, leaving audiences with hope for the fate of the modern woman. And today, as in the past, womankind has not lacked examples of liberated women to emulate: Emma Goldman, Greta Garbo and Isadora Duncan all denounced marriage and the double standard, and believed their right to freedom included sexual independence; but still their example has not affected the lives of millions of women who continue to marry, divorce and remarry, living out their lives dependent on the status and economic power of men. Patriarchy still holds the average woman prisoner not because she lacks the courage of an Isadora Duncan, but because the material conditions of her life prevent her from being anything but an object.

In the *Elementary Structures of Kinship,* Claude Levi-Strauss gives to marriage this universal description, 'It is always a system of exchange that we find at the origin of the rules of marriage.' In this system of exchange, a woman is the 'most precious possession'. Levi-Strauss continues that the custom of including women as booty in the marketplace is still so general that 'a whole volume would not be sufficient to enumerate instances of it.' Levi-Strauss makes it clear that he does not exclude Western Civilization from his definition of 'universal' and cites examples from modern wedding ceremonies. (The marriage ceremony is still one in which the husband and wife become one, and 'that one is the husband'.)

The legal proscription against rape reflects this possessory view of women. An article in the 1952–53 *Yale Law Journal* describes the legal rationale behind laws against rape:

> In our society sexual taboos, often enacted into law, buttress a system of monogamy based upon the law of 'free bargaining' of the potential spouses. Within this process the woman's power to withhold or grant sexual access is an important bargaining weapon.

Presumably then, laws against rape are intended to protect the right of a woman, not for physical self-determination, but for physical 'bargaining'. The article goes on to explain explicitly why the preservation of the bodies of women is important to men:

> The consent standard in our society does more than protect a significant item of social currency for women; it fosters, and is in turn bolstered by, a masculine pride in the exclusive possession of a sexual object. The consent of a woman to sexual intercourse awards the man a privilege of bodily access, a personal 'prize', whose value is enhanced by sole ownership. An additional reason for the man's condemnation of rape may be found in the threat to his status from a decrease in the 'value' of his sexual possession which would result from forcible violation.

The passage concludes by making clear whose interest the law is designed to protect. 'The man responds to this undercutting of his status as *possessor* of the girl with hostility toward the rapist; no other restitution device is available. The law of rape provides an orderly outlet for his vengeance.' Presumably the female victim in any case will have been sufficiently socialized so as not to consciously feel any strong need for vengeance. If she does feel this need, society does not speak to it.

The laws against rape exist to protect rights of the male as possessor of the female body, and not the right of the female over her own body. Even without this enlightening passage from the *Yale Law Journal*, the laws themselves are clear: In no state can a man be accused of raping his wife. How can any man steal what already belongs to him? It is in the sense of rape as theft of another man's property that Kate Millett writes, 'Traditionally rape has been viewed as an offense one male commits against another – a matter of abusing his woman.' In raping another man's woman, a man may aggrandize his own manhood and concurrently reduce that of another man. Thus a man's honour is not subject directly to rape, but only indirectly, through 'his' woman.

If the basic social unit is the family, in which the woman is a possession of her husband, the superstructure of society is a male hierarchy, in which men dominate other men (or patriarchal families dominate other patriarchal families). And it is no small irony that, while the very social fabric of our male-dominated culture denies women equal access to political, economic and legal power, the literature, myth and humour of our culture depict women not only as the power behind the throne, but the real source of the oppression of men. The religious version of this fairy tale blames Eve for both carnality and eating of the tree of knowledge, at the same time making her gullible to the obvious devices of a serpent. Adam, of course, is merely the trusting victim of love. Certainly this is a biased story. But no more biased than the one television audiences receive today from the latest slick comedians. Through a media which is owned by men, censored by a state dominated by men, all the evils of this social system which make a man's life unpleasant are blamed upon 'the wife'. The theory is: were it not for the female who waits and plots to 'trap' the male into marriage, modern man would be able to achieve Olympian freedom. She is made the scapegoat for a system which is in fact run by men.

Nowhere is this more clear than in the white racist use of the concept of white womanhood. The white male's open rape of black women, coupled with his overweening concern for the chastity and protection of his wife and daughters, represents an extreme of sexist and racist hypocrisy. While on the one hand she was held up as the standard for purity and virtue, on the other the Southern white woman was never asked if she wanted to be on a pedestal, and in fact any deviance from the male-defined standards for white womanhood was treated severely. (It is a powerful commentary on American racism that the historical role of Blacks as slaves, and thus possessions without power, has robbed black women of legal and economic protection through marriage. Thus black women in Southern society and in the ghettoes of the North have long been easy game for white rapists.) The fear that black men would rape white women was classic paranoia. Quoting from Ann Breen's unpublished study of racism and sexism in the South, '*The New South: White Man's Country*', Frederick Douglass legitimately points out that, had the black man wished to rape white women, he had ample opportunity to do so during the Civil War when white women, the wives, sisters, daughters and mothers of the rebels, were left in the care of Blacks. But yet not a single act of rape was committed during this time. The Ku Klux Klan, who tarred and feathered black men and lynched them in honour of the purity of white womanhood, also applied tar and feathers to a Southern white woman accused of bigamy, which leads one to suspect that Southern white men were not so much outraged at the violation of the woman as a person, in the few instances where rape was actually committed by black men, but at the violation of his property rights. In the situation where a black man was found to be having sexual relations with a white woman, the white woman could exercise skin-privilege, and claim that she had been raped, in which case the black man was lynched. But if she did not claim rape, she herself was subject to lynching.

In constructing the myth of white womanhood so as to justify the lynching and oppression of black men and women, the white male has created a convenient symbol of his own power which has resulted in black hostility toward the white 'bitch', accompanied by a fear on the part of many white women of the black rapist. Moreover it is not surprising that after being told for two centuries that he wants to rape white women, black men have begun to actually commit that act. But it is crucial to note that the frequency of this practice is outrageously exaggerated in the white mythos. Ninety percent of reported rape is intra- not inter-racial.

In *Soul on Ice*, Eldridge Cleaver has described the mixing of a rage against white power with the internalized sexism of a black man raping a white woman.

> Somehow I arrived at the conclusion that, as a matter of principle, it was of paramount importance for me to have an antagonistic, ruthless attitude toward white women . . . Rape was an insurrectionary act. It delighted me that I was defying and trampling

upon the white man's law, upon his system of values and that I was
defiling his women – and this point, I believe, was the most
satisfying to me because I was very resentful over the historical fact
of how the white man has used the black woman.

Thus a black man uses white women to take out his rage against white
men. But, in fact, whenever a rape of a white woman by a black man
does take place, it is again the white man who benefits. First, the act
itself terrorizes the white woman and makes her more dependent on
the white male for protection. Then, if the woman prosecutes her
attacker, the white man is afforded legal opportunity to exercise overt
racism. Of course, the knowledge of the rape helps to perpetuate two
myths which are beneficial to white male rule – the bestiality of the
black man and the desirability of white women. Finally, the white
man surely benefits because he himself is not the object of attack – he
has been allowed to stay in power.

Indeed, the existence of rape in any form is beneficial to the ruling
class of white males. For rape is a kind of terrorism which severely
limits the freedom of women and makes women dependent on men.
Moreover, in the act of rape, the rage that one man may harbour
toward another higher in the male hierarchy can be deflected toward
a female scapegoat. For every man there is always someone lower on
the social scale on whom he can take out his aggressions. And that is
any woman alive.

This oppressive attitude towards women finds its institutional-
ization in the traditional family. For it is assumed that a man 'wears
the pants' in his family – he exercises the option of rule whenever he
so chooses. Not that he makes all the decisions – clearly women make
most of the important day-to-day decisions in a family. But when a
conflict of interest rises, it is the man's interest which will prevail. His
word, in itself, is more powerful. He lords it over his wife in the same
way his boss lords it over him, so that the very process of exercising his
power becomes as important an act as obtaining whatever it is his
power can get for him. This notion of power is key to the male ego in
this culture, for the two acceptable measures of masculinity are a
man's power over women and his power over other men. A man may
boast to his friends that 'I have 20 men working for me.' It is also
aggrandizement of his ego if he has the financial power to clothe his
wife in furs and jewels. And, if a man lacks the wherewithal to acquire
such power, he can always express his rage through equally masculine
activities – rape and theft. Since male society defines the female as a

possession, it is not surprising that the felony most often committed together with rape is theft. As the following classic tale of rape points out, the elements of theft, violence and forced sexual relations merge into an indistinguishable whole.

The woman who told the following story was acquainted with the man who tried to rape her. When the man learned that she was going to be staying alone for the weekend, he began early in the day a polite campaign to get her to go out with him. When she continued to refuse his request, his chivalrous mask dropped away:

I had locked all the doors because I was afraid, and I don't know how he got in; it was probably through the screen door. When I woke up, he was shaking my leg. His eyes were red, and I knew he had been drinking or smoking. I thought I would try to talk my way out of it. He started by saying that he wanted to sleep with me, and then he got angrier and angrier, until he started to say 'I want pussy', 'I want pussy'. Then, I got scared and tried to push him away. That's when he started to force himself on me. It was awful. It was the most humiliating, terrible feeling. He was forcing my legs apart and ripping my clothes off. And it was painful. I did fight him – he was slightly drunk and I was able to keep him away. I had taken judo a few years back, but I was afraid to throw a chop for fear that he'd kill me. I could see he was getting more and more violent. I was thinking wildly of some way to get out of this alive, and then I said to him, 'Do you want money? I'll give you money.' We had money but I was also thinking that if I got to the back room I could telephone the police – as if the police would have even helped. It was a stupid thing to think of because obviously he would follow me. And he did. When he saw me pick up the phone, he tried to tie the cord around my neck. I screamed at him that I did have the money in another room, that I was going to call the police because I was scared, but that I would never tell anybody what happened. It would be an absolute secret. He said, 'okay', and I went to get the money. But when he got it, all of a sudden he got this crazy look in his eye and he said to me, 'Now I'm going to kill you.' Then I started saying my prayers. I knew there was nothing I could do. He started to hit me – I still wasn't sure if he wanted to rape me at this point – or just to kill me. He was hurting me, but hadn't yet gotten me into a stranglehold because he was still drunk and off balance. Somehow we pushed into the kitchen where I kept looking at this big knife. But I didn't pick it up. Somehow, no matter how much I hated him at that moment, I still couldn't imagine putting the knife in his flesh, and then I was afraid he would grab it and stick it into me. Then he was hitting me again and somehow we pushed through the back door of the kitchen and onto the porch steps. We fell down the steps and that's when he started to strangle me. He was on top of me. He just went on and on until finally I lost consciousness. I did scream, though my screams sounded like whispers to me. But what happened was that a cab driver happened by and frightened him away. The cab driver revived me – I was out only a minute at the most. And then I ran across the street and I grabbed the woman who was our neighbour and screamed at her, 'Am I alive? Am I still alive?'

Rape is an act of aggression in which the victim is denied her self-determination. It is an act of violence which, if not actually followed by beatings or murder, nevertheless always carries with it the threat of death. And finally, rape is a form of mass terrorism, for the victims of rape are chosen indiscriminately, but the propagandists for male supremacy broadcast that it is women who cause rape by being unchaste or in the wrong place at the wrong time – in essence, by behaving as though they were free.

The threat of rape is used to deny women employment. (In California, the Berkeley Public Library, until pushed by the Federal Employment Practices Commission, refused to hire female shelvers because of perverted men in the stacks.) The fear of rape keeps women off the streets at night. Keeps women at home. Keeps women passive and modest for fear that they be thought provocative.

It is part of human dignity to be able to defend oneself, and women are learning. Some women have learned karate; some to shoot guns. And yet we will not be free until the threat of rape and the atmosphere of violence is ended, and to end that the nature of male behaviour must change.

But rape is not an isolated act that can be rooted out from patriarchy without ending patriarchy itself. The same men and power structure who victimize women are engaged in the act of raping Vietnam, raping black people and the very earth we live upon. Rape is a classic art of domination where, in the words of Kate Millett, 'the emotions of hatred, contempt, and the desire to break or violate personality,' take place. This breaking of the personality characterizes modern life itself. No simple reforms can eliminate rape. As the symbolic expression of the white male hierarchy, rape is the quintessential act of our civilization, one which, Valerie Solanis warns, is in danger of 'humping itself to death'.

Women and Children Last

When I wrote this article in 1972, my daughter was only four years old; my work had only just begun to be published, and I worked at several part-time jobs. Our life then was difficult. Though my life has changed, the conditions I described here for women and children have not improved. Because of the economy, and the present administration's attack on government aid, these conditions have become worse. America lets her children suffer neglect, malnutrition and starvation. This essay was published in 1973 by Ramparts Magazine. [*Under the title 'Confessions of a Single Mother', which I did not like!*]

'Woman with a broken foot and a two-and-a-half-year-old child needs a woman to help three hours a day to make meal, get child ready for bed.' When I read that ad in our local women's newsletter, I felt I had been there before. I remembered the last time I had a serious illness, sitting in bed with my red telephone book, leafing through the pages for someone who might help take care of my daughter. I shudder at the memory. Where can I begin to explain?

I am writing about women who are divorced or who never married, women who are raising children alone. Only 35 percent of this nation is made up of nuclear families, yet the illusion persists that to live in a nuclear family is 'normal'. Though the number of families headed by women is rising more rapidly than the number of all families, we are still pariahs. Our economic survival is marginal. Our needs are not met or even recognized.

Needs. Like what does a mother do when she has a broken foot? Or what does a mother do when she has to go to work and her child is sick? I remember the day my daughter woke up with a stomach ache and I took her to the doctor for a urine sample. I had cancelled a morning hour of teaching, thus forgoing my salary. (I, like many single mothers, work part-time, and therefore have no sick leave.) At the doctor's office my daughter could produce no urine. We agonized for an hour and a half. 'You'll have to come back later in the day,' the receptionist told me. But my daughter's stomach ache had vanished, and I had hoped to take her to day-care and return to work. 'Can't I get the sample at home?' I asked. 'I can't come back today, I have to work.' The receptionist picked up a buzzing phone before she darted righteously at me, 'Your daughter's health should come first.' 'She has to eat, too,' I mumbled as we hurried out the door.

We are always doing something wrong. If we go to work, someone is available at every hour to make us feel guilty for not being at home with our children. If we live on welfare we are the object of derisive political commentary, of the unending curiosity of social workers, of the Kafkaesque illogicality of bureaucratic rules. In either case we are likely to be poor. We are likely to be tired to the point of illness, and despite all our efforts, we are likely to be the silent witnesses to the sufferings of our children.

Statistics yield up some part of the truth. There are 5.6 million families in the U.S. headed by women, more than one family in ten. Almost half of these families live in poverty whether the mother is working or not.

And there are more statistics, which tell the same story. For instance, we make up 35 percent of all families living in poverty. Of families earning under $2000 yearly, 63 percent are headed by women, but of families earning $10,000 or more yearly, only two percent are headed by women.

But these figures only represent probabilities. They show nothing of the struggle to survive, the battle a woman goes through, with the divorce courts, the county welfare office, the job market, to find day-care, to somehow get through each day, each year, and feed herself and her children.

This is supposed to be a child-centred nation. We pride ourselves on a tender, even mawkish attitude toward children. And it is a special point of the American male ethos that a man, no matter how indifferent he may be to his neighbour's children, supports his own family. Yet once there is a divorce, the average American male seems to be able to shed his paternal concern as naturally as a reptile shedding his coat in the proper season.

According to popular myth, almost always disadvantageous to women, men after divorce are hounded into poverty by avaricious, lazy and luxury-seeking females. The facts argue differently. According to a report written by the Citizen's Advisory Council on the Status of Women, 'The rights to support of women and children are much more limited than is generally known and enforcement is very inadequate . . . fathers by and large are contributing less than half the support of children in divided families; and that alimony and child support awards are very difficult to collect.'

The logic of the court is based on an assumption which is not in fact true: equality of the sexes. The court assumes that the earning powers and time to use those earning powers of both the mother and the father of the children are equal. The idea that a mother might be paid for her child rearing and housekeeping activities is one totally foreign to the court.

The implications of these assumptions in the lives of real people usually result in poverty for the mother and her children, but not for the children's father. Let us take Mr and Mrs Smith for an example. Mr Smith earns about $640 a month, the national average for a full-time male worker in 1968. He is ordered by the court to pay $125 for the support of his child. If one deducts that amount from his salary, Mr Smith is left with $515 a month, with which to support himself alone.

Mrs Smith and her child are not quite so well off. Of course she cannot live on $125 a month, so she invests this child support payment in full-time day-care (which usually costs from $100 to $150 a month) and she seeks employment. Notwithstanding the fact that unemployment is a third higher for women than for men, let us say she finds a job and begins to earn the median national salary for a full-time working woman in 1968, that is about $370 a month. (In fact the average salary for a woman with children is somewhat lower: $333 a month.) Thus, both Mrs Smith and her child live on less than 4/5 of what Mr Smith alone has.

I had my own experience with the California divorce courts. As I sat in court awaiting our case, watching the other divorce cases before us, my faith in blind justice began to wane, and by the end of the day it was dead. While my female lawyer and I sat surrounded by male lawyers, we listened as the male judge counselled a man and wife to continue living together under the same roof in separate bedrooms as a solution to the man's money troubles. The wife was opposed to this; the husband not. Her lawyer pleaded that the husband's presence seriously disturbed the children and that, in a fight, he tended to violence. None of this cut any ice with the judge, who was principally concerned about the husband's credit rating.

Under this judge's pervasive male logic, I fared no better. He was told that I was going to graduate school, teaching part-time, and writing for a small living, but still having financial difficulty. He suggested, as a solution, that I take my three-year-old daughter out of day-care, and save that cost. He saw no reason why I could not continue work for my Master's degree, teach, write, and watch after a three-year-old at the same time. I stared around his silent, orderly courtroom, protected from disturbance by armed guards, antiseptically clean, obedient to his every judicial command, and wished suddenly for the room to be filled with babies and toddlers and kindergarten children, screaming, turning over the shiny flag stands, gurgling scatological nonsense to this man in black robes, despite all the rappings of his little gavel. The dream faded and the judge told me, with a fatherly smile on his lips, that *his* wife never had any day-care.

But Mrs Smith and I must count ourselves blessed, for many women, though they may receive a court order for child support, never actually receive any money.

A friend of mine, another single mother, after separation from her husband, was stranded during the winter in a house so flimsy one could see daylight through cracks in the walls. She needed blankets and shoes for her children; they all had colds. She called legal aid and was referred to a lawyer. Her lawyer advised her to open an account at Montgomery Ward and charge whatever she needed to her husband's name. She did.

Eventually her case came to court and her husband was ordered to pay child support of $150, $50 for each child. But he left the state and never sent anything for the children except an occasional box of toys. From one of these boxes, she managed to track down her ex-husband, but when she informed the court, they did nothing.

Finally she went on welfare and was presented with two large bills. One from Montgomery Ward for $200 and one from her lawyer for $300. Her welfare grant was $176.

Rarely is child support or alimony adequate enough for a woman and her children to live on, even if it is paid, and so to stay off welfare most women must find work. But before she can accept work, a mother must find decent day-care, and her search is often fruitless. In Berkeley, supposed to be a city providing better than average services for children, although 10,000 children need day-care, facilities exist for only 2000. An article in the *New Republic* estimates that nationally, 50 percent of the children of working parents are left in unlicensed centres, with relatives or alone.

Recently I heard a story about a child, part of that 50 percent, who is the playmate of a friend's children. Her mother had been attending secretarial school during the day, hoping that better skills might find her work. Her welfare grant left no money for babysitting, so she left her five-year-old daughter at home alone. She had taught the child how to cook her own breakfast and one morning, when the little girl was alone, the stove failed to ignite; she leaned over the burner and the gas fumes exploded. Her clothes caught fire. Fortunately she ran down the hallway in her burning clothing and jumped into a shower. She saved her life, but now, from her waist to her neck, she has only scar tissue. Her nipples were burned off entirely.

I had my own experience with an unlicensed day-care centre. Because my daughter's regular day-care teacher was on vacation, I was searching for a temporary centre, and went one day to observe 'The Boat', an informal arrangement described as 'free' experimental, spontaneous and every other word one associates vaguely with Summerhill.

I knocked at the screen door and after several minutes was told to come in by what sounded like a child's voice. My three-year-old daughter and I walked into a group of ten or more children whose ages varied from infancy to about six years. They were sitting in a semi-circle, oddly, doing nothing at all, except to stare at us in mute hostility. My daughter quickly clung to the end of my blouse and disappeared behind my legs.

I called somewhere into the guts of the house for an adult, hoping that the children would begin to play with the toys scattered about the room to talk to each other, or even to scream. They remained silent until a tall bearded man appeared. He, like the children, did not smile but instead gave us a surly distrustful look. Before we could speak, one of the children, an older, thin, dark boy spilled his soda pop on the floor. Though the spill was clearly an accident, the man called out in an angry voice, 'Goddamn it, what did ya have to do that for? What a drag!' The child obediently answered that he would clean up the mess and ran toward the kitchen. 'Yeah, but that doesn't help me man!' the man answered, irrationally. I began to feel intimidated.

In a rather choked voice I explained to him that I had come because I might want to leave my daughter there. I asked if any activities were

ever planned for the children, waving my hand to indicate the group
that still sat and stared in silence, as if they were our jury. He looked
at me in amazement, and then looked away, as if his attention were on
the inner eye, and proceeded to lecture me about allowing children
freedom (he said, 'do your own thing') and not forcing them to read
(not 'laying trips').

I tried to engage him in conversation, but unfortunately, aside from
an abundance of white, male, hip argot, he was inarticulate. He had
never read Summerhill, and he admitted, had not 'been around'
children for very long.

In the course of our talk, all of the children, except for my
daughter, had run out the screen door into a front yard that was not
fenced. I watched them disperse over the neighbourhood. 'You don't
have a fence?' I asked, as subtly as I could manage. 'We don't believe
in fences,' he asserted defiantly.

By now, my daughter was crying to me, 'Don't leave me, Mommy.'
As we walked together to our car, we passed by the children, now at
least animate, playing a game of tag over the neighbourhood lawns. A
baby in diapers, part of the group, was making a shaky way toward
the sidewalk, and a moving truck was barrelling down the street at 30
miles an hour.

Where public day-care and extended care (after school) facilities
exist, the places are few and far between. Like most public services
for children, the waiting list can be as long as a childhood.

And the mother who is looking for work is faced with this example
of Catch-22 – in order to be put on a waiting list, she must be
employed. Yet, in order to be employed, she must have day-care.
(Recently I found myself in a shouting match with my food stamp
worker. She told me I could not deduct the cost of child care from my
income while I was looking for a teaching position.)

And if a woman on welfare is seeking training so that she can get off
welfare, her welfare grant provides nothing for child care. With a
matching grant from the Department of Health, Education and Welfare, a handful of parents at Grove Street College have set up a
day-care centre to look after their children while they are in school.
The existence of this centre is constantly in question because money
must be raised from the community by the parents themselves. The
parents are already going to school, caring for children and running
the centre, and the community has very little money.

Still, the centre allows one woman to try to get past the welfare system. Janet is a young black woman with a two-and-a-half-year old son. She is a student at Grove Street College, learning business and secretarial skills. Though she earns high grades in language, history and sociology as well, she is deadly realistic about the employment possibilities for women.

She puts her son in the Grove Street Centre while she is in class, and in turn, contributes several hours of her week working in the centre. She does most of her studying in her two-room apartment with her son, frequently interrupting her work to pull him out of trouble, change a diaper, or give him a slap on the wrist.

She and her son live on a welfare grant of $176 a month. She pays $100 for rent, $26 for $64 worth of food stamps, and then the gas, water and garbage bills. She has no money left for transportation; she and her son hitchhike back and forth to school.

While we were talking one evening in her kitchen she got a telephone call from someone who wanted to buy her couch. In a bad moment she had put it up for sale, but now she changed her mind. Without her couch, by now already fourth hand, she would have only two kitchen chairs to sit on. But she was worried about an optometry bill. Medical had turned down her request for glasses. Since she does not drive, they told her, she did not need to see clearly.

If Janet finds a job as a secretary, she may have a starting salary of $550. At first glance, that sounds like an immense improvement over $176.

But one must deduct expenses. To begin with, $125 a month for day-care, and another $20 for babysitting. (She probably, at the very least, has to hire a sitter for the rush hour, since most day-care centres close at five pm). She will have car payments if she has a new car, or repair bills, if she has a second-hand car, gas and insurance, all amounting to at least another $100. Her food bill will be high since she cannot spend a great deal of time cooking or shopping, probably at least $80. Her rent will be at least $175 (if she does not stay in her current, ramshackle apartment in one of Oakland's industrial areas). Added to that she will have utility bills of $30. And then, if she is a secretary, she has to dress well. Stockings alone cost $10 a month, cleaning another $10, clothes at least $15.

But when her expenses are added up, they already exceed her income! And we have made no provisions for taxes, medical bills, dental bills, books, movies, toys, a television, furniture, anything in life which yields a little pleasure.

Did you know, for instance, that both zoos in the Bay area charge admission? That all the public pools in Berkeley charge at least $.50 a day for children and $1.00 for adults. Not to mention art classes, or summer camp.

But she will not have much time to spend money. She will be free of the welfare system – she will not have to reveal every detail of her life to a stranger, nor subject every personal decision to the scrutiny of the State – but that is where her freedom will end. She will have no time for freedom. She will have to be up by 6.30 in order to have her child to a day-care centre by 7.30 and herself to work by 8.00 am.

She will work until 5.00, unless she is asked to work over-time (a request secretaries often cannot refuse). She may, if she does not have to commute, be home by 5.30. Then she has to pick up her son, shop, prepare dinner, do the dishes, bathe her child, read him a story, put him to bed. She might be finished by 9.00 pm, free to pay the bills, mend clothes, do a wash, answer mail, or even fall asleep.

On the weekends she can vacuum, scrub the kitchen floor, clean the bathroom, or work in the garden. Even if she or her child do not get sick, she has a difficult life. Still, she will be living in a house that isn't standing at a forty-five degree angle. And she will have a large part of her dignity back. She will not have to tell her employer every detail of her life, itemize every penny she spends, or yield to his suspicious glance her bank books, rent slips and birth certificate.

Another friend of mine, a poet and a writer, didn't make it in her attempt to get off welfare. She told me the whole story one morning over a cup of herbal tea, while our children played with blocks in the next room. (I will call her 'Sarah' and her son 'Mark'. I am using no real names in this story; welfare recipients all know the value of anonymity.)

For the first month after Mark was born, Sarah lived on welfare. She decided that she wanted to work, but since she had no secretarial skills, she had to accept piece work as a process server, earning $2.00 for each process. Because she had to maintain a car and support a live-in babysitter, she found she was working 80 hours a week. She never saw her son.

After almost a year of this existence, she decided to go back to school. She hoped that with a degree she could find work that meant more to her and gave her more time to be with her son. She reduced her working hours by half, to forty hours a week, applied for and received a bank loan, and enrolled for fifteen units of undergraduate study. Within two weeks, living on this schedule, she suffered a complete mental breakdown. Friends who witnessed her during that time told her she would sit in a corner and cry. She does not remember.

She was hospitalized for a short time and then she went home, to live with her family. While her mother took care of her son, she was able to rest.

After she got back on her feet, she returned to school with a second bank loan and help from her parents. She did very well; she was close to graduation with an A minus average. She had wanted to continue an academic career, and began to apply for graduate scholarships; her parents were not wealthy and could no longer support her. 'That's when discrimination against women really hit me,' she said. All of her male friends, many of whom had poorer academic records, received offers for scholarships. She received none. She quit school.

She is living on welfare again now. She lives with other women who share food, and the work of keeping a house and child care with her. They are an island of disbelief in a culture that believes children are private property.

'God bless the child who's got his own.'

In this society, to be a mature adult is to be cynical, is to understand that reverence exists only in relation to power, is to know that whenever a group, like the very young or the very old, is vulnerable, they are the least powerful, and in truth, sentimentality to the contrary, the least revered. (Consider that among the nation's poor, the elderly and children under sixteen make up the largest sector.)

In our society, consequently, it is a child's parents who must speak for her, or for him. And thus, the child who has a father does better in this world because women have no power. Even among women, the woman who is raising children alone has a soft voice, or no voice at all. She is too busy struggling for survival to make herself felt as a political presence. She is both silent and invisible. Yet her silence, our silence, helps to keep us in our place.

The child who is a victim of this powerlessness does not always experience direct prejudice. Though in many parts of this country a child may still be taunted or excluded because her mother was never married, or his parents are divorced, in many places, overt hostility has disappeared. Yet the child experiences a more subtle and perhaps more difficult kind of exclusion. Children do not need swimming lessons, a Saturday at the movies, summer camp, or braces on their teeth. But when they grow up in a world where other children are given these things as a matter of course, what do they feel? A sixteen-year-old may be able to understand budgets and frugality and the job market, but can a three-year-old, a seven-year-old? Do they feel they are less loved, or do they feel as I did, myself the child of a divorce, that the children with newer clothes are somehow intrinsically superior?

And the effect of inadequate day-care, schooling and after school care may be even more devastating. For it is during childhood that the adult psyche develops. What may be simply unhappiness in an adult's life, in a child's life can cause irreparable damage. Yet there is no evidence that day-care in itself is bad for children; indeed, the facts argue the contrary, that children in loving and creative day-care develop both emotionally and intellectually at a much faster rate than do children at home. In a sense, children kept at home alone with their mothers are being deprived of social contact.

I have come to believe that the contention that children should remain in the home with their mothers until school age is, in the mouths of many people, simply a rationalization because society does not want to be bothered. Good day-care centres cost money, and take a great deal of effort. In the same year, President Nixon vetoed a bill for child-care claiming that he wanted to protect the nuclear family, and initiated a programme which would force welfare mothers to put their children into day-care centres and seek work. This later plan, ironically, is now under criticism from the Department of Health, Education and Welfare because the cost of day-care and job training would, to quote the *S.F. Chronicle*, 'exceed the value to society of the work such mothers would perform.' Clearly no one was concerned about the welfare of the children.

This is a nation, and a world power, run by and for the benefit of a minority, mostly grown-up white men, who complain louder than all the children in the world about a meagre welfare programme while they themselves steadily waste the world's resources in pollution and warfare.

Those of us who care for children must begin to make ourselves heard.

Feminism and Motherhood

What follows was written in 1974 for **Momma,** *the newspaper for single mothers, in answer to a request for a feminist theory of motherhood. These notes are a collection of insights, the beginnings of a theory, records of pieces of my life. When I wrote this, I had been divorced for six years. My daughter was eight years old. There is no formal theory here; the work is incomplete; more needs to be written over a much longer period of time. And so I call these pieces of a future work: 'Notes on the Subject of Feminism and Motherhood'.*

On this subject – Feminism and Motherhood – very little has been written.

I am hesitant to begin anywhere. My words come up out of frustration. They are often blurted out. And then I do not record them. What is said must be so right. Guilt surrounds me. I am angry at my mother for not mothering me. There, it is said. I am angry – this is harder to say – at my daughter for always interrupting me. Generation after generation it is the same story. My daughter says to me one night, 'You don't like me because I always bother you.' I carry this around with me, these words, a sorrow so deep to express it would be to fly apart.

I have been asked if I had the choice again, would I have a child? This is an absurd question. I am not the same person I was before I had a child. That young woman would not understand me.

What did you learn from having a child?
    I learned vulnerability. So simple, really, the simplicity of it amazed me, tears, my daughter's tears, her pain, her fears, and that I could comfort her, that her body relaxed against mine, that she

learned to smile from me, that she was wholly unashamed of her hungers, her tempers, that there was no line of explanation between joy and sorrow but experience itself. The vulnerability and the clear logic of her flesh was a revelation to me. One morning, shortly after her birth, I lay on top of the bed crying because I realized one day I would have to explain death to her. Clearly in all her innocence, she did not deserve death.

'I think you are having diarrhoea,' my friend said to her. And Becky began to cry as if she were terrified. 'No, no,' she said, 'I don't have that. Only old people get that.' She ran to the hallway to hide. My friend and I quarrelled. She thought I spoiled her, gave into her crying, and that was often true. But often not. If there are two adults, I am always her defender.

I ran after her and, kneeling, grabbed her with both my hands. 'Becky,' I said (only guessing at what I thought was wrong), 'diarrhoea has nothing to do with dying. Everyone gets diarrhoea. It's a kind of ca ca.' Slowly she understood. Slowly she separated the two words in her mind. That a pun could cause such terror!

Is it because no one shares the daily work of raising a child with me? I ask. Or have I changed? Is it because I have too much work and too little time? Or because I myself feel unloved. Or tired. Now I am quarrelling with myself and I am not accusing myself of spoiling her. I don't listen enough, I tell myself. I don't spend enough time with her; I have this argument with myself as I try to make telephone calls, do laundry, write out the bills, grade papers, type poems or letters, and she is running in and out of the room with questions and demands. I call them interruptions.

Very little has been written on the subject of motherhood.

What did you learn from having a child?

I was alone all day in the house with an infant. I began to watch daytime television. I watched soap operas. Women are always having surgery on daytime TV. I began to identify with those women. I began to feel as if I had had a lobotomy. I had always relied on being able to sleep long hours before. Now my daughter woke me every three hours. I had loved conversation before. Now I was alone in a house with an infant most of the time. And when I went out, always with my child and husband (I did not exist apart from them), I found I had lost my speech. I was inarticulate. I imagined people thought me stupid. I felt stunned, dumb. But there was something I had wanted to tell. Something profound.

I learned what it is like not to be able to speak.

Birthing, raising my daughter through infancy to childhood was a hard process of knowledge, a kind of physical endurance for us both, bearing knowledge of survival; of the simplest facts of eating, sleeping, and the struggle to exist. All around me floated archetypal mothers, Italian Madonnas, the red velvet framing their breasts as unstained as their smiles, young, carefree-looking women running in slow motion across fields, swooping to caress angelic children, unbearably lithe models grinning over clean babies in clean blankets. I could not see through them. My own experience waited blind and dumb, unspoken.

I don't have a feminist theory of motherhood. I have only these notes, these paragraphs, some insights. Curiously, they take the form of another woman's writing about motherhood, *Momma*, by Alta: she has two young children. They take the form of René Clair's 'Leaves of Hypnos', the journal he wrote during the French Resistance. We are part of a resistance. For necessity does not stop long enough for us to analyze. We have only brief illuminations which we must record between interruptions, set down side by side, hoping to make sense of it all some day later.

And scrutiny is painful. Society's suggestion of guilt is involved. And too much suffocation. Too many contradictions. So that when a woman is finally free of her children's needs, she wants to forget. She does not want to face or express her rage. And rage must come before analysis. Even now I feel I want to escape this. It is said, 'I do not want to think about my children now.'

The way people don't want to think about poverty, or sickness or death. Or that mothers and children are not always protected. That a woman and her children are entitled to a roof, clothing, food is not birthright; to have these necessities a woman must be married to the father of her children, and he must be able and willing to provide for them. Children without fathers are called 'bastards' and most often live in poverty. On the question of the protection of women and children, one must ask which women and children are protected and why.

> July 16 . . . I told the children that I didn't have any bread, that
> they would have to drink their coffee plain . . . Everything that I
> find in the garbage I sell. . . I returned home, or rather to my
> shack, nervous and exhausted. I thought of the worrisome life that
> I led. Carrying paper, washing clothes for the children, staying in
> the street all day long. Yet I'm always lacking things. Vera doesn't
> have any shoes and doesn't like to go barefoot. (Carolina Maria de
> Jesus, *Child of the Dark*)

And if society does step in to take the place of the father, the woman
who accepts this aid must be humbled. Every detail of the welfare
system conspires to rob one of one's dignity, as if the troubles and the
weariness that belong to women raising children alone and in poverty
were not enough.

> My spirit never recovered from that insult, just like my heart never
> recovered from my husband's desertion, just like my body never
> recovered from being almost starved to death. I started to wither
> in that winter and each year found me more hacked and worn
> down than the year before. (Alice Walker, 'The Revenge of
> Hannah Kemhuff')

Over and over in what literature exists about mothers raising children
in poverty, one reads about the destruction of the spirit and the
bodies of those women.

> Money, she is thinking, sicknesses. Streets. Dirt. The children, my
> children. What is happening to them, what will be? My babies, my
> children. Outside no answer. Only the smell of earth, expectant of
> rain, the mysterious blue light that is on everything, the trees
> moving palsied against the sky, and strident, strained, breaking,
> the sound of a freight starting up. My children, the children.
>   Heavy to take up again, being poor and a mother. (Tillie Olsen,
> *Yonnondio*)

I remember that on hearing of the despoiling of Michelangelo's
'Pietà', I was not displeased. Part of me wanted that serene, unlined,
youthful face of the Madonna to be obliterated, or at least cracked, to
show some sign of having lived a life that is not easy.

Because even the life of the mother who is not poor is not easy.

Children in any circumstances demand a great deal of time and care, a large part of the life of the mother. The definition of motherhood in our culture is one in which the mother sacrifices herself to the child. She sacrifices her self. Her self is lost. The child becomes the centre of her life; the child's needs placed before her needs, until often, she lives in her child, through her child, placing her spirit in the child's body, until the merging of her self with the child's is complete.

> A young man begs his mother for her heart, which a betrothed of his has demanded as a gift; having torn it out of his mother's proffered breast, he races away with it; and as he stumbles, the heart falls to the ground, and he hears it question protectively, 'Did you hurt yourself, my son?' (Jewish Folk Tale as quoted in 'Portnoy's Mother's Complaint', by Pauline Bart, in *Woman in Sexist Society*)

When the children grow up and leave home, if the mother has sacrificed her self to them, she now loses it entirely. The person she gave her self to has now abandoned her. Her loss is absolute.

> It was not that she had not loved her babies, her children. The love – the passion of tending – had risen with the need like a torrent; and like a torrent drowned and immolated all else . . .
>
> On that torrent she had borne them to their own lives, and the river bed was desert long years now. Not there would she dwell, a memoried wraith . . . (Tillie Olsen, *Tell Me a Riddle*)

And we pretend that this sacrifice of years of the mother's life is for the child's benefit. But who benefits? Most children grow up to find their families are strangers, that they are people to visit out of a sense of obligation at best, or at worst, to hate and fear as destructive, and we have grown to accept this relationship between the adult child and the parent. We call this alienation natural.

Another insight to fit in a feminist analysis of motherhood: the sacrifice of the mother which is supposed to be for the child's benefit can destroy the child. If the mother sacrifices her self, so does the child sacrifice a self. Her love devours the child. Her value becomes repression, her protection, dominance.

And why is it in the case of women that we always blame the individual and not the social structure. That we see failure in discrete lives and do not question 'the way things are'.

The more I begin to look at my life as a woman, the more I take the stance of a startled anthropologist. Why does rape happen so frequently? Why do men rape women and not women men? Why do women and not men raise children? Why are the children and the mother unhappy? And finally, why are women blamed for this unhappiness?

In any given period of history, the laws of child custody have reflected conventional morality. In the 19th century a woman having a lover would lose her children to her husband, but the same behaviour in the husband would not even be grounds for divorce. In certain states of the Union a woman can today lose custody of her children for what is called 'promiscuity'. Homosexuality, still a taboo everywhere, is almost everywhere considered grounds for society to take the custody of a woman's children from her.

Over and over again I put the pieces together trying to find an analysis: that the paradigm mother, 'the Madonna', was a virgin; that motherhood implies a kind of asexuality; that mothers are symbols of purity. And I come to the conclusion, one conclusion, that the mother is required to make one other sacrifice. She must sacrifice her sexuality. (And this denial of her self is perhaps one of the most severe, most damaging, not only because of the physical pleasure found through sexuality, but because it is, in this society, the mode through which we reach other beings outside language, the only way we love with our physical selves, and it is from our sexuality and through it that we find one of our deepest senses of the self.)

And I ask again who is responsible for sexual repression and who benefits from it. And I remember a passage from a 'Diary from Dixie', a journal written by the wife of a white slave owner. She writes of the irony that he has punished their two daughters for reading novels when he considered it his right to regularly rape the women who worked as slaves on his plantation.

And I think of these lines from *A Woman Is Talking to Death* by Judy Grahn:

> *I read this somewhere, I wasn't there:*
> *In feudal Europe, if a woman committed adultery*

her husband would sometimes tie her down, catch a mouse and trap it
under a cup on her bare belly, until
it gnawed itself out, now are you
afraid of mice?

But the experts on child-rearing, the Ginotts and the Spocks, are forever concerned with damages to children in this closed system. The negligences, rages, injustices of the mother are never explained. In their accounts, it is as if the mother simply lacked skill or human understanding. Dr Ginott suggests that a mother who vented her rage at her son should have 'confined herself to one sentence . . .' I read the word 'confined' and I think – anger confined, sexuality confined, movement confined, thoughts confined. And that in Dr Ginott's columns only the children have names.

And yet I take the part of the child, too. The wild child. I remember my fury at the constrictions placed upon me as a child. I remember the look of innocence on my daughter's face, and how I wanted her life to be perfect; how I wanted her to suffer nothing that I suffered . . . And that when I realized I'd given birth to a girl child my heart opened to myself and all the suffering of women seemed unreasonable to me.

And the sacrifice I make as a mother is not what my daughter wants; she asked me one night, 'Why don't you get a baby-sitter and go to a movie?'

> *At home*
> *my daughter waits,*
> *the innocent jailer*
> *together*
> *we grow pale*
> *doing dishes,*
> *and answering the telephone.*

If children benefit from the suffering and sacrifice of women, that is only an incidental fact, not the cause. Sacrifice and suffering are the definition of womanliness in our culture.

When I was twenty, I had an abortion before the laws in California were changed. He had to work quickly and hence without anaesthesia because he was afraid of discovery. I was four months pregnant and the abortion lasted for forty-five minutes. For the first half hour I screamed. Finally, too tired to yell, I began to sing. When the abortion was over, impressed with my performance, the doctor told me, 'Now you are a woman.'

And I think men do not relate to children or to infants but to the idea of children and the idea of motherhood. They do not want to touch the blood of birth or the body of the child.

> Were they not all of them weak women? Wearing crinolines the better to conceal the fact; the great fact; the only fact; but, nevertheless, the deplorable fact; which every modest woman did her best to deny until denial was impossible; the fact that she was about to bear a child? (Virginia Woolf, *Orlando*)

Everywhere motherhood is mystified. Pregnancy, the body of it, menstruation, the blood of it, the lining of the uterus that would have nourished an embryo, concealed. Even contraception, the prevention of birth, denied and withheld.

> The cramped three-room apartment was in a sorry state of turmoil. Jake Sachs, a truck driver scarcely older than his wife, had come home to find the three children crying and her unconscious from the effects of a self-induced abortion . . . The doctor and I settled ourselves to the task of fighting the septicemia . . . It did not seem possible there could be such heat, and every bit of food, ice and drugs had to be carried up three flight of stairs . . . At the end of three weeks, as I was preparing to leave the fragile patient to take up her difficult life once more, she finally voiced her fears, 'Another baby will finish me, I suppose?'
>
> 'It's too early to talk about that,' I temporized.
>
> But when the doctor came to make his last call, I drew him aside, 'Mrs Sachs is terribly worried about another baby.'
>
> 'She well may be,' replied the doctor, and then he stood before her and said, 'Any more such capers, young woman, and there'll be no need to send for me.'
>
> 'I know, doctor,' she replied timidly, 'but,' and she hesitated as though it took all her courage to say it, 'what can I do to prevent it? . . .'
>
> He laughed good-naturedly. 'You want to have your cake and eat it too, do you? Well, it can't be done.'

Then picking up his hat and bag to depart he said, 'Tell Jake to sleep on the roof.'

I glanced quickly at Mrs Sachs. Even through my sudden tears I could see stamped on her face an expression of absolute despair. We simply looked at each other, saying no word until the door had closed behind the doctor. Then she lifted her thin, blue-veined hands and clasped them beseechingly. 'He can't understand. He's only a man. But you do, don't you? Please tell me the secret, and I'll never breathe a word to a soul. Please! . . .'

The telephone rang one evening three months later, and Jake Sachs's agitated voice begged me to come at once; his wife was sick again and from the same cause . . . Mrs Sachs was in a coma and died within ten minutes. . . (Margaret Sanger, *An Autobiography*)

And often, even the children themselves become invisible. Children seldom appear in a courtroom. Their needs are not considered admissible evidence. All that appears is the mother who seems to be pleading for herself: she is accused of avarice or malice.

And still the labour of mothers is unpaid.

I read somewhere that by and large fathers contribute less than half the support of children in divided families and that alimony and child support are hard to collect.

He did not have the same response to infants that I did. Most men don't like infants, everyone said. And so when our daughter cried at night, I woke up and fed her and changed her alone. When I asked for help, her father said, let her cry, he said, I was making work for myself, and when I let her walk around without a diaper, he said that he would never clean up the mess. I could not let her cry. I loved to see her walking about the house with no clothing; I loved her delight in herself. Men are like that I was told. *They don't like babies.*

We talk about money, and my friend who teaches in a school for disturbed children tells me, 'It is the same down the line. Women with children get the lowest welfare cheques; child-care workers are paid the lowest salaries, and our school is always begging for money.'

And I have more questions which may bear on a feminist theory of motherhood. Why are the two largest groups of the poor in this country the very young and the very old? Why is it that most of the families living in extreme poverty are headed by women? Why does the wealthiest country in the world have trouble paying for its schools? Who does the family benefit? Men, women, or children? Who invented the word for bastard? A man? A woman? A child? *Why don't men like babies?*

This has been a well-kept secret: biology does not link the mother and the child. My mother and I learned this. After we were separated for several years, we found we were strangers.

There is nothing mysterious about my love for my daughter. We are on the same side, she and I, fighting for a little tenderness, and for our material survival.

One day she discovered she had toes. One day she solved the mystery of her own voice. She discovered language. She taught herself how to use a spoon. She found out that objects fall unfailingly toward the earth, all objects, bananas and pillows as well as plates. I was there. I witnessed this awakening.

The link between child and parent is not an irreversible fate of biology. After the divorce, my daughter and her father spend long hours alone together. They become close. He develops subtle understandings. He mothers.

To have all the decisions of state rest in the hands of those who do not understand or respond to the needs of children, who do not perceive the vulnerability of flesh, or who perceive that vulnerability with fear – this must be dangerous.

> We will glorify war – the world's only hygiene – militarism, patriotism, the destructive gesture of freedom-bringers, beautiful ideas worth dying for, and scorn for women. (F.T. Marinetti, *Futurist Manifesto*, 1909)

I learned to love babies as a child because I could touch them and hold them. I could make them laugh. They gave and accepted love easily. I wanted a baby. I wanted to be the mother that I wanted.

And I find I am angry that men cannot take care of children and I am angry that they cannot be tender to women.

> *& all those years nobody loved me*
> *except her & I screamed at her & spanked*
> *her*
> *& threw her on the bed & slammed the*
> *door when*
> *i was angry & desperate for her*
> *father's love,*
> *& I cant undo all those times i frightened her*
> *& she loved me, she still loves me,*
> *i cant undo needing &*
> *being tortured with loneliness*
> *until I cried out at her,*
> *who loved me even in my needy loneliness. & how*
> *do mothers, unloved, love their children?*
> *the wonder is that we do, we*
> *do not leave the little girl, we*
> *do not destroy*
> *we cry out in terror we love*
> *our little girls*
> *who must have a better life . . .*

Alta, 'Placenta Praevia,' in
Momma: A Start on All the Untold Stories

My daughter comes home and I am on the telephone when she walks in; she tries to talk to me but I ask her to be quiet and finally she goes to take a bath. My friend on the telephone comes to visit. I have to say things to someone, words my daughter is too young to understand. She comes downstairs after her bath and begins what is called 'pestering' me for a glass of orange juice. I know this is not what she really wants but I can't give her what she really wants so I make orange juice as I go on talking. I am needing love – this is what I talking about so urgently – and my daughter is needing love and I am tired for both of us. She comes and sits with my friend and me and does not interrupt any longer. She sits quietly with a book on her lap and falls asleep. I carry her to bed, and finally, later, when I am alone in the house, I go up to my daughter's room, I sit on her bed and I kiss her and I press my face against her face and I hope that the sweet look on her face is some aknowledgement that the love I am able to give her now is somehow received.

In these months while I am so intensely absorbed in my thoughts, writing so many poems, so many new connections and illuminations racing through my mind, trying to struggle through old ways of pain, to earn a living, when I am tired, never free from work, teaching, deadlines, organizing a conference, and dealing with endless paperwork that sits in a pile in the middle of my desk, taking care of the house that seems to fall apart daily around us, my daughter keeps asking me, 'Mommy, do you like me?'

'Foxes,' she said as she crawled into bed with me. 'I'm afraid I'll dream of foxes again.' Just this once, I was letting her fall asleep in my bed, because of her nightmare of the night before. 'Sometimes,' I say carefully, 'when we dream about a fox, or an alligator or a gorilla, it's really something else we're afraid of. You know there aren't any foxes around here where we live,' I pointed out to her dubious eyes. 'Maybe there is something you're afraid of?' She nods. 'Can you tell me what it is?' I ask. 'Foxes,' she says.

And then one day, she got me to listen to her version of how the world started. There was a bird. The bird gave some of his magic to a woman. She made a son and then married her son and gave him some of her power and they made the world. Now, the bird kept some of his power and so he could live forever. He's alive today in South America, living in a cage. He doesn't want to come out of his cage, but he hopes people will come to visit him, or take him somewhere, though nobody does and that's why he's sad.

Sometimes strangers point out her beauty to me. And then it is not pride I feel. It is longing. Longing to be with this creature, to respond to her, free of the heavy necessity that shackles us together all of the time that I fear (though I try every day to obviate this destiny) will make her have to turn away from me one day in an alienation we have grown to call natural and I in an effort to preserve myself will try not to look over my shoulder at my past for very long, as so many women do, and are lost.

> *because the line dividing*
> *lucidity from darkness*
> *is yet to be marked out*

Adrienne Rich,
'From an Old House in America', in *Poems: Selected and New*

We have only pieces of an analysis and the barest fragments for any vision of the way things could be. That the experience of mothering changes one; that it is learned; that men, in our culture, do not learn this; that women are not in power; that some children are called bastards; that the children of fathers who will feed them and who can are well fed; that those without fathers are more often not well fed; that a mother is asked to give up her life for her children; that mothers are idealized; that mothers are hated; that children are unhappy . . . that women go mad; that the order of life as we live it now is dangerous.

And the fact is that whether I know what it is or not to be liberated, I am not liberated. The means necessary for liberation are not here. My life is still not that different from the lives of centuries of women who have raised children before. But the small differences are significant. I have some time to write and think, even if it is not enough. And I can be honest. If we who are raising children now speak the truth, finally we will be able to see.

> *This eye*
> *is not for weeping*
> *its vision*
> *must be unblurred*
> *though tears are on my face*
>
> *its intent is clarity*
> *it must forget*
> *nothing*

Adrienne Rich,
'From the Prison House', in *Diving into the Wreck*

And I take the part of the mother and of the child which is to believe in the future, and yes, what one sees clearly is usually a way of life that is passing.

Woman and Nature

I wrote Woman and Nature: The Roaring Inside Her *over four years, beginning in 1974. It was published in 1978. The form for* Woman and Nature *was forged from circumstance.*

I was a poet writing about philosophy, about the scientific world view and about technology. It exists in a realm between essay and poem, between reality and myth. Though the book contains analytic ideas, it moves by the force of echoes and choruses, counterpoints and harmonies. In one way, the book is an extended dialogue between two voices (each set in different type face), one the chorus of women and nature, an emotional, animal, embodied voice, and the other a solo part, cool, professorial, pretending to objectivity, carrying the weight of cultural authority. Yet, though the book is shaped by the conflict between these two voices, it sings more than it argues.

The whole book is made up of four separate books. 'Matter' begins with a history of scientific, religious and philosophical notions about nature or matter, juxtaposed chronologically with a history of ideas about women. And the rest of the first book explores the manifestations of these notions as they have been applied in our culture to Land, Timber, domesticated animals, our bodies. The second book, 'Separation', speaks of the unnatural divisions which must proceed from a thought that opposes male and female, body and mind, heaven and earth. 'Passage' is a short book about transformation. The last book, 'Her Vision', mirrors back the subject matter of the first two books, but now in a different voice, and in a different way of seeing. Timber becomes Forest, and The Zoological Garden, the story of a caged lion, becomes The Lion in the Den of the Prophets. Selections from 'Matter', 'Separation' and 'Her Vision' follow.

PROLOGUE

He says that woman speaks with nature. That she hears voices from under the earth. That wind blows in her ears and trees whisper to her. That the dead sing through her mouth and the cries of infants are clear to her. But for him this dialogue is over. He says he is not part of this world, that he was set on this world as a stranger. He sets himself apart from women and nature.

And so it is Goldilocks who goes to the home of the three bears, Little Red Riding Hood who converses with the wolf, Dorothy who befriends a lion, Snow White who talks to the birds, Cinderella with mice as her allies, the Mermaid who is half fish, Thumbelina courted by a mole. *(And when we hear in the Navaho chant of the mountain that a grown man sits and smokes with bears and follows directions given to him by squirrels, we are surprised. We had thought only little girls spoke with animals.)*

We are the bird's eggs. Bird's eggs, flowers, butterflies, rabbits, cows, sheep; we are caterpillars; we are leaves of ivy and sprigs of wallflower. We are women. We rise from the wave. We are gazelle and doe, elephant and whale, lilies and roses and peach, we are air, we are flame, we are oyster and pearl, we are girls. We are women and nature. And he says he cannot hear us speak.

But we hear.

MATTER

Mutability on the earth, it is said, came to the Garden of Eden after the Fall. That before the Fall there was immortal bliss on earth, but that after the Fall 'all things decay in time and to their end do draw'

That the face of the earth is a record of man's sin. That the height of mountains, the depth of valleys, the sites of great boulders, craters, seas, bodies of land, lakes and rivers, the shapes of rocks, cliffs, all were formed by the deluge, which was God's punishment for sin.

'The world is the Devil and the Devil is the world,' it is said.

And of the fact that women are the Devil's Gateway it is observed that sin and afterwards death came into the world because Eve consorted with the devil in the body of a serpent.

That the power of the devil lies in the privy parts of men.

That women act as the devil's agent and use flesh as bait.

That women under the power of the devil meet with him secretly, in the woods (in the wilderness), at night. That they kiss him on the anus. That they offer him pitch-black candles, which he lights with a fart. That they anoint themselves with his urine. That they dance back to back together and feast on food that would nauseate 'the most ravenously hungry stomach'. That a mass is held, with a naked woman's body as an altar, faeces, urine and menstrual blood upon her ass. That the devil copulates with all the women in this orgy, in this ritual.

That these women are witches.

That 'Lucifer before his Fall, as an archangel, was a clear body, composed of the purest and brightest air, but that after his Fall he was veiled with a grosser substance and took a new form of dark and thick air.'

1382 Thomas Brawardine in *Treatise on the Proportions of Velocities in Moving Bodies* proposes a mathematical law of dynamics universally valid for all changes in velocity.

1431 Joan of Arc, aged 22, 'placed high on the fire so the flames would reach her slowly,' dies.
(She is asked why she wears male costume.)

1468 The Pope defines witchcraft as *crimen exceptum*, removing all legal limit to torture.

1482 Leonardo da Vinci moves to Milan, and begins his notebooks on hydraulics, mechanics, anatomy; he paints *Madonna of the Rocks*.
(Does she see the body of St Michael, they ask her? Did he come to her naked?)

1523 One thousand witches burn in a single year in the diocese of Como.

1543 Vesalius publishes *De Humani Corporis Fabrica*.

1543 Copernicus publishes *De Revolutionibus Orbium Coelestium*.
(She is asked if she is in a state of grace. She is asked if St Margaret speaks English.)

1571 Johannes Kepler born.

1572 Augustus the Pious issues *Consultationes Saxionicae*, stating that a good witch must be burned because she has made a pact with the devil.
(She confesses that she falsely pretended to have revelations from God and his angels, from St Catherine and St Margaret.)

1585 Witch burnings in two villages leave one female inhabitant in each.

1589 Francis Bacon is made clerk of the Star Chamber.
(He says that nature herself must be examined.)

1581–1591 Nine hundred burned in Lorraine.
(That nature must be bound into service, he persuades.)

1600 Gilbert's *De Magnete* published.

1603 William Harvey assists at the examination of the witches.

1609 Galileo, on hearing a rumour of the invention of a glass magnifying distant objects, constructs a telescope.
(It is urged that nature must be hounded in her wanderings before one can lead her and drive her.)

1609 Kepler publishes *Astronomia Nova*.

1609 The whole population of Navarre is declared witches.
(He says that the earth should be put on the rack and tortured for her secrets.)

1615 William Harvey lectures on the circulation of the blood at the Royal College of Physicians.

1619 Kepler publishes his third law, *De Harmonice Mundi*.

1619 The first black slaves are introduced in America.
(She is asked if she signed the devil's book.
She is asked if the devil had a body.
She is asked whom she chose to be an incubus.)

1622 Francis Bacon publishes *Natural and Experimental History for the Foundation of Philosophy*.

1622–1623 Johann George II, Prince Bishop, builds a house for the trying of witches at Bamberg, where 600 burn.

1628 One hundred and fifty-eight burned at Würzburg.

1637   Descartes publishes *Discours de la Méthode*.
(She is asked what oath she made. What finger she was forced
to raise. Where she made a union with her incubus. What food
she ate at the sabbat. What music was played, what dances were
danced. What devil's marks were on her body. Who were the
children on whom she cast spells; what animals she bewitched.
How she was able to fly through the air.)

1638   Galileo publishes *Two New Sciences*.

1640   Carbon dioxide obtained by Helmont.

1644   Descartes publishes *Principia Philosophiae*.

1666   Newton procures 'a triangular glass prism to try the celebrated
phenomena of colours.'

1670   Rouen witch trials.

1687   Newton publishes *Principia*.
(She confesses that every Monday the devil lay with her for
fornication. She confesses that when he copulated with her she
felt intense pain.)
(She confesses that after having intercourse with the devil she
married her daughter to him.)

1704   Newton publishes *Opticks*.

1717   Halley reveals that the world is adrift in a star swirl.

1738   Dean of Faculty of Law at Rostock demands that witches be
extirpated by fire and sword.

1745   Witch trial at Lyons, five sentenced to death.

1749   Sister Maria Renata executed and burned.

1775   Anna Maria Schnagel executed for witchcraft.
(She confesses she passed through the keyhole of a door. That
she became a cat and then a horse. She confesses she made a
pact with the devil, that she asked for the devil's help.)
(We confess we were carried through the air in a moment.)

MULES

> . . . So de white man throw down de load and tell de nigger man
> tuh pick it up. He hand it to his womanfolks. De nigger woman is
> de mule uh de world so fur as Ah can see. . .
>
> Zora Neale Hurston, *Their Eyes Were Watching God*

*We are the mules. Offspring of the he-ass and the mare. We cannot
procreate our own kind together; nature did not create us: we were bred
for domestic labour. Though we work hard, our very name signifies
obstinacy and stupidity. Yet that is the very nature of our work,
obstinate and stupid. We have the strength of staying power. Though
our labour is necessary and though we were bred for that purpose, no
one envies us; no one yearns to do the work we do as finely as we do it.
We are despicable. If we go on, cleaning the toilets, washing the floors,
dusting the furniture, lugging the groceries, cutting the beans, folding
the laundry, if we go on, bearing the children, washing their faces, their
asses, their noses, carrying their faeces away, feeding them from our
own bodies, if we go on, our hair pulled up in bandannas, our hands
smelling of garlic, our noses filled with dust, our backs bent close to the
earth, our ears hearing only inarticulate cries, our eyes hard with
obstinate labour, our mouths shut for all but necessity, our brains only
calculators for simple quantities, three cups of flour, 10 yards of
flannel, 14 pounds simmered in butter, vinegar and rags, water and
rags, pins in the soap, vegetables on Tuesday, cotton in hot water, wool
in cold, if we go on, changing the sheets, administering dosages, we are
despicable, and if we stop in our tracks, speech not having been bred in
us, we articulate nothing, our nature is mysterious, mulish, but that is
what we are bred for, we are a useful beast, you who feed us and house
us in exchange for our labour say, but difficult to handle, still, men
count mules among their riches and among their godlike accomplishments, to have ordered nature, to have made an animal.*

And we know we are not logical. The mule baulks for no apparent
reason. For no rhyme or reason. *We remember weeping suddenly for
no good reason.* Spiteful and kicking, angry out of nowhere, like a
hurricane, with almost no warning, and incomprehensible, brutish.
  *And despite all the solutions we apply and all the scrubbing of cloth
and wood and porcelain, still there are always stains; and no matter
how often we wash, washing the smell of excrement from our hands so
we may prepare food, washing the smell of food from our hands, still*

the odour stays. And because she is bestial, not fit for thought, she is clumsy with the dullness of labour.

But the mule does have a certain grace. She is sure-footed. She can turn, with the plow harnessed to her, her weight pulling the blade through the soil, on the steep side of a mountain, not sliding or stumbling at the incline. She can follow men up through the steepest mountain pass, carrying food and water. (So that the mule-driver is as necessary to an army as is the gunner.) And is this grace bred into her?

Bred or not, it is the grace of labour. It at least is a strength and has that spare beauty of function, of things that are what they are, the definition, the line, the movement, essential.

And if we find this grace through our labour, with our fingers finding the loose thread in the garment, our ears late at night hearing the cries no one else hears, catching the milk in the pot as it begins to boil, the body bent over rocking, rocking, the pieces of cloth sewn together in patterns, the taste of thyme with rosemary and the different odour of oregano, or the grace, the grace of crisis, the fever, the steady application of cold cloths, the grace of economy, the soup of leftovers, the ruse of the bed covering in a skirt, or the seeing of the barely seeable, the unnamed, the slight difference in the expression of the eyes, the mood, the slow opening, the listening, the small possibility, barely audible, nodding, almost inarticulate, yet allowing articulation, words, healing, the eyes acknowledge, this grace of the unspoken, spoken in movement, the hand reaches, the blanket is wrapped around, the arms hold this mulish daily grace, without which we do not choose to continue, and if we find this, we have something of our own.

This is our secret grace, unnamed, invisible, surviving.

THE SHOW HORSE

The Bit

> Be ye not like to horses and mules which have no understanding: whose mouths must be held up with bit and bridle, lest they fall upon thee.
>
> *The Book of Common Prayer*

The right thumb of the rider holds the centre of the bridle in front of the horse's face and above her head so that the bit is in front of the horse's mouth. The right hand is placed under the horse's jaw. If the horse does not open her mouth when the bit touches her teeth, if she clenches her teeth, the rider presses his left forefinger in the toothless bars of the lower jaw, which will make the horse open her mouth and accept the bit. The thicker the bit, the milder its effect on the mouth of the horse. The bit should neither pull up the corners of the mouth nor touch the teeth. The noseband must be tight but not so tight that the horse cannot breathe. And she must be able to accept tidbits from the rider's hand. The throat latch, however, should be fastened loosely.

Nature

> [The horse] is by nature a very lazy animal whose idea of heaven is an enormous field of lush grass in which he can graze undisturbed until his belly is full, and after a pleasant doze can start filling himself up all over again.
>
> Captain Elwyn Hartley Edwards,
> *From Paddock to Saddle*

> A perfect hostess in a household with servants gives the impression that she has nothing whatever to do with household arrangements, which apparently run themselves. In a servantless household, she has the cleaning, marketing and as much cooking as possible done in advance, so that an absolute minimum of her time is spent on these chores while her guests are with her.
>
> Emily Post, *Etiquette*

It is the horse's extreme sensitivity to pain, especially in the mouth but also all over the body, which allows the rider to control her with the pressure of his own weight, the movements of his legs, and with the aid of the bit, the bridle and the rein, the riding whip, the long whip and the spur.

It is the timorous nature of the animal coupled with this sensitivity that allows her to be trained. The horse is not aggressive; her only defense is to flee. Therefore the horse reacts to pain by running away from the pain. If the rider stands at the horse's head and taps her flank with a long whip, the horse will move away from the discomfort.

In addition, the horse has a prodigious memory, is a social animal, has a desire to please and a need for security, and all these qualities are used in her training. Her faults are nervousness, laziness and an excitability that is at times unpredictable.

Education

> Differences emerge too in the instinctual disposition which gives a glimpse of the later nature of women. A little girl is as a rule less aggressively defiant and self-sufficient, she seems to have a greater need for being shown affection and on that account to be more dependent and pliant.
>
> Sigmund Freud, *'Femininity'*

> To train horses, it is essential that we have a very clear understanding of the way in which their small minds work and appreciate how limited they are in this department.
>
> Captain Elwyn Hartley Edwards,
> *From Paddock to Saddle*

> Oh how lovely is her ignorance!
>
> Jean Jacques Rousseau, *Emile*

The horse is not designed for carrying weight; she has a structure similar to a rectangular box with a leg at each corner, and the rider places his weight on the weakest part, the unsupported centre. Her legs and feet are not designed for trotting on hard roads or galloping. And jumping is entirely unnatural to the horse. But through an arduous process of training, the body ill-designed for this task can become a carrier of weights and learn to adjust her own balance for that purpose.

Therefore the body of the horse must be reshaped. A horse in the correct form has a rounded top line accompanied by a lowered head and neck and hind legs engaged beneath the body; to achieve this form the teacher uses exercise, strapping, and encourages higher head carriage. Thus formed, the horse carries weight and can develop paces, balance and movements at the bidding of first the teacher and then the rider.

The horse has a natural curvature of the spine, perhaps as a result of the fetal position of the unborn foal. This curvature prevents the animal from moving on a straight line so that the hind feet follow exactly the track of the forefeet. Therefore the horse is trained in exercises to correct this natural crookedness by increasing the flexibility in the lumbar vertebrae. This straightening improves the mechanical efficiency of the horse.

Grooming

She is brushed all over her body with a dandy brush in the direction that the fur grows. She is brushed with the body brush in round, scrubbing movements. She is polished with a linen cloth until she shines.

Her eyes, her lips, her nostrils, under her tail, are washed. Bits of sand, dust, manure, pebbles, mud, grass, weeds, are taken from her hoofs with a pick. Oil is rubbed into her foot.

She is clipped. (So that she does not have the naked look of a fresh cut, this is done before the show.) The scissors move against the fur, leaving only her mane, her tail and a saddle mark.

(The groom places a saddle on her back and clips around it so that when the saddle is removed, a saddle of fur remains on her back.)

And now that she is clipped her rider must protect her. The grease that was natural to her, that protected her from the cold and the wet, has been removed. She is vulnerable to the weather. He must provide for her a warm woollen blanket to put under her and a lined rug to put over her.

She may have her fetlocks clipped for showing in summer.

On certain occasions, good form requires that her mane and her tail be braided. Her hair is sewn or tied with ribbons.

Dressage

Girls ought to be active and diligent; nor is that all; they should also be early subjected to restraint. This misfortune, if it really be one, is inseparable from their sex; nor do they ever throw it off but to suffer more cruel evils. They must be subject, all their lives, to the most constant and severe restraint, which is that of decorum: it is, therefore, necessary to accustom them early to such confinement, that it may not afterwards cost them too dear; and to the suppression of their caprices, that they may the more readily submit to the will of others.

Jean Jacques Rousseau, *Emile*

She must not swing her arms as though they were dangling ropes, she must not switch her self this way and that; she must not shout and she must not, while wearing her bridal veil, smoke a cigarette.

Emily Post, *Etiquette*

The teacher should insist that the horse stand still and on all four legs during the process of mounting and until asked to move on by the rider. Fidgeting on the spot or moving on without command must not be tolerated.

Alois Podhajsky, *The Riding Teacher*

The movements that the show horse executes have no use in themselves but exist as part of the show of dressage, manifesting how obedient she is, how well she keeps her balance, how complete is the mastery of her rider.

To 'Go Large' she rides straight along the walls of the riding school, taking the corners precisely on an arc of a circle of three steps' diameter.

The 'Circle' is performed in either half sector of the school by inscribing a circle of sixteen to eighteen metres.

A 'Volte' is the smallest circle the horse may perform; it is six steps in diameter and may be done in the corners, along the walls or on the centre line. The volte is performed only once.

The 'Half Volte and Change' consists of a half circle and a straight line on which the horse is led at an angle of 45 degrees back to the wall, where her position is changed.

'Serpentines all along the wall' may be ridden as single or double loops. For the single loop, the horse, after passing the second corner of the short side, is taken on a single track approximately five metres from the wall, thus describing a flat arc, and halfway through the school she is taken back in the same manner. For the double loop the curve of the single is repeated, but the horse does not move from the wall more than three metres. Both arcs must be of the same size.

The 'Half Pass' is performed on parallel tracks, usually on a diagonal of the school. The horse's head is bent slightly at the poll in the direction she is going. The rest of her spine is held straight. If her shoulders move laterally more than her haunches, she will move on circular tracks, and this is classic direct rotation. If her haunches move more than her shoulders and on circular tracks, she does a classic inverse rotation.

A common fault in the half pass occurs when the horse's quarters are pushed ahead of the shoulders. Another occurs when the horse falls onto the leading shoulder in loss of balance owing to her not being straight.

Difficulties in training a horse to perform are these: nervousness or laziness, qualities which it has been decided are part of the horse's nature. Calmness and patience are recommended for the former. For the latter, the long whip.

Physical problems may be a long back or weak hindquarters, making it either difficult or painful for the horse to carry a rider or train for long hours. These may be eliminated partially by gymnastic training. Another difficulty is the oversensitive mouth of most high-spirited horses: this necessitates a light use of the bit.

If the horse lets her tongue hang out, this is counted as a serious fault. This may be prevented by a manipulation of the bit.

Whenever the horse performs well, the rider offers her a lump of sugar.

The collaboration of horse and rider is essential to performance. When it is possible, a nervous horse should be led by a calm rider and a phlegmatic horse by a nervous rider.

Love

> Love gets its name *(amor)* from the word for hook *(amus)* which means to capture or to be captured.
>
> Andreas Capellanus, *The Art of Courtly Love*

Though she loves her stable because of the comfort, because she can always count on it to be there, because it is her private world and it is where she rests and is fed, she waits there. It is in the stable that she waits for her rider. It is only when her rider appears that she leaves her stable, that she moves. She loves to please her rider. It is her rider who rubs her flanks, who carries bits of food in the white flesh of his palm, who speaks to her softly, kindly. It is her rider who has trained all her movements, her rider who tells her what she must do from one moment to the next. Her rider who possesses a secret knowledge of a series of memorable movements whose purpose she cannot decipher, a knowledge above her capacity to understand, her rider who knows how to produce food and pleasure, for she is so entirely stupid and helpless that she cannot even feed herself without his aid, let alone know what or where to go, to do. The horse has no wish for freedom. She waits the occasional visits of her master, who day after day seems more powerful, more wise, taking on a majesty the horse would never dream of for herself. When he is in her presence, her thoughts are riveted on him. She likes no one else to ride her. Is this not love the horse is feeling? But she is mute. The rider has named her and so he must also name her feelings. He decides that she loves him.

SEPARATION

The Zoological Garden

> Wild, wild things will turn on you
> You have got to set them free.
>
> Cris Williamson, 'Wild Things'

In the cage is the lion. She paces with her memories. Her body is a record of her past. As she moves back and forth, one may see it all: the lean frame, the muscular legs, the paw enclosing long sharp claws, the astonishing speed of her response. She was born in this garden. She has never in her life stretched those legs. Never darted farther than twenty yards at a time. Only once did she use her claws. Only once did she feel them sink into flesh. And it was her keeper's flesh. Her keeper whom she loves, who feeds her, who would never dream of harming her, who protects her. Who in his mercy forgave her mad attack, saying this was in her nature, to be cruel at a whim, to try to kill what she loves. He had come into her cage as he usually did early in the morning to change her water, always at the same time of day, in the same manner, speaking softly to her, careful to make no sudden movement, keeping his distance, when suddenly she sank down, deep down into herself, the way wild animals do before they spring, and then she had risen on all her strong legs, and swiped him in one long, powerful, graceful movement across the arm. How lucky for her he survived the blow. The keeper and his friends shot her with a gun to make her sleep. Through her half-open lids she knew they made movements around her. They fed her with tubes. They observed her. They wrote comments in notebooks. And finally they rendered a judgment. She was normal. She was a normal wild beast, whose power is dangerous, whose anger can kill, they had said. Be more careful of her, they advised. Allow her less excitement. Perhaps let her exercise more. She understood none of this. She understood only the look of fear in her keeper's eyes. And now she paces. Paces as if she were angry, as if she were on the edge of frenzy. The spectators imagine she is going through the movements of the hunt, or that she is readying her body for survival. But she knows no life outside the garden. She has no notion of anger over what she could have been, or might be. No idea of rebellion.

It is only her body that knows of these things, moving her, daily, hourly, back and forth, back and forth, before the bars of her cage.

HIS CERTAINTY:
HOW HE RULES THE UNIVERSE

Quantity

> Mathematics is thought moving in the sphere of complete abstraction from any particular instance of what it is talking about.
>
> Tobias Danzig, *Number, The Language of Science*

> Granted, granted that there is no flaw in all that reasoning, that all I have concluded this last month is as clear as day, true as arithmetic. . .
>
> Raskolnikov in Dostoyevsky, *Crime and Punishment*

He says that through numbers 1 2 3 4 5 6 7 we find the ultimate reality of things 8 9 10 11 He says 12 13 14 that quantities are the most rigorous test of things 12 13 He says God created numbers and our minds to understand numbers 14 15 16 He says the final proof 16 17 is always a sum 18 19 20 (Counting. She is counting. The number of seconds in a minute, the number of minutes in an hour, the number of hours) He measures the distance from his land to his neighbour's land. He measures his wealth. He numbers his wives. He numbers his children 21 22 23 24 25 26 He weighs what will be traded (1 Faning Mill $17.25, 1 red-faced cow $13.25, 1 yearling calf $4.25) He calculates the worth of what he has (1 plough £1.60, 1 Wench and child $156.00, 8 fancy chairs $9.25) He assesses the value of what is his. (He measures the gallons of milk she produces. He measures the board feet they yield. He measures the hours she works, the value of her labour.)

He tells us how big he is. He measures his height. He demonstrates his strength. He measures what he can lift, what he can conquer. He calculates his feelings. He numbers his armies. *He measures our virtue. He counts the reason why we fell.* (570 through poverty, he says, 647 through loss of their parents or their homes, 29 orphaned with elder brothers and sisters to care for.) *He counts the reasons why we fell from grace.* (23 widowed women with small children, 123 servant girls seduced and discharged by their masters.) *He tells us how strong he is.* He counts the sperm in his seminal fluid. He numbers his genes. . . . (She numbers the seconds. She numbers the hours. She numbers the days.) 27 28 29 30 31

Counting. They count. They count one billion suffering from

hunger.   32 33 34 35   They count twelve thousand dying of starvation.   36 37 38 39   He counts the number of children being born.
40 41 42   He measures the growth of food.   43 44 45   He calculates
the sum.   46 47 48   He says that through quantities we find ultimate
reality. (She is counting the number of days in a week. The number of
months in a year.)

He tells us how rich he is. He is counting his possessions and all he
might possess. He measures his intelligence. He measures the coal in
the ground. He calculates his life expectancy. He estimates the oil in
the sea. He adds up the value of his life. He measures productive
acres. He calculates the value of his existence.   49 50 51 52 53

He tells us how long he will live. He measures his neighbour's land.
He numbers their children, the bellies of their cows, the spans of their
horses, the numbers of their bridges, their cities, their hospitals, their
armies. He counts their dead. He counts his dead. He calculates. He
calculates the sum. *He gives us the final proof.*

54 55 56 57 58 59 60   (She has numbered each second of each
hour of each day of each year. She has been counting.)   61 62 63 64
65 66 67 68 69 70 71 72 73 74 75 76 77 78 79 80 81

He counts   82 83   necessity. He counts what he imagines to be
necessary. He says six combat divisions are necessary; he counts
thirteen   training   divisions   as   necessary,   four   brigades,   two
manoeuvre area commands.   84 85 86 87 88 89   He says 1,700
ballistic   missiles   are   needed   and   seven   hundred   bombers.
90 91 92 93 94   He counts bombs, he counts 70,000 bombs. 95 96
He says when people. He counts the number of people. He says when
people have nothing they starve. He counts four hundred million on
the edge of starvation. He says when starving people are fed. He
counts ten million children risking death from starvation. When
starving people are fed, he says, they reproduce. He counts.
97 98 99 100 101   (She has numbered her children. She has
counted the days of their lives. On this day, she can say, this one
learned to pronounce her name. In this month, she can say, this one
learned to walk. She has counted the moments.)   102 103

104 105 106   He has counted.   107   He has counted the effects.
108 109   One roentgen, he says   110 111   shortens a life by 3.5 days.
112 113 114   One hundred roentgens will shorten a life   115 116
by one year   117   and one thousand roentgens by ten years.   118 119
120 121 122123124125126127   Counting. They have counted the
targets. Of 224 targets they count, 71 were cities. They count the
bombs.   128 129 130   They count 263 bombs and 1446 megatons.

131 132 133 They count the dead to be 42 million. They imagine 42 million to be dead. They count the injured to be 17 million. They imagine 17 million injured.

134 135 136 137 *He tells us how powerful he is.* 138 139 And they count what they imagine will survive. They count 23 percent of electrical machinery. They estimate 28 percent of fabricated metal products. They say 29 percent of rubber products. 30 percent of apparel. 34 percent of machinery. 40 percent of chemicals. 51 percent of furniture. 138 139 140 141142143144145146

(Counting. She has counted on this life continuing. She has counted on continuing. Each day she has counted, each day she has done what she must, done what she must to go on.)

147148149   57 percent of food, 60 percent of construction, 89 percent of mining, 94.6 percent of agriculture. Counting. He is counting how much. He is counting how much tragedy is acceptable. He imagines ten roentgens of radiation. 150 151 152 He imagines the birth of one million defective children. Counting. He counts 153 154 155 156 157

Counting. We count each second. No moment do we forget. We live through every hour. We are counting the number he has killed, the number he has bound into servitude, the number he has maimed, stolen from, left to starve. We measure his virtue. We count the value of our lives. We are counting the least act of the smallest one, her slightest gesture, as we count the ultimate reality of her breath barely visible now in the just cold air, 1, 2, 3, we say, as it shows itself in small clouds, 4, 5 and 6, and disappears from moment 7, 8, 9 to moment.

HER VISION

Flying

> . . . ye was taken out of bed to that meeting in a flight.
> Bessie Henderson, Crook of Devon, 1661

In those years, whatever we wanted it seemed we could not have. Nothing in our lives was ever fortunate. We had the meagerest portions of things, and when things were rare, we went without. That is our lot in life, we told ourselves. And we stopped wanting. Only we longed, and we grew so accustomed to the pain of longing that we called this our nature. We put this into our songs. We said disappointment was part of life. Even in our imaginations, all our attempts began to fail. But one day all this changed. On this day we met a woman who was used to getting what she wanted. She ate large portions and her body was big. She let us know there were other such women. We were bewitched. We began to dream we were like this woman. Her very smile invited us to be like her. And that is how we were finally initiated.

We began to think we might get what we want. Our longing turned into desire. Do you know how desire can run through the limbs? How wanting lets your eyes pierce space? How desire propels even the sleeping? How a resolve to act can traverse this atmosphere as quick as light? We were alive with desire. And we knew we could never go back to those years of longing. This is why, despite the threat of fire and our fear of the flame, we burst out through the roofs of our houses. Desire is a force inside us. Our mouths drop open in the rushing air. Our bodies float among stars. And we laugh in ecstasy to know the air has wishes; the stars want. 'Yes,' we call out, full of ourselves and delight. 'Yes,' we sing. 'We fly through the night.'

Consequences (What Always Returns)

> And I pray one prayer – I repeat it till my tongue stiffens – Catherine Earnshaw, may you not rest as long as I am living! You said I killed you – haunt me, then! . . . Be with me always – take any form – drive me mad! Only *do* not leave me in this abyss, where I cannot find you! Oh God! It is unutterable! I *cannot* live without my life! I *cannot* live without my soul.
>
> Emily Brontë, *Wuthering Heights*

> To have risked so much in our efforts to mould nature to our satisfaction and yet to have failed in achieving our goal would indeed be the final irony. Yet this, it seems, is our situation.
>
> Rachel Carson, *Silent Spring*

We say you cannot divert the river from the riverbed. We say that everything is moving, and we are a part of this motion. That the soil is moving. That the water is moving. We say that the earth draws water to her from the clouds. We say the rainfall parts on each side of the mountain, like the parting of our hair, and that the shape of the mountain tells where the water has passed. We say this water washes the soil from the hillsides, that the rivers carry sediment, that rain when it splashes carries small particles, that the soil itself flows with water in streams underground. We say that water is taken up into roots of plants, into stems, that it washes down hills into rivers, that these rivers flow to the sea, that from the sea, in the sunlight, this water rises to the sky, that this water is carried in clouds, and comes back as rain, comes back as fog, back as dew, as wetness in the air.

We say everything comes back. And you cannot divert the river from the riverbed. We say every act has its consequences. That this place has been shaped by the river, and that the shape of this place tells the river where to go.

We say he should have known his action would have consequences. We say our judgment was that when she raised that rifle, looking through the sight at him, and fired, she was acting out of what had gone on before. We say every act comes back on itself. There are consequences. You cannot cut the trees from the mountainside without a flood. We say there is no way to see his dying as separate from her living, or what he had done to her, or what part of her he had used. We say if you change the course of this river you change the shape of the whole place. And we say that what she did then could not be separated from what she held sacred in herself, what she had felt when he did that to her, what we hold sacred to ourselves, what we feel we could not go on without, and we say if this river leaves this place, nothing will grow and the mountain will crumble away, and we say what he did to her could not be separated from the way that he looked at her, and what he felt was right to do to her, and what they do to us, we say, shapes how they see us. That once the trees are cut down, the water will wash the mountain away and the river be heavy with mud, and there will be a flood. And we say that what he did to her he did to all of us. And that one act cannot be separated from another. And had he seen more clearly, we say, he might have predicted his own death. How if the trees grew on that hillside there would be no flood. And you cannot divert this river. We say look how the water flows from this place and returns as rainfall, everything returns, we say, and one thing follows another, there are limits, we say, on what can be done and everything moves. We are all a part of this motion, we say, and the way of the river is sacred, and this grove of trees is sacred, and we ourselves, we tell you, are sacred.

THE LION IN THE DEN OF THE PROPHETS

She swaggers in. They are terrifying in their white hairlessness. She waits. She watches. She does not move. She is measuring their moves. And they are measuring her. Cautiously one takes a bit of her fur. He cuts it free from her. He examines it. Another numbers her feet, her

teeth, the length and width of her body. She yawns. They announce
she is alive. They wonder what she will do if they enclose her in the
room with them. One of them shuts the door. She backs her way
toward the closed doorway and then roars. 'Be still,' the men say. She
continues to roar. 'What does she roar?' they ask. The roaring must
be inside her, they conclude. They decide they must see the roaring
inside her. They approach her in a group, six at her two front legs and
six at her two back legs. They are trying to put her to sleep. She swings
at one of the men. His own blood runs over him. 'Why did she do
that?' the men question. She has no soul, they conclude, she does not
know right from wrong.'Be still,'they shout at her. 'Be humble. trust
us,' they demand. 'We have souls,' they proclaim, 'we know what is
right,' they approach her with their medicine, 'for you.' She does not
understand this language. She devours them.

Naming

*Behind naming, beneath words, is something else. An existence named
unnamed and unnameable. We give the grass a name, and earth a
name. We say grass and earth are separate. We know this because we
can pull the grass free of the earth and see its separate roots – but when
the grass is free, it dies. We say the inarticulate have no souls. We say
the cow's eye has no existence outside ourselves, that the red wing of the
blackbird has no thought, the roe of the salmon no feeling, because we
cannot name these. Yet for our own lives we grieve all that cannot be
spoken, that there is no name for, repeating for ourselves the names of
things which surround what cannot be named. We say Heron and
Loon, Coot and Killdeer, Snipe and Sandpiper, Gull and Hawk,
Eagle and Osprey, Pigeon and Dove, Oriole, Meadowlark, Sparrow.
We say Red Admiral and Painted Lady, Morning Cloak and Question
Mark, Baltimore and Checkerspot, Buckeye, Monarch, Viceroy,
Mayfly, Stonefly, Cicada, Leafhopper and Earwig, we say Sea Urchin
and Sand Dollar, Starfish and Sandworm. We say mucous membrane,
uterus, cervix, ligament, vagina and hymen, labia, orifice, artery,
vessel, spine and heart. We say skin, blood, breast, nipple, taste,
nostril, green, eye, hair, we say vulva, hood, clitoris, belly, foot, knee,
elbow, pit, nail, thumb, we say tongue, teeth, toe, ear, we say ear and
voice and touch and taste and we say again love, breast and beautiful
and vulva, saying clitoris, saying belly, saying toes and soft, saying ear,
saying ear, ear and hood and hood and green and all that we say we are
saying around that which cannot be said, cannot be spoken. But in a*

moment that which is behind naming makes itself known. Hand and breast know each one to the other. Wood in the table knows clay in the bowl. Air knows grass knows water knows mud knows beetle knows frost knows sunlight knows the shape of the earth knows death knows not dying. And all this knowledge is in the souls of everything, behind naming, before speaking, beneath words.

The Anatomy Lesson (Her Skin)

> It is only real feelings that possess this power of transferring themselves into inert matter.
>
> Simone Weil, *First and Last Notebooks*

From the body of the old woman we can tell you something of the life she lives. We know that she spent much of her life on her knees. (Fluid in the bursa in front of her kneecap.) *We say she must have often been fatigued, that her hands were often in water.* (Traces of calcium, traces of unspoken anger, swelling in the middle joints of her fingers.) *We see white ridges, scars from old injuries; we see redness in her skin.* (That her hands were often in water; that there must have been pain.) *We can tell you she bore several children. We see the white marks on her belly, the looseness of the skin, the wideness of her hips that her womb has dropped.* (Stretching in the tissue behind the womb.) *We can see that she fed her children, that her breasts are long and flat, that there are white marks at the edges, a darker colour of the nipple. We know that she carried weights too heavy for her back.* (Curvature of the spine. Aching.) *From the look of certain muscles in her back, her legs, we can tell you something of her childhood, of what she did not do.* (Of the running, of the climbing, of the kicking, of the movements she did not make.) *And from her lungs we can tell you what she held back, that she was forbidden to shout, that she learned to breathe shallowly. We can say that we think she must have held her breath. From the size of the holes in her ears, we know they were put there in her childhood. That she wore earrings most of her life. From the pallor of her skin, we can say that her face was often covered. From her feet, that her shoes were small* (toes bent back on themselves). *That she was often on her feet* (swelling, ligaments of the arch broken down). *We can guess that she rarely sat through a meal.* (Tissue of the colon inflamed.) *We can catalogue her being: tissue, fibre, bloodstream, cell, the shape of her experience to the least moment, skin, hair, try to see what she saw, to imagine what she felt, clitoris, vulva, womb, and we can tell you that despite each injury she survived. That she lived to an old age. (On all the parts of her body we see the years.) By the body of this old woman we are hushed. We are awed. We know that it was in her body that we began. And now we say that it is from her body that we learn. That we see our past. We say from the body of the old woman, we can tell you something of the lives we lived.*

Sadism and Catharsis:
The Treatment Is the Disease

Within the past five years women have organized to protest the proliferation of pornography. In 1978 thousands of women marched through San Francisco to fill the streets at Broadway and Columbus, a neighbourhood of nightclubs featuring nude women, 'adult' bookstores, pornographic cinemas. The following article was published by the Bay Guardian *in 1979. It was part of the early work I did for my book* Pornography and Silence, *but it did not appear there. In* Pornography and Silence *I decipher pornographic texts as symbolic codes which give us an understanding of the fear and hatred of women, and of racism.*

Catharsis, catharsis it is grimly implied, is the true role of pornography. There would be *more* rape, I hear the threat under the reasoning tone, were there not pornography. Be grateful. Be grateful. Oh, but what a depressing picture of the world believing this voice gives me. I imagine men filled with the desire for violence, the need for violence growing in them every day, as natural as hunger or thirst, controlled only by small, placating attention, bits of nourishment. I imagine the average male in the corner of a cage growling with menace. Here, his tenders say, let us give him these photographs of men beating women, of men holding knives up to women's throats, breasts, vulvas, of women's mouths gagged, their legs chained. This will appease him, they say, these images will bring him peace.

Drawn here in a woman's hand, this outline of male nature as essentially rapacious and brutal appears less glamorous than usual. But this is not my image. I have only copied the self-portraits of men; it is the same picture of male nature that can be found, for instance, in the work of Norman Mailer.

His hero in *The American Dream* is far more violent than the man I have imagined. He goes beyond appeasement, past metaphorical catharsis. Only the real act can save him from the forces inside him; he murders his wife. As if this murder were what he had always wanted (the failure to murder his failure to be) the murder itself becomes a healing.

With his hands around his wife's throat, on the point of killing her, Mailer's hero envisions a door and on the other side of the door, 'heaven was there, some quiver of jewelled cities shining in the glow of a tropical dusk . . .' Yet he does not move toward this shining glow consciously. Rather, a kind of primal force in him takes to murder, and he likens this force to the power of his sexual feelings, 'some black-biled lust, some desire to go ahead not unlike the instant one comes in a woman against her cry that she is without protection . . .' Her death proceeds from him as if it were an inexorable historical process confirmed in its justice by the good it does him . . .

> and *crack* I choked her harder, and *crack* I choked her again, and *crack* I gave her payment – never halt now – and *crack* the door flew open and the wire tore in her throat, and I was through the door, hatred passing from me in wave after wave, illness as well, rot and pestilence, nausea, a bleak string of salts. I was floating. I was as far into myself as I had ever been and universes wheeled in a dream . . . I opened my eyes, I was weary, with a most honourable fatigue, and my flesh seemed new.

And this imagining of Mailer is in its turn not his own because it comes from a long tradition of heroes who are violent to women: Raskolnikov, Bigger Thomas, in fantasy; Eldridge Cleaver, Caryl Chessman, in fact. And the theme of male violence appears everywhere, the strange yet not surprising narcissism of the Hell's Angels, the rapaciousness and the threat of rapaciousness of armies; it creeps into one's consciousness when one pulls the curtains closed at night, or locks the door. And yes, it is true, men are violent. I have read the statistics. But still, I begin to doubt. An uncanny feeling comes to me after I see the image projected again and again on different screens. Perhaps this image is in itself precious; perhaps the violence itself takes place in the service of this image. Perhaps underneath violence is the desire to appear violent.

Even science labours to keep this image of man as a menace alive; to prove it. The words of Robert Ardrey: 'The territorial imperative is as blind as a cave fish, as consuming as a furnace, and it commands beyond logic, opposes all reason, suborns all moralities, strives for no goal more sublime than survival . . .' Lionel Tiger's descriptions of the aggressiveness and dominance of male masques, Darwin's theories of the struggle for existence, Herbert Spencer's social Darwinism, all part of a large work of defence. Man is violent, they protest, almost hysterically, man will always be violent.

Be grateful, I hear them telling us, look what we sacrifice to you, our true nature, our redemption. But the imperative to violence in us (as blind as a cave fish) must be fed something, some tidbit, or else even we, with our good intentions, will be able to do nothing against it. And so pornography in the light of these protestations becomes almost an act of mercy. For just as it prevents terrible actual violence, we are told, it is a kindness to those men who wage war against their own natures, a sop to their own mighty urges.

Like much of the thought of this male civilization, the story ends in tragedy. What an abysmal bitterness. A civilization of discontent. A nature forever held back, to be satisfied simply with appeasement, the transcendence, the shining glow of tropical dusk behind the door of real rape and murder, to be forever denied. And what is more, this old story implies that this denial has taken place for the sake of women. Somehow it is because we like to have our kitchen floors clean, because we are fussily gentle and given to soft fabrics, if not a kind of softness in the head, men have to contain the grandness of their true natures. (Lionel Tiger writes that the equivalent of childbirth for the male includes 'perhaps even the violent mastery and destruction of others.')

Underneath the argument that pornography is cathartic, then, is a terrible nostalgia and a grief for the imagined loss of this primal violence. And so the double message. The speaker who utters opposite truths out of each side of his mouth. The Janus head. Gemini. The twin love of violence and fear of violence in the warning, don't take away pornography or the beast will be unleashed.

I do not believe what this head is saying to me. In the first place, the head is severed. And it is not Salome who holds it up for admiration. The head has detached itself from the body and blames the body now for its own beastliness. For it is the head, the intellect, which has imagined this violence to be part of male nature and then must speak and protest and defend and prove because the head needs this violence as the body does not. What leads me to feel this, to sense it out? The hysteria. The hysteria of these arguments, which I must now move through delicately and slowly, unwrapping a tangled and distorted web: this hysteria is a sign to me that the violence is unreal, has been fabricated by the severed head. And of course the head is hysterical. Without the body, it must feed on images alone.

What if we imagined our true natures, male and female, as undeniably tender?

Tenderness as deaf as moss, as enveloping as fog, it lives past words, opposes nothing, feeds all perception, cares for no concern past feeling . . . That laced through our profoundest stories are moments of confrontation when the soul of the heroine is overwhelmed because she perceives the depths of her ability to love and this takes the greatest courage, tests her being. Oh, but this is softminded. This in the culture of pornography, which is the culture of sadism, is the height of softmindedness.

Hysteria. For instance, the head claims out of one side of its mouth that pornography leads to nothing. Produces no behaviour, they would say in the social science texts. That pornography does not make or encourage men to rape women, or in any way to reproduce the acts of cruelty they see. But out of the other side of its mouth, the head tells us that pornography allows many men to achieve (and this in itself is an interesting word, 'achieve') sexual release. This is not logical. Yet, in working through the knots of this hysteria, let me attempt to make it logical.

Perhaps what is being said by the two sides of the mouth is that pornography excites some behaviour but not all behaviour. That, to be precise, a pornographic magazine, with a drawing of a nude woman whose face is enclosed in a horse's bit, whose body is roped and suspended, will excite a man to sexual pleasure, but not to the desire to bind and bridle a woman.

Let us forget for a moment that the article which this drawing accompanies suggests that, 'The world of restraint devices with its treasure trove of straps, harnesses and buckles, provides an acceptable way to act out their dream with a minimal risk of injury.' Let us forget that these words surround the illustration in this case because here the argument is different. Here the argument is not for any acting out as 'an acceptable way' to fulfill fantasy (leading, of course, to minimal injury). Here the argument is that simply to see a photograph or read a story about 'restraint devices' (oh, how the language domesticates these horrors) is acceptable and leads to only minimal injury, if any injury at all.

And so that image, of the body of a woman unclothed and bound and in pain, which excited feeling in the body, the head says, introduces no corresponding idea of violence.

But this is the head speaking. And, of course, the image of violence does not make the body feel violent. A body feels violent only when physically frightened, threatened in its being. It is the head that requires images of violence, that is excited by them, that *wants* them. And this same male head convinces the body that it needs those images, pictures of women's bodies, and tyrannises its own body, restrains and misshapes the bodily responses to these ends, to its far more complicated purposes. The head exploits the body's simple desire for pleasure and uses this for its own unsimple desires.

And the head that requires this violence will push the body further and further, for its demands, like the limitless world of images, can be inexorable. And so the head, while deftly constructing an ineffable association between the undeniable ways of the body and the tortuous binding of a woman, at the same time, out of the other side of its mouth, denies that such a thing as association exists. Says that a man may look at a picture of a woman bound and gagged and feel sexually, but feel no desire to bind or gag or cause pain.

In fact, the argument is that her body and the binding around her body have opposite effects on the same man. By her body, he is moved to action. He can 'achieve' sexual pleasure. But her binding has an opposite effect. This does not stir him to action. This ends in the image, purges him of any striving toward action, placates him in his primal desire for violence.

What a tangle this head with its mouth speaking from two sides has created. It has obscured the perfectly obvious; that to put any two images together is to create an association. That to put violence and women's bodies together, to associate sexuality and violence fabricates a need. (But, of course, the head must conceal simple observations because it is the head which fabricates needs, and in order to make a need felt, it is important that the need be believed, and, therefore, it must never be known that the need is fabricated.) Advertisers in the last decades have spent millions of dollars to create associations between their products and sexual pleasure in order to fabricate a need for those products. In this case the product is brutality toward women.

But I come back to the idea of catharsis. Because I have experienced catharsis. I have had catharsis pass through my mind and enter my body and have seen my body be sick and then be well as my mind was healed of what I held too long within myself without seeing.

And so why should it not be true that seeing pornographic photographs could purge a man of his need for violence, even if the mind has created the need? If it is a mental need, born of fantasy, fantasy should be able to answer that need.

But this has not been my experience, nor is this the shape of catharsis, for catharsis is not an end in itself. That deep experiencing of old, sometimes long-buried emotions bears a fruit, and the fruit is knowledge. If there were really to be a catharsis experienced regarding sexual violence toward women, the need for that violence would disappear or if it reappeared, be only a shadow of itself and renamed, linked to its source, its origin.

How I wish Freud had begun his practice on young men, treating their hysteria, their fatal attraction to war, rape, dominance. How I wish he had treated the fathers who were accused of raping their daughters for whatever illness brought them to these acts. But this is the central problem, and why I write these pages and why our lives as men and women have taken the shape they have in this civilization. Such behaviour as war and rapaciousness has not been seen as proceeding from illness. Such behaviour has been termed normal, if not 'animal', wild, untrammelled, uncivilized perhaps but not pathological. But this behaviour is not seen as illness. Who sees? The severed heads are seeing. Freud himself was a severed head. He would not see himself.

And, of course, this behaviour is normal in the sense that it is practised by most men. As has been widely documented, first in Phyllis Chesler's *Women and Madness*, but now in many other places, male healers of the mind are themselves very often rapists and they rape their clients in the name of wellness. There is such a phenomenon as an illness which is created by and sustained by a culture; and one of those illnesses accounts for a great deal of the range of masculine behaviour, including rape and sadism and the enjoyment of images of brutality toward women and the apologia for that brutality which constitutes much of our culture. Freud was not above this illness. What he saw, he saw through the lens of this cultural madness.

So how understandable it is that he treated mostly women, that he *saw* hysteria in women, so that the very term hysteria has come to connote a young female patient. When I think of catharsis, naturally the cases of the young women whom Freud treated come to mind. A woman who had fits of choking; one who had a morbid fear of snakes, whose arms were paralysed; a woman who had attacks of dizziness and fear of heights. A young woman who would not eat or drink. In order to make them well, the doctor brought these women to their memories. The death of a friend who was never mourned, the death of a father who was hated, a mother who forced her daughter to eat food which had sat for two hours and was cold. Feelings which could not be recognized or lived to their full extent and *never named* living on in the head, finally expressed by the body as distortions.

In all these cases it was not the mere experiencing of choking or dizziness or fear or paralysis or nausea or revulsion that healed illness. In each case the origin of these symptoms themselves could be revealed as unreal and the real source of illness be precisely named. Knowledge, ultimately, is what healed. Had these women gone on experiencing nausea or dizziness or fear or paralysis, moreover accompanied by the belief that these symptoms were somehow causes or accumulated passions which would subside with some indulgence, one might presume that the symptoms would have gotten worse, for the continual indulgence in them would strengthen a belief in them and thus take each psyche farther away from a real knowledge of herself.

But this is precisely what pornography, which the severed heads claim is cathartic, does. It is dangerous to confuse the therapeutic experience with the experiencing of the symptoms of one's illness. But such is an old habit, an old trick of systems of oppression, whether they be psychic or social. What George Orwell called the politics of language; to name peace war or war peace. This is what Mary Daly calls reversal. The truth only hidden in what is said. The wolf in sheep's clothing. Language itself, which can be the healing agent, takes us farther away from what we know to be true, and we are severed from our own knowledge and so obsessed with the distorted ghost of truth.

And then once possessing this knowledge, one desires to be free. This is the first emotion. I have felt it. In *Tribute to Freud*, H.D. wrote of her investigations of dream states and memories, 'I am drifting out to sea. But I know I am safe, can return at any moment to Terra Firma.' This is the clarity one wants, not the freedom to be ill to the extremity of one's illness, but the freedom which comes from being free of illness, free of an obsession with the past.

Pornography and Silence

PROLOGUE

One is used to thinking of pornography as part of a larger movement toward sexual liberation. In the idea of the pornographic image we imagine a revolution against silence. We imagine that eros will be set free first in the mind and then in the body by this revelation of a secret part of the human soul. And the pornographer comes to us, thus, through history, portrayed as not only a 'libertine', a man who will brave injunctions and do as he would, but also a champion of political liberty. For within our idea of freedom of speech we would include freedom of speech about the whole life of the body and even the darkest parts of the mind.

And yet, though in history the movement to restore eros to our idea of human nature and the movement for political liberation are parts of the same vision, we must now make a distinction between the libertine's idea of liberty, 'to do as one likes', and a vision of human 'liberation'. In the name of political freedom, we would not argue for the censorship of pornography. For political freedom itself belongs to human liberation, and is a necessary part of it. But if we are to move toward human liberation, we must begin to see that pornography and the small idea of 'liberty' are opposed to that liberation.

These pages will argue that pornography is an expression not of human erotic feeling and desire, and not of a love of the life of the body, but of a fear of bodily knowledge, and a desire to silence eros. This is a notion foreign to a mind trained in this culture. We have even been used to calling pornographic art 'erotic'. Yet in order to see our lives more clearly within this culture, we must question the meaning we give to certain words and phrases, and to the images we accept as part of the life of our minds. We must, for example, look again at the idea of 'human' liberation. For when we do, we will see two histories of the meaning of this word, one which includes the lives of women, and even embodies itself in a struggle for female emancipation, and another, which opposes itself to women, and to 'the other' (men and women of other 'races', the 'Jew'), and imagines that liberation means the mastery of these others.

Above all, we must look into the mind that I will call 'the chauvinist mind', which has defined this second use of the word 'human' to exclude women, and decipher what the image of woman, or 'the black', or 'the Jew', means in that mind. But this is why I write of pornography. For pornography is the mythology of this mind; it is, to use a phrase of the poet Judy Grahn, 'the poetry of oppression'. Through its images we can draw a geography of this mind, and predict, even, where the paths of this mind will lead us.

This is of the greatest importance to us now, for we have imagined, under the spell of this mind, in which we all to some degree participate, that the paths this mind gives us are given us by destiny. And thus we have looked at certain behaviours and events in our civilisation, such as rape or the Holocaust, as fateful. We suspect there is something dark and sinister in the human soul which causes violence to ourselves and others. We have blamed a decision made by human culture on our own natures, and thus on nature. But instead, what we find when we look closely at the meaning of pornography is that culture has opposed itself in violence to the natural, and takes revenge on nature.

As we explore the images from the pornographer's mind we will begin to decipher his iconography. We will see that the bodies of women in pornography, mastered, bound, silenced, beaten, and even murdered, are symbols for natural feeling and the power of nature, which the pornographic mind hates and fears. And above all, we will come to see that 'the woman' in pornography, like 'the Jew' in anti-Semitism and 'the black' in racism, is simply a lost part of the soul, that region of being the pornographic or the racist mind would forget and deny. And finally, we shall see that to have knowledge of this forbidden part of the soul is to have eros.

But the pornographic mind is a mind in which we all participate. It is the mind which dominates our culture. A mind which speaks to us through philosophy and literature, through religious doctrine and art, through film, through advertisement, in the commonest gestures, in our habits, through history and our ideas of history, and in the random acts of violence which surround our lives. And that is why this book must be written as 'we', using this plural voice, as if we were a group of beings who shared some fate. For although we are assigned different parts in the pornographic drama – myself as pariah, perhaps you as conqueror, or you as victim – we are all imagined in this mind and the images of this mind enter all our minds.

A woman's mind ought to be surprised by pornography, for most women do not read pornography. We do not even enter those places or neighbourhoods where it is sold. Still, when we first see these images, this mythos, this language, we are shocked only by a shock of recognition. We knew all these attitudes before (though we did not know, or did not want to know, his mind would 'go so far'). We read on the jacket of an American book that the narrative speaks of 'Captive Virgins and Heroic He-Men'. Another book, entitled *Fatherly Love,* describes two adolescent girls who become the lovers of older men. In the language of a French pornographer we read of a woman that 'the state her heart and mind might be in absolutely doesn't matter.' In a pornographer's voice we come upon the confession that 'I use a woman out of necessity as one uses a round and hollow receptacle for a different need'. We see a pornographic film in which women are transformed into animals, and whipped into submission by a trainer.

For the pornographic mind is the mind of our culture. In pornography we find the fantasy life of this mind. So, in a reviewer's observation that both D.H. Lawrence and Henry Miller 'had a definite physical love for women and a definite spiritual love for men', we can find ourselves in equal proximity to both pornography and church doctrine. The pornographer reduces a woman to a mere thing, to an entirely material object without a soul, who can only be 'loved' physically. But the church, and the Judeo-Christian culture, give us the same ethos. For we read in church doctrine that the man is the head and the wife the body, or that woman is the known, whereas man is the knower. At one end of this spectrum or another, as pornographer, in fantasy, as the beings on whom these images are projected, our minds come together in culture, as we are shaped by the force of images and through the events which these images effect.

Let us consider six lives, for instance, six lives famous to us and filled with emblematic meaning for our own lives. The life of the writer Kate Chopin. The life of the painter Franz Marc. The life of the pornographer the Marquis de Sade. The life of the actress Marilyn Monroe. The life of a man who raped a young woman and cut off her arms, Lawrence Singleton. And the life of Anne Frank. We know of these lives that only accident has kept us from living out their tragedies. On some level of our minds, without thinking, without questioning, we have assumed that the shapes of these lives were inevitable, just as the shape of our culture appears to us, in our dream of an existence, as inevitable.

But let us retell these lives in a different light. And let us now consider, as we hear each brief story, that the tragedies in these histories were caused not so much by nature as by the decisions of a mind we shall call pornographic, the mind which is the subject of this book.

The painter Franz Marc was born in Munich on 8 February, 1880. His father was a landscape painter and Franz studied painting at the Munich Academy as a young man. In 1903 he travelled to Paris and was moved by the work of the Impressionists. He became conscious of the problems of form. He had an empathy for the life of nature, which he sought to find an expression for in his work. He loved the paintings of Van Gogh. Later he edited *Der Blaue Reiter,* one of the great documents of modern art, with the objectivist Vasily Kandinsky, and he lived at the centre of a group of painters known as the Blue Rider School. He was famous for his brilliantly sensual paintings and his allegories of the lives of animals. But gradually he moved away from natural forms and began to seek a way to dismantle the sensual, material world so that he might create a world of 'pure spirit'. Believing the war would purge the corruption of the material, he joined the German army in 1914 and in 1916, at the age of 36, he was killed.

Kate O'Flaherty Chopin, the American writer, was born in St Louis, Missouri, exactly 29 years before the birth of Franz Marc, on 8 February, 1851. She was educated at the Sacred Heart Academy in St Louis and received 'no special training that might have prepared her for authorship'. She married a cotton manufacturer and lived with him in New Orleans until 1880, when he retired. Now she moved with him to a plantation in a French hamlet in Louisiana and her life was completely 'given over to the rearing of a family'. Her husband died in 1882 and she moved back to St Louis. At the age of 36 (the same age Franz Marc was when he died in a battlefield at Verdun), 'seemingly with no premeditation', she began to write of her years spent on Louisiana plantations. She published a novel and then a collection of short stories and sketches, which made her famous. She had an inborn sense of the dramatic and a capacity to make her characters 'intensely alive'. Yet she achieved her effects more through accuracy than by an overlay of 'romantic glamour'. Her last published book, *The Awakening,* was received with storms of protest because within its pages it spoke openly of a woman's sexual passion. The novel was taken from circulation at the Mercantile Library in St Louis. And she was denied membership in the Fine Arts Club. The St Louis *Republic* wrote that the book was 'too strong drink for moral babes and should be labelled "poison".' And *The Nation* decided that this account of the 'love affairs of a wife and mother' was trivial. Because of the overwhelming hostility of public reaction to this book, she ceased to write. And five years after the publication of *The Awakening*, she died.

Donatien Alphonse François Sade, the Marquis de Sade, was born in Paris on 2 June, 1740. In 1754, befitting his class (he was the descendant of one of the best Provençal families), he began a military career. He abandoned this career at the end of the Seven Years' War, in 1763. In this same year, although he was in love with another woman, whom he claimed had given him venereal disease, he followed the wishes of his father and married the elder daughter of the Comte des Aides in Paris. As governor general of Bresse and Bugey and lord of Saumane and La Coste, he led what he himself described as the life of a 'libertine'. Several times he was convicted of acts of violence against women. In 1772, for example, he imprisoned five girls, raped them, and gave them a drug which poisoned them. One of the girls he had kept prisoner was severely injured. And another died. For these kidnappings, he was sentenced to death. He was reprieved from this sentence, however, and then arrested again for another crime. Continually he was arrested, and continually he escaped or used his influence to obtain a release. But only to commit the same crimes of kidnapping, imprisonment, or violence again, so that he would again be arrested. Finally, in 1777, he was arrested once more and after a trial, another escape, and a rearrest, spent six years in a prison in Vincennes. After this he was imprisoned at the Bastille and finally at Charenton. It was during the years of his life spent in incarceration that he wrote most of his work, pornographic fantasies and essays, including the novels *Juliette* and *Justine*, for which he became famous and from which the word 'sadism' was coined. In 1801, when he was 60 years old, de Sade was arrested for having written *Justine*. This was the first time he was imprisoned for his writing. He was transferred from one prison because he sexually assaulted other prisoners. In the last years of his life, in Charenton, he had an affair with a fourteen-year-old girl, 'who was essentially sold to him by her mother'. He died in prison in 1814, at the age of 74.

Marilyn Monroe, originally named Norma Jean Mortensen (and

later Norma Jean Baker), was born on 1 June, 1926, in Los Angeles, California. She spent her childhood in foster homes and orphanages. She began her career as a photographers' model. Her nude photograph on a calendar led to a film debut in 1948, followed by larger and larger roles in films. She was publicised in her early career as a 'beautiful but dumb blonde', and became famous as a 'sex symbol'. After she achieved this fame she began to study at the Actors Studio in New York City. In 1962, at the age of thirty-six, and at the height of her career, she ended her life by taking an overdose of sleeping pills.

Lawrence Singleton was born in July 1928 in Tampa, Florida. He was one of eight children born to a working-class family and raised in a strict Southern Baptist tradition. He quit school in the eleventh grade and began work on the railroad. Later he joined the merchant marine and worked his way up to the highest rating given by the US Coast Guard, that of 'unlimited master'. He was certified to command any ship carrying passengers or freight. He was married twice. His first wife died of cancer. In the summer of 1978, his daughter left home because he beat her when he was drunk. In September 1978, he picked up a fifteen-year-old hitchhiker, raped her, and cut off her arms. On 20 April, 1979, he was convicted of rape, sodomy, oral copulation, kidnapping, mayhem, and attempted murder, and sentenced to fourteen years in prison. In 1980, as this book is being written he is serving his time in San Quentin prison.

Anne Frank was born on 12 June, 1929, in Frankfurt. She was a victim of the anti-Semitism of the Nazi regime. Her diary, written while she was hiding, 'made her the personification of the martyred Jewish young'. She is remembered by her teachers as a talkative, 'movie-loving', 'dreamy' girl. Faced with deportation, on July 9, 1942, the Franks went into hiding in the back room and office of the father's business. They lived there until they were arrested by the Gestapo on 4 August, 1944. Anne Fránk was sent to a succession of camps. She died in Bergen-Belsen in March 1945. After her death, her father, who was the sole survivor of the family, found her diary, in which we can still read the words: 'In spite of everything, I still believe that people are really good at heart'.

And now let us tell the story of pornography as if it were a part of the story of these lives, and as if, indeed, the tragedy of these lives were all our suffering. For pornography, in its intensified mythology, simply expresses the same tragic choice which our culture has made for us, the choice to forget eros.

SACRED IMAGES

Transgression

> . . . all the members that had been thrust into her and so
> perfectly provided the living proof that she was indeed prosti-
> tuted, had at the same time provided the proof that she was
> worthy of being prostituted and had, so to speak, sanctified her.
>
> *The Story of O*

We are perhaps surprised to find that the metaphysics of Christianity
and the metaphysics of pornography are the same. For we are
accustomed to thinking of history in a different light. We imagine the
church fathers as the judges of and inquisitors against the
pornographers. We imagine the pornographer as a revolutionary of
the imagination, who bravely stands up to speak of the life of the body
openly while the church pronounces on the evils of the flesh. We
remember Tertullian's words that even 'natural beauty ought to be
obliterated by concealment and neglect, since it is dangerous to those
who look upon it.' And in the wake of these words, we imagine the
display of bodies in a pornographic magazine to be an act of
liberation. We remember the words of St Paul: 'It is good for a man
not to touch a woman, or the idea of Augustine that the sexual organs
are tainted with lust. Or we go back further in time, to the Romans
who preceded Christian thought with their own asceticism and hatred
of the body. We hear Democritus define a brave man as one who
overcomes not only his enemies but his 'pleasures'. We hear Epicurus
intone that sexual feeling 'never benefitted any man'. We remember
the Stoics' warning against passion in marriage, or Plotinus and his
student, Porphyry, who despised desire as evil, or the Neoplatonists,
who practiced celibacy as a virtue. And to these voices we oppose the
voice of the pornographer, who we imagine defends the body, loves
flesh, worships desire, would explore all the possibilities of sexual
joy. Thus we begin to think of pornography as a kind of transgression
against 'holy' prudery.

Certainly the pornographer is obsessed with the idea of transgression. The Marquis de Sade, for instance, finds transgression more
pleasurable than pleasure itself. He tells us, 'Crime is the soul of lust'.
He tells us that 'there is a kind of pleasure which comes from the
sacrilege or the profanation of the objects offered us for worship'.
And of his life, Simone de Beauvoir writes, 'No aphrodisiac is so
potent as the defiance of Good.' Throughout pornography the priest

or the nun, therefore, is turned into a lecherous or a prostituted figure. In Aretino's *Dialogue of the Life of a Married Woman*, a wife pretends to be near death so that she can commit adultery with the priest whom she has called for her last confession. In another classic pornographic novel, *Le Bain d'Amour*, a couple make love in a pew, and the scene of their passion alternates with descriptions of the mass. One of the more famous episodes of de Sade's *Justine* takes place in a monastery, where the monks abduct, rape, and commit sadistic acts on women. But to this we must add the enacted pornography in a brothel, in which, for example, a prostitute is asked to dress as a nun to please her client.

In his history of the creation of *Playboy* magazine, Gay Talese tells us that in the earlier years of its existence in Chicago, the *Playboy* office lay in the shadow of a great church, Holy Name Cathedral. Writing ironically of this juxtaposition, he tells us: 'great cathedrals cannot be . . . maintained without sufficient numbers of sinners to justify them.' But when we look at the history of pornography, and the pornographer's obsession with transgressing the morality of the church, we begin to understand that pornography, and the pornographic idea of sin, could not exist without the great cathedrals.

We begin to see pornography more as if it were a modern building, built on the site of the old cathedrals, sharing the same foundation. And if one were to dig beneath this foundation, we imagine, one might see how much the old structure and the new resemble one another. For all the old shapes of religious asceticism are echoed in obscenity. And every theme, every attitude, every shade of pornographic feeling has its origin in the church.

But this, finally, is the nature of rebellion. For to run away from the enemy is to call upon oneself the fate of one day meeting that enemy in oneself. A rebellion ultimately imitates that which it rebels against, until the rebel comes to understand himself. And no form of culture seems so blind to its own nature as pornography. The pornographic fantasy has that shape of the mind familiar to us in the madman, and in the totally naive liar, who contradict their speech with their gestures, who speak at cross purposes to their intent, and yet who tell us, even in their lies, the truth about their secret thoughts. Here we encounter the dream life of an otherwise duplicitous being.

So a veil is drawn over the real life of pornography. What advertises itself as nakedness is shrouded. What is called frankness is denial. What is called passion is the death of feeling. What is called desire is degradation. And the pornographic mind hallucinates. The two who are called lovers are really one soul divided. And what is called a transgression against the church fathers is finally loyalty. Just as St Jerome, in his attempt to flee from a woman's body, found the images of dancing girls intruding on his vision even when he lived alone in the desert of Chacis, so, too, perdition, sin, and hell haunt the pornographer even in his most extreme acts of rebellion.

The Revelation of Flesh

> *Beauty stands*
> *in the admiration of weak minds*
> *Led captive.*
>
> John Milton, *Paradise Regained*

The moment at which a woman begins to remove her clothing and thus to reveal her body is an event of high drama in pornography. It is rehearsed in the imagination. Elaborate means lead us to its eventuation, and the striptease is the pinnacle both of fantasy and of actual effort, a simultaneous realization in which culture and the material world become one. For the desire which runs through pornographic literature, to see the naked body of a woman, has about it the quality of the desire to see a miracle performed. The hero of *Le Bain d'Amour*, for example, strains with all the ardent frustration of a saint toward his holy vision:

> In his mind he lifted up the chaste petticoats of his friend Louise and tried with all the power of his will to conjure up an exact image of the dusky spot between the lily white nudity of her virgin thighs and stomach and that silky triangle, the mystery of which perturbed him so much.

In the industry of pornography, the preoccupation with an almost magical knowledge which is mythically withheld from a man's eyes by a woman's clothing takes on the aura of a search for the holy grail. Everywhere the revelation of a woman's flesh is advertised as if the true nature of a woman's body were a carefully guarded secret. Thus a film produced by the Mitchell brothers is called *Inside Marilyn Chambers*. This atmosphere of magic and secrecy informs the sale of slides of women's bodies, still photographs, calendars, magazines with fold-out pictures, fetishes of women's bodies shaped as swizzle sticks (which become nude when manipulated), endless varieties of burlesque events. It is part of the design of women's underclothing meant to titillate, veil, and reveal, or of the structure of a gesture, or of a story with a double entendre whose hidden meaning will reveal itself to the seeker. Inside this scenario of the revealed secret live all the stereotypical ideas we have of male and female behaviour, of modesty and deceit, aggression and rejection, seduction and rape.

Consider the myths which surround this revelation. We believe a woman is naturally modest, ashamed of her own body, afraid by nature to reveal her flesh. And on the other hand, we believe the sight of this flesh has a transformative effect on the mind of a man. That if a woman shows a bit of her legs, or her shoulder, or even leans over so that a man may see where her breasts meet, that a man will be overcome with desire for her, and compelled almost, by this sight, to rape her. (A judge in Utah, for instance, overturned a jury's verdict of guilty against a rapist because his victim was 'flimsily dressed'.) Thus behind female modesty there lurks the shape of an awesome female power.

For if a woman by her beauty can make a man into a rapist, she can also transform him in other ways. Her overwhelming seductive power can lead him into the world of flesh and the devil. Desiring her, he forgets his soul. He moves into eternal perdition. And in this eternal perdition, he loses the eternal life of his spirit. The full weight of an earthly mortality falls upon his consciousness.

But we can read in this religious scenario another language and another range of meanings, which belong to the life of the psyche. When a woman's beauty brings a man into the realm of the material, he must live in his body. He must know himself as matter. Therefore, he must give up the illusion that his mind controls his body, or that culture controls nature. Rather, inside the experience of sexual knowledge, he learns that culture and nature, meaning and love, spirit and matter, are one. And in this he loses the illusion that culture has given him against the knowledge of the vulnerability of his own flesh.

And now if we move from the language of the psyche back to mythology, we can read myth in a new light. We have a new understanding, for example, of the story of Actaeon. We see him enter the forest looking for animal prey. He is the controller of nature; he is the hunter. But by accident, or we might say through *fate*, by the natural occurrence of circumstances, he comes upon the goddess Diana as she is bathing in a pool. We know that he is stunned by her beauty. And we also know that this moment of beauty will lead to his death.

For the beautiful goddess will reach her hand into the water (a pool in which, like Narcissus, he must be able to see *his own reflection*), she will splash his face with this watery face, and he will turn into an animal. Now we know the rest of his story. As a stag, he runs through the forest. But the scent of his animal body is detected by his own hunting dogs. And thus these animals, which were his own (and which belonged to his psyche), will now tear him to pieces.

The idea that the sight of a woman's body calls a man back to his own animal nature, and that this animal nature soon destroys him, reverberates throughout culture. We find it in the most ancient sources. In the Biblical story of creation, we discover Eve, who has spoken with a serpent, seducing Adam into eating an apple, the forbidden fruit of knowledge. Through this seduction, the commentators tell us, 'Eve brought death into the world.'

And this mythology entered the reasoning minds of the monks who shaped an ideology for the burning of witches. Thus in the *Malleus Maleficarum*, Sprenger and Kramer write that when men see and hear women, they 'are caught by their carnal desires', for a woman's face is 'a burning wind' and a woman's voice is 'the hissing of serpents'.

We meet the same idea, that a woman's beauty causes a man death (and in the same Biblical imagery), in these lines by Swinburne:

> *Thou hast a serpent in thine hair*
> *In all the curls that close and cling*
> *And oh that breast flower!*
> *Oh love, thy mouth, too fair*
> *To kiss and sting!*

And again in these lines by the Italian Renaissance poet Giambattista Marino:

> *Black thou art, but beautiful, O thou*
> *Love's charming monster among nature's*
> *Beauties, dark is the dawn near thee.*

Faulkner tells us again and again that 'men are helpless in the hands of their mothers, wives and sisters'. Poe writes of the dying Berenice: 'And now – I shuddered in her presence, and grew pale at her approach.' Balzac crafts the tale of Pauline, who, after she murders her lover by making love to him, utters the words: 'He is mine. I have killed him.'

And Balzac's tale is mild compared to the pornographic story we read from medieval France called 'Of a Girl Who Was Ill of the Plague and Caused the Death of Three Men Who Lay with Her, and How the Fourth was Saved and She Also.' Here a woman's strength is fed by the deaths of three men. Each man makes love to her while she is ill, and each man contracts the plague from her and dies. But after enjoying each lover she becomes stronger, until she's well.

Yet again, we realize that the death of a pornographic hero has more than one meaning. First, of course, it has a simple literal meaning. Even on the surface of the tale we read the old religious fear that 'where there is death, there too is sexual coupling'. And this death takes us to a second level of meaning, where we encounter the fear of the knowledge of the body and of the power of nature, which must lead us to acknowledge mortality and vulnerability. But beneath this level is still another meaning. For the idea of physical death, terrifying in itself, can also symbolise another death. And this is the death of a self-image. Culture imagines itself to be invulnerable to nature. A man who believes culture's illusions believes that he is invulnerable to nature and that he controls nature. But the sight of a woman's body reminds him of the power of his own body, which is nature, over his mind, which is culture. Thus, for a few moments, his self-image dies and he is *humiliated*.

In the pornographic novel *Fatherly Love*, we find a clear description of this humiliation. Here a man appears to lose control of himself. He is overwhelmed by desire. At the sight of a woman's body he begins to masturbate. And as he continues to masturbate, the pornographic heroine, who we must remember only speaks the words of the pornographic psyche itself, tells him, 'Don't you feel ashamed of yourself? Don't you feel humiliated standing there in public, masturbating in front of a girl you've never seen before?' When the hero, who angrily continues to masturbate, says that he does not feel ashamed, this humiliation continues and is equated with sexuality itself. Cunnilingus becomes a means for degradation. Telling a man she has not washed herself in weeks and that she 'just took a piss', she invites him to put his mouth to her, 'knowing how filthy it is'. She tells him, 'I can't believe any man – even your type – would be that low.'

Here is not a man who humiliates a virgin by making her a whore. Rather, it is a whore who humiliates a man. But the pornographic mind retaliates against this imagined humiliation. Participating in the church's fantasy that it is a woman's body which destroys a man's soul, now the pornographic mind takes out its revenge against that same body which has humbled it. For this is the underside and the secret message in the pornographic revelation of beauty: its purpose is to rob the female body of both its natural power and its spiritual presence. So in the striptease, culture realizes its revenge against nature. The mystery of the female body is revealed to be nothing more than flesh, and flesh under culture's control.

At once promising and giving the reader his revenge, an advertisement for a pornographic magazine emblazons these words next to the nude body of a woman: 'If women have been a mystery to you,' the words promise, 'let *Chic* Magazine unveil their mysteries. *Chic*'s ladies have nothing to hide . . . They know all and show all . . . You'll know all!' Here, then, is her knowledge, her mystery, her power, her secret. Just this flesh which she reveals because she is paid to do so. Beneath her pose, one can hear the voice of the pornographer whispering, 'This is all she is; she is a *thing*.'

But we need not imagine this voice of derision. Over and over, through classical culture, and through pornography, the pornographic mind tells us that woman's mysterious beauty is simply nothing. We read this in Alexander Pope's 'Rape of the Lock'. We discover it in these lines by the seventeenth-century poet Robert Gould:

> *Strip but this Puppet of its gay Attire*
> *Its gauzes, Ribbons, Lace, Commode and Wire*
> *And tell me then what 'tis thou dost admire? . . .*
> *Open her secret Boxes; Patches here*
> *You'll horded find, her Paints and Washes there:*
> *Love's artful twigs, where the chatt'ring Ape*
> *Sits perched and hasn't the Judgement to Escape . . .*

We find the same formula for the annihilation of beauty in the words of the pornographic writer Juvenal: 'In good time she discloses her face; she removes the first layer of plaster and begins to be recognizable.'

But the pornographic revelation of beauty goes beyond ridicule. When the pornographer models a figure of a woman, when he fashions her portrait, or captures her in his camera, he is possessing her. And now, by this possession, he controls the one who has captured him, who has ensnared and enchanted him, who causes his death and shames him. He has made himself safe from her power.

The man who stares at a photograph of a nude woman is a voyeur. He can look freely and turn away when he wishes. He can run his hands over the two-dimensional surface, but he will not be touched. He can know the body of a woman, and yet encounter a knowledge which will not change him. We read that the sight of a woman contains 'the image of everything which rises up from the depths'. But the voyeur, when he sees a photograph of a woman's body, keeps these depths at a distance. An invisible line separates him from the image he perceives. He will not be overwhelmed by the presence of her flesh. He need not encounter the knowledge of his own body. He can hide from the deepness of his own soul.

Of the extraordinary appeal of *Playboy* magazine's first centrefold models, Gay Talese writes:

> She was their mental mistress. She stimulated them in solitude, and they often saw her picture while making love to their wives. She was an almost special species who exists within the eye and mind of the observer and she offered everything imaginable. She was always available at bedside, was totally controllable . . . she behaved in a way that real women did not, which was the essence of fantasy.

For we must understand here again that the nude woman in the pornographer's mind is really only a denied part of himself which he refuses to recognise. But this is part of himself which has a will to live, a will to expression, to being. This part of himself returns, and threatens to destroy his illusion of himself. If he is to entertain the existence of desire at all in his mind, desire must come to him in a form that he can control.

Yet desire always transforms us. We are enchanted by beauty. We are indeed overwhelmed by feeling. The mind's attempt to silence the soul must have another effect than silence. Part of the pornographer's mind remembers what the pornographic mind would forget. Even the desacralised and humiliated images of pornography must remind the pornographer of his lost self. Even by his means of control, the images he has created, he feels himself losing control. But this is the nature of obsession. The obsessive act must be repeated. And thus the pornographer must invent more images and fantasies, more ingenious devices through which to assert the superiority of his mind over matter.

He puts the body of a woman on a pack of playing cards, for example. And thus he can handle her with ease. He can put her in his pocket. And he is the dealer. In his hands, fate is decided. He has reversed natural order. He reprints millions of copies of photographs of women's bodies and distributes these all over the world. And he exerts his power in other ways too. In a centrefold depicting the bodies of nude women which he calls 'Beaver Hunt', he displays these photographs on pink tiles, and places a man's foot next to them, so that the foot on the page looks like the foot of a man who looks at the pictures, and the toe of this foot alone is larger than each woman's whole body. But as if this display of power through size is not enough, he humiliates these images further by surrounding them with cigarette ash and stamped-out cigarettes. And in another mode of fantasy, a novel in which beautiful women are saddled, ridden, and whipped, he exclaims, 'What a picture of loveliness under complete domination!'

Over and over again, the pornographer must reverse his own humiliation, his own enslavement, his own terror. Fearing that he will be transformed if he looks on beauty, the pornographer takes possession of a woman's body. Fearing that he will die of his own desire, he places her loveliness under his control. And fearing that her presence will destroy his soul, he destroys her soul and makes of her an object. And then, fearing the object he has made, he destroys her.

THE DEATH OF THE HEART: FROM FANTASY TO EVENT

> All great simple images reveal a psychic state.
>
> Gaston Bachelard

We know the heart to be the centre. The place where body and soul meet, where reason gives way to passion. And the trembling of desire we feel in our bodies, which comes from the heart, is also the spirit's trembling. In this trembling, the body expresses the soul, and perhaps it is this trembling that tells us the body is captured and ruled by the spirit's longing.

But where is this heart in the pornographer's vision of ourselves? The heart is here, but she is held captive. We find this shape of the red valentine, for instance, depicted on the cover of a pornographic magazine for February, the month of Valentine's Day. Before a glistening red background, a woman in a glossy photograph kneels before us. She wears red glasses in the shape of hearts. And she is in chains. But this is the task of pornography – to chain and imprison the heart, to silence feeling.

Two tales come down to us from a long history of a civilization and they both tell the story of a civilization's sacrifice of innocence and vulnerability in the body of a young woman. Yet one, Euripides' *Iphigenia,* is a great tragedy; the other, *Justine,* is pornography. What separates the two is feeling.

To watch Agamemnon send his daughters to death is almost unbearable. We are outraged. We hope. With Clytemnestra, we pray and plead for her life. And when she dies we weep, as if one loved, or a part of ourselves, were lost. But one never weeps as a witness to pornography. No death in pornography touches us with sorrow. Justine's suffering fails to move us. We cannot imagine loving Justine, and we let her die with no protest, because as we enter the mind of the Marquis de Sade, our own hearts are silenced.

All death in pornography is really only the death of the heart. Over and over again, that part of our beings which can feel both in body and mind is ritually murdered. We make a mistake, therefore, when we believe that pornography is simply fantasy, simply a record of sadistic events. For pornography exceeds the boundaries of both fantasy and record and becomes itself an act. Pornography *is* sadism.

This sadism has many forms. A woman who enters a neighbourhood where pornographic images of the female body are displayed, for instance, is immediately shamed. Once entering the arena of pornography, she herself becomes a pornographic image. It is *her* body that is displayed. And if she is interested in pornography, this interest becomes the subject of pornographic speculation. If she is shocked and turns away from the pornographic image in disgust, she becomes the pornographic 'victim'. She cannot escape pornography without humiliation. And we know humiliation to be the essence of sadism. It is thus that pornography exists as an act of sadism toward all women.

But now let us add to this that there is nowhere in culture where a woman can evade pornography. She cannot have come to age without seeing at least one of these images. And, we know, when images enter the mind, they remain there forever as memory.

Yet pornography (which appears to know its own cruelty to women) is also cruel to the souls of men. In the pornographic mind, women represent a denied part of the self; in this mind a woman is a symbol for a man's hidden vulnerability. Here disguised in a woman's body are his own feelings, and his own heart. When Agamemnon sacrifices his daughter, he also gives up his own tenderness. And as part of this choice, he takes on the armour of a warrior. But when we witness Agamemnon's choice, we regret it. In *Justine*, when feeling is slaughtered, it is slaughtered twice. Once in the ritual portrayed to us. And a second time within us. For this second sacrifice of feeling is accomplished through language and imagery which horrifies, disgusts, and finally numbs us.

Now one learns why it is that pornography is so often ugly. One of its functions, one of its reasons for being, is to offend sensibility. We find the ugliness of obscenity in a magazine such as *Hustler*, for instance, in which the publisher writes of the need to 'dig . . . turds' out of another man's 'rectum'. (Without making a conscious connection between cruelty and ugliness, we understand that these two qualities belong together.) In the same magazine, a cartoon appears which depicts a man about to be executed. We accept the crude caricature of his features, his body, the way he is made repulsive to us. We know without knowing why that this style is appropriate to the message of the cartoon. The man stares at two electric chairs, one of which reads 'Regular', the other, 'Extra Crispy'. This is the language of the sadist; ugliness is his style. We are shocked, but shocked away from feeling. For while beauty evokes feeling, ugliness numbs us. The pornographer's art is meant to dull our feelings, and his own.

Even where the language or style of pornography takes on the skill and superficial grace of great art, even where it *is* artful, it never partakes of that quality of beauty which makes us *feel*. Thus de Sade's language is elegant and skilful, but through another means, it creates the same effect on us as ugliness. In *Justine*, a Monsieur Rodin, who has been the headmaster of a school for children, decides to put his daughter to death for 'the progress of science'. But unlike the evocative language of Euripides' tragedy, this language works to deaden any response we might have to this sacrifice. Thus her father speaks to us of the death of his daughter:

> anatomy will never reach its ultimate state of perfection until an examination has been performed upon the vaginal canal of a fourteen- or fifteen-year-old child who has expired from a cruel death; it is only from the contingent contraction we can obtain a complete analysis of a so highly interesting part.

In her essay on pornographic literature, Susan Sontag writes that this flatness of tone we discover in obscene writing is not an 'index of principled inhumanity'. And yet de Sade, through a self-portrait of the artist as sadist, which he draws in the words of his character Rodin, tells us exactly the opposite. Defending the murder of his daughter for the progress of science, Rodin argues: 'When Michelangelo wished to render a Christ after Nature, did he make the crucifixion of a young man the occasion for a fit of remorse? Why no: he copied the boy in his death agonies. But where it is a question of the advance of our art, how absolutely essential such means become!' In *The Story of O*, another 'artful' example of pornography, where we find the same flatness of language, we discover the same attitude toward feeling. When a character named Jacqueline is horrified and upset by the scars the heroine has received from her floggings, O first ridicules her, and then vows to punish her. And this logical argument against compassion, this ridicule, and this threat are equally intended for the reader. For when one reads pornography, one enters into a sadomasochistic relationship with an author in which one is punished, humiliated, and terrified through language.

In the sadomasochistic ritual, the sadist must appear to have no feeling. Projecting his feeling onto his victim, he tries simultaneously to elicit and destroy feeling. In his mind, he is both actor and acted upon, writer and reader. Wilhelm Stekel, in his massive study of sadomasochism, writes:

> The sadist pictures to himself what is happening in the mind of his object, whose resistance he calls forth and breaks. Only this feeling of himself into the affective life of the object brings him the expected pleasure. But this object is merely a reflection of his different psychic and sexual components, and the scene represents a play with himself.

Thus fantasy lies at the very heart of any sadistic event. And at the centre of pornographic fantasy lies a real event. The reader plays the denied self of the pornographic writer and the writer plays out the denied self of the reader, and for both, feeling is destroyed.

In *The Past Recaptured*, a work which is not pornography, but is instead a profound portrait of the sadomasochistic dilemma, Marcel Proust describes sadism as it is performed within a male whorehouse. His hero, M. de Charlus, has paid to be beaten and humiliated, but he is dissatisfied with his treatment. The young man who whips him

appears to be insincere when he tells him, 'No, you worthless trash
. . . since you bawl and crawl on your knees, we're going to chain you
to the bed. No pity!' As the young male prostitutes stand in the
reception room of the brothel, in an effort to appear sadistic they
impersonate 'Bellevue toughs'. They must give the impression to
their clients that any of them would 'do it with his own sister for 20
francs'. As part of their performance, they speak of brutal sexual
exploits, boast of murder and theft, brag about life as soldiers in the
trenches ('some days a hand grenade goes right through you'). Above
all, the aesthetic which they must create for their patrons is one of
hardness, unfeelingness, invulnerability. (And M. de Charlus is
disappointed again when he hears the young man speak of his parents
as 'dear old mother and father'.)

The house of prostitution is in itself an illustration of pornography's
transformation into reality. For the whorehouse is simply an obscene
illusion acted out in space and time; it is four-dimensional pornography. Here the 'client' (as does the patron or the reader of
pornography) asks to be brutalized. He complains at the presence of
sentiment or softness. He wishes his sexual partner to act out coldness
and harshness. And in this one can sense the shadow of a whole
culture. Outside explicit pornography, culture has created 'hard'
heroes, in the writer, the actor, the public persona. We expect
Norman Mailer to shock and offend our sensibilities. We celebrate
Charles Bukowski for what we label crudeness. We seek the imper-
viousness of Brando. And all this 'toughness' is part of an aesthetic
which we believe to be sexually exciting.

Of the flatness of language and the absence of emotion in pornography, Sontag writes that the 'arousal of a sexual response in the
reader *requires* it.' Yet now we must begin to question this
conventional idea of sexuality. For perhaps, like the statement of the
sadomasochistic patient – made over and over in clinical studies – that
he *seeks* feeling, this may be one of those unconsidered thoughts we
accept as canon whose real truth is revealed to us when they are
reversed. Let us remember, for instance, that it is extremely difficult,
perhaps next to impossible, to experience any sensation without an
emotion. Memory attaches itself to smell, to touch, to colour. As
Stendhal tells us: 'Each time the soul is moved by two affections at the
same time, then, in the future, every time it feels one of them again, it
feels the other also.' A therapist who attempts to heal the mind
through the body uses this knowledge. The body holds memories of
feelings from the past. To be touched, to move, to breathe, all these

experiences of the body bring intense feelings to consciousness. A woman is touched on a certain place on her back, and she remembers an old grief from her childhood she had forgotten. After moving and breathing, sinking deeper in the knowledge of his body, a man begins to weep and scream as he relives an incident from his youth. In his analytical work, Wilhelm Reich found that the emotional amnesias, called 'blocks', and muscular tensions were in fact, to use his language, 'functionally identical'. Freud's first patients were 'hysterically paralysed'. Their bodies were literally paralysed with unexpressed emotions. Thus paralysis in the body was a metaphor for an emotional paralysis.

Nothing brings the soul to feel so much as physical sensation, for emotions live in the body; we know a whole physical language of emotion. The body cries tears in sorrow, convulses with laughter in mirth, becomes flushed and hot in anger. The pornographer argues to us that pornography gives him back his sexual feeling. But the truth is more complex. In truth, what has made a man impotent *are* his feelings, because *he is afraid to have them*. He would avoid knowledge of himself. And in the language of the body, this fear and denial of a part of himself is expressed as impotence. For he is literally afraid to experience sensation, especially sexual sensation, which is an intense physical feeling, and therefore an intense emotional feeling. This is the real history of his impotence.

If 'the arousal of sexual response' requires the deadening of feeling, this fact does not belong to the nature of sexuality. It is the nature of sexuality to arouse feeling, and of feeling to arouse sexuality. Rather, 'the arousal of sexual response' requires the deadening of feeling in a man who is already impotent, and who has already chosen to 'forget' his emotions. This man might instead have chosen to remember. He might have sought to be healed by memory. (Or his culture might have offered him this choice in its very idea of sexuality.) But instead, driven by his own ambivalence, wanting and not wanting his feeling back, his own body still expressing the desire for eros, he solves his dilemma through brutality. He is brutal to all that might be emotionally sensitive in himself. He destroys the emotional part of himself, in himself or in a projected image of himself. For he is terrified of what he denies.

In one who is afraid of feeling, or of the memory of certain emotions, sexuality in itself constitutes a terrible threat. The body forces the mind back toward feeling. And even when the mind wills the body to be silent, the body rebels and plagues the mind with 'urgency'. And the body, seeking to be open, to be vulnerable, seeking emotional knowledge, is threatened, punished, and humiliated by the pornographic mind. All these acts are intended to deaden the heart. To make the heart retreat long enough so that the body, which perhaps has reached a fever pitch, can 'release' sensation. And yet we must not be too quick to believe that this 'urgency', and this 'release', this fever pitch, this demandingness, belong to the body alone. For the separation between body and mind is unnatural. The body speaks the language of the soul. In the body's fevered longing is perhaps a deep desire for that self to come to consciousness, to be remembered. For an experience of the heart is also an experience of the mind. The body and heart cry out like a long neglected child, pleading, 'Pay attention to me.' But the pornographic mind, hoping for silence from the heart, responds with punishment. And now, if the body is 'relieved', it is because at least the mind has given some sign that it is aware of the body's existence. Like the neglected child, the body is glad even for this destructive gesture from the mind.

But the real intent of sadomasochism and of sadomasochistic pornography is to sever the connection between mind and body. And it is precisely because this severance is unnatural that it must be violent and terrifying. Because the body, in its desire to become a part of consciousness, is persistent. Like any living thing, it would survive, and survive in consciousness also. Just as the sadomasochist tells us he seeks feeling, when indeed he is afraid of feeling, so also the pornographer, who says he would bring sexuality into consciousness, and who says that he desires the freedom to speak of sexuality, in fact wishes to suppress and silence sexual knowledge. This is the message of the brutality of pornography: the pornographer is a censor.

Liberty and Liberation

Pornography is filled with heroes who are seeking liberty. But the meanings of the word 'liberty' are not simple. Within the range of meanings this word has, one discovers two definitions completely opposed to one another. The first reference to liberty listed in the *Oxford English Dictionary* speaks of an 'exemption or release from captivity, bondage or slavery'. But from this definition the word 'liberty' evolves into an entirely different concept. It soon becomes 'the faculty or power to do as one likes', and then freedom from the control of 'fate or necessity', then 'leave, permission', then 'an unrestrained use of or access to', then 'licence', and then 'to take liberties or be unduly familiar' (as, for example, when 'the poor man had taken liberty with a wench'), and then the word 'liberty' comes to mean a privilege granted by a sovereign, and then it means privilege over one's domain,* and finally, 'at one's power or disposal'. And giving us an example of this usage of the word 'liberty', the dictionary quotes: 'I nowe had her at my liberte I sholde make her to deye a cruell deth.'

In the pornographic mind, 'liberty' moves through all of those meanings. The pornographer begins by telling himself that he wishes liberation. To himself and to the world, he poses as a man who would simply liberate his sexuality from an imprisoning morality. And yet it is his own mind which holds him captive. And this is a mind which would have a power over nature which exists only in fantasy. The pornographer wants the power to 'do as he likes'. But in order to have freedom from natural limitation, the pornographer must obtain privileges which do not exist in nature; this mind must be given power by the authority of culture, which it holds sovereign. And now, by the right of this power, the pornographic mind conceives of nature as part of its domain and makes nature at its power and disposal.

But in the pornographic mind, woman *is* nature. She represents natural fate. And so, in the name of freedom, the pornographer imagines he must control her. And to control her he must take away her liberty. He must imprison her. He may even take the 'liberty' of murdering her. But above all, this man, who pleads to us that he only wishes for 'freedom of speech', must silence 'woman'.

Pornography expresses an almost morbid fear of female speech. A pornographic magazine publishes this poem next to an illustration of a pornographic 'device' in which to encase a woman:

> *It sculptures her breasts and it narrows her waist*
> *And it shows off her gorgeous behind*
> *And the helmet which over her head has been placed*
> *Keeps her deafened and silent and blind*

An advertisement in another magazine promises a doll as the 'bedpartner that doesn't talk back – just obeys'. Even the sexual act, in pornography, seems to exist less for pleasure than to overpower and

---

*And here we might remember that in the sixteenth, seventeenth, and eighteenth centuries, a white man's 'domain' included his wife, his children, and his property.

silence women. Hands, feet, penises, are thrust like weapons into women's mouths. Orgasm itself becomes a retaliation against a woman's words. From a novel by Henry Miller, for example, we read this scene:

> 'Shut up, you bitch,' I said. 'It hurts, doesn't it? You wanted it, didn't you?' I held her tightly, raised myself a little higher to get it in to the hilt, and pushed myself until I thought her womb would give way. Then I came – right into that snail-like mouth which was wide open.

And to this list of pornographic fantasies we add a series of still photographs which appear in a pamphlet published in Amsterdam. Here a woman is strapped to a table. She is naked. And a man in the uniform of a doctor stands at her side. He places a tube in her rectum, and a tube with a funnel in her mouth. But we have seen these postures before. We recognise them as history, as actual events. In the nineteenth century, women in the female suffrage movement were strapped down to tables with tubes thrust in their mouths. And this force-feeding took place as a retaliation and punishment against the political movement for a woman's freedom of speech and equal social power.

Inside and outside explicit pornography, a woman's expression of her will to freedom is met with violence or a threat of violence. In 1850, an editorial in the *Saturday Review* argues against female suffrage, that as a means to recover 'the lost rights of man', men should resort to the 'argument of the black eye'. And this recommendation is enacted in the pornographic novel. In *The Skin Flick Rapist*, for example, as she is being raped, a woman begins to protest. '. . . you men,' she says, 'aren't really concerned about women. You're only concerned about what you can drag out of their bodies. You're not concerned about them as total entities, as human beings.' The hero responds by taping her mouth. And then he beats her.

But we can find a deeper shade of the meaning of the pornographic silencing of women in this scene. Just as she is protesting against his treatment of her, and pleading for her own beingness, the heroine accuses the hero of being a 'mama's boy' who is 'weak-kneed' and 'gutless'. When the pornographer creates a female character, he creates a 'doll' through whom he himself speaks, and thus we know it is his *own* fear that he is weak, that he is tied to his mother. Nature terrifies him. Therefore, when a woman declares to him that she is human, her very beingness evokes his fear. Thus, when a woman asks to be treated as a human being, as an equal, he imagines that she is calling him 'weak'. And when she protests that he doesn't care about her feelings, he imagines she wants to reduce him to the powerlessness he felt as a child with his mother.

Throughout Western literature one finds a tradition of male struggles against the female attempt to weaken men. This is the story of Ulysses and the Sirens; it is the story of Samson and Delilah; of John the Baptist and Salome. In each of these legends, men are not only weakened – their very lives are endangered. In this mythos, not only is male freedom based on female silence, but a man's *life* depends on the death of a woman.

That male freedom and vitality require the death of women is a major but hidden theme of the modern novel. We find it in *Crime and Punishment,* in *Native Son*, in *An American Tragedy*, in *An American Dream,* and countless other works. In *An American Tragedy*, as the hero, Clyde Griffiths, watches his lover drown, he calls out to himself: 'You deserve to *live*! And her living will make your own life not worthwhile from now on!' And Norman Mailer expresses this theme when he writes, in *An American Dream:* 'Deborah had gotten her hooks into me . . . living with her I was murderous; attempting to separate, suicide came to me.' As he murders her, he describes himself to us as a victim who acts only in self-defence: 'It was as if killing her, the act had been too gentle, I had not plumbed the hatred where the real injustice was stored. She had spit on the future, my Deborah, she had spoiled my chance, and now her body was here.' His hands on his wife's throat, moments before her death, he glimpses the promise of heaven beyond her existence, 'some quiver of jewelled cities shining in the glow of a tropical dusk.'

Mailer's novel *An American Dream* is virtually a reversal of Dreiser's *An American Tragedy*. In Dreiser's book, because the hero wishes to marry the daughter of a rich man and rise in society, he feels entrapped by his promise of marriage to a woman in his own social class. While in Mailer's book, his hero is married to the daughter of a rich man, and feels himself to be under her power. After he murders his wife, he becomes the lover of a woman in the lower classes. Dreiser's novel comments on and grieves for the corruption of Clyde Griffiths' soul. And the hero's intention to murder his lover inevitably causes his own death. But in Mailer's work, the murder of a woman bears no consequences. His hero escapes punishment victoriously. We are left with the impression that he committed a *just* murder.

In the pages of pornography, one finds a mechanism of the mind, through which the victim becomes the murderer. The Marquis de Sade even describes the mechanism for us through the plot of his novel *Justine*. Over and over again, Justine, who is the victim of every kind of crime, is accused by her persecutors of having committed *their* crimes. In each instance, their word is believed over hers and she is found guilty, imprisoned, and prepared to be executed. Justine even takes the identity of the criminal into herself, for by these accusations she feels herself to have been 'dreadfully humiliated'.*

Yet when we remember that the 'woman' in pornography is simply the pornographer's dark self projected onto a female character, Justine's dreadful humiliation takes on a symbolic meaning. For it is the female aspect of the self who is punished in pornography – punished and then blamed for her own punishment. The pornographer's fear of his own sexual feelings is written implicitly into every scene in which a man binds and silences a woman. When the pornographer silences a woman, part of himself dies. That place in his body dies where gentleness sings, where the child's fear hides, where the heart lives. And as he is committing this ritual murder, the pornographic hero turns on his victim and blames her for this death. He calls her frigid. He claims she has rejected him. She has driven him to this act. In the same way, as the pornographer himself ritually murders his own feeling by doing violence to the *image* of a woman, he turns on the woman who is horrified by this violence and he calls her a prude. He cries out that she threatens his liberty. That it is she who would silence his sexual feelings, and who would enslave him. For he is a man at odds with himself, who cannot recognise the prudery he fears as his own prudery, who does not see that he is his own master, nor that he is his own slave.

*We find the same reversal of moral order and of shame in rape (that event which is surely pornography enacted). The woman who is raped is often accused of perjury in a courtroom. Her word is not believed. Moreover, part of the defence of a man accused of rape has been to accuse a woman of being a 'whore', of being licentious or amoral. Even a woman who has been raped but who has not gone through a rape trial feels ashamed of what has happened to her, as if this violence against her revealed something of her own nature.

Illusion and Delusion: Culture's Desire to Replace Reality

> The most striking difference between ancient and modern sophists is that the ancients were satisfied with a passing victory of argument at the expense of reality.
>
> Hannah Arendt, *The Origins of Totalitarianism*

> It was necessary to make the difficult decision to make this people disappear from the face of the earth.
>
> Heinrich Himmler, October 1943

Certain ideas have the power to transform our lives. 'The nexus between idea and act,' Lucy Dawidowicz writes (of the history of the Holocaust), 'has seldom been as evident in human history with such consistency as in the history of anti-Semitism.' Yet that anti-Semitism should have been the central idea for an effective political movement surprised us. Before Hitler's rise to power and his genocidal acts, we did not take the political and social consequences of anti-Semitic ideas seriously. (Thus, in the early twentieth century, one did not take the French writer Céline's call to 'massacre all the Jews' seriously.) One does not think of the pornography of racism as 'ideas'. The central idea of anti-Semitism, for instance, that 'the Jew' cunningly plots our destruction, has no weight for our minds once it is stripped of the delusionary state which supports it. We understand racism to be a brand of madness. And were pornography not a kind of mental addiction, an enthralled fantasy, who would seriously credit its 'ideas'?

Underneath our conventional understanding of pornography, we somehow know that the man who *believes* pornography must be mad. We can see the shape of the insanity of this mind in Huysmans' portrait of Gilles de Rais:

> He sobs as he walks, haunted by ghosts that rise up unexpectedly before him, looks around and suddenly discovers the obscenity of age-old trees. It is as if nature transforms itself before him, as if it was his presence that spoils it . . . He sees the tree as a living thing, but reversed, head down, buried in the hair of the roots. The legs of this being stick up in the air, spread themselves, divide once more into so many crotches that become smaller and smaller, the farther away they get from the trunk; there between those legs, a branch is buried in frozen debauchery.

We say to ourselves, 'This is the thinking of a madman; his ideas cannot affect reality.' And in this way, we dismiss the power of these ideas to affect history.

And yet it is precisely because of the madness of the anti-Semitic or pornographic idea, and precisely because it is a delusion, that it must assault reality and try to change it. A man 'believes' in anti-Semitic propaganda, or the pornographic ideology, because the illness of his mind *requires* that he believe these ideas to be true. Yet illness is of its very nature resistant. Thus, when a madman is told that he does not see the world correctly, and when he is given evidence against his prejudices, he will refuse to see the truth, and he will even distort this evidence to support his own delusion. But most significantly, he will even change reality so it supports his mad idea of the world. This is what anti-Semitism and pornography require of their believers. *The deluded mind must try to remake the world after an illusion.*

When we understand that it is in the nature of the pornographic idea to attempt to replace reality with itself, the fact that many pornographic fictional works disguise themselves as scientific 'documents' appears to us in a new light. A fictional work entitled *Teenage Sadism* is subtitled 'A Documentary Casebook'. It is published as part of the 'Dr Guenther Klow Library'. The author, a 'Dr Dean Copeland', is described as 'one of the foremost authorities on sexual deviancy among today's uninhibited young people'. Despite a disclaiming paragraph inside the first page warning that any 'similarity between real persons and these characters is coincidental', we are told in the introduction that the stories are 'graphic true life accounts'. A magazine filled with photographs of women chained and beating one another announces itself as a 'Casebook in Lesbianism'. Another fictional collection is called *The Multiple Climaxing Woman* and bears the subtitle 'In-depth Case Histories'. In a magazine we find a fictional 'study' entitled 'Rape: Agony or Ecstasy?' Here we read the fictional statistic that 'nearly one-half of all women who are forcibly raped experience orgasm during the assault', and we encounter the fictional conclusion that 'the emotional impact of forced intercourse . . . is an aid to orgasm.' In this way pornographic fantasy masquerades as fact.

Perhaps it is the pornographer's desire to replace reality with fantasy which ultimately leads him to prefer the image and the symbol over what is real. We read from Gay Talese in *Thy Neighbor's Wife*, for instance, that Hugh Hefner spent much of his adolescence obsessed with photographs of women. In the 1940s, he decorated the walls of his bedroom with photographs cut from the pages of *Esquire* magazine. And reading his sexual history, we suspect that as a young man, he had a far more passionate sex life with images than with real women.

In Talese's detailed sexual history of this man, we learn that at 18 his sexual experience 'precluded masturbation' and he had 'not experienced sexual intercourse' by the age of 22. We might understand this slowness as a natural condition of the rebellion he was making from his fundamental Methodist background. And yet one cannot help but notice that throughout his life he was fascinated, and even obsessed, with the photographed, the documented, the filmed, the *observed* experience of reality. When Talese recalls for us Hefner's childhood, we do not hear a scene of masturbation or childish exploration described. Rather, the memory that he could recall 'decades later', and the experience with which, as a child, he was 'mesmerised', was essentially voyeuristic. Thus we learn that as a 13-year-old boy, while attending a Boy Scout meeting, he saw a young girl getting undressed 'through the half-raised shade of the window next door'. And later we read that before his marriage he photographed his fiancée in the nude. And that when he had an affair outside his marriage, he filmed himself 'making love to his girl-friend'. And we learn that Hefner has kept cartons of photographs and films of himself, along with documents and mementoes which record his entire personal life.

Telling us that the magazine Hefner created 'had re-created him', Talese describes Hefner in the early days of *Playboy* as a man who 'virtually lived within the glossy pages'. We learn that he marvelled over the photograph of one young woman because 'her skin did not glisten with perspiration' (and of course, we discover that as a youth, Hefner 'perspired freely'); that, in the words of Gay Talese, he seemed 'to be getting as much pleasure from what he was seeing as from what he was feeling'; that he kept portfolios of all the women who ever modelled for his magazine; that he regarded these women, in some way, as his 'possessions'. All these attitudes speak to us of a certain architecture of the mind. Here is the essence of the voyeuristic experience. Above all, the voyeur must see and not feel. He keeps a safe distance. He does not perspire and his photographs do not glisten with sweat. He is not touched by reality. And yet in his mind, he can believe he possesses reality. For he has control over these images he makes and he shapes them to his will.

One finds the same architecture in the design of Hugh Hefner's house. For he has isolated himself completely from nature. His house has no windows. Nothing unpredictable or out of his control can happen to him there. Sunrise makes no difference to him. He rises and sleeps at odd hours. Seasons do not affect him. And he never has to leave the house. Food emanates from a kitchen supplied with a staff day and night. Inside the house he has a projection room, a swimming pool (with an underwater bar), a fully equipped office. Here he is never compelled by a need which cannot be immediately answered. And even within this house, as if one layer of protection from the world were not enough, his bedroom contains another self-sufficient and man-made world, with a desk, and food supplies, and a bed which is motorised so that it not only changes positions but also carries him about the room. Thus he never has to leave his bed. In this passive manner, he can have total control over nature.

Yet can the pornographer be satisfied with this degree of control? Within Hefner's bedroom and over this bed he has a camera which will photograph him as he experiences coitus. The pornographer must replace even his own experience with a cultural record of his experience. For otherwise, how can nature be completely controlled? The attempt to control her must be like the labour of Sisyphus, a task which promises despair and rage. For nature will always make herself felt. Even if we hide the sunrise from ourselves, or escape knowledge of rainfall, of hunger, or death, we cannot escape nature in ourselves. We feel. Here is the great and terrible irony of that soul which would escape itself. Like Gilles de Rais, running from himself into the woods, even as we escape ourselves we confront ourselves. When we turn away, all that we have denied rises up like a ghost to terrify us. We are trapped.

The philosopher of language Ludwig Wittgenstein writes that 'Symbols appear to be of their nature unsatisfied.' And yet it is not the nature of the symbol itself to deceive us, nor to act as the escape from reality in which, eventually, we are imprisoned. As Susan Sontag reminds us, we have been used to thinking (in the tradition of Plato and Feuerbach) that the problem lies with the nature of imagery itself; we complain that human beings have become dependent on images of reality rather than reality. And yet this way of thinking exists inside our collective amnesia. We have forgotten that an image can reflect and reverberate with reality. We forget that an image can enchant us precisely because it opens our souls to a greater know-ledge of the real. We forget that the beauty of an opening rose can make our hearts 'open'. We forget that in the image we can find an embodiment of what we thought was unknown; that the image, instead of entrapping us, can open a door in our own minds, into our own nature and into the nature of nature. And we do not see that instead of an imagery filled with the power of reality, pornographic culture has chosen an imagery which tries to deny reality.

It is because of this denial that, finally, we must find the pornographic image dissatisfying. This dissatisfaction colours all of pornography with a kind of anger. For the pornographer imagines he has been betrayed. His promises have not been fulfilled. Henry Miller writes, for example: 'Paris is like a whore. From a distance she seems ravishing, you can't wait to have her in your arms. And five minutes later, you feel empty, disgusted with yourself. You feel tricked.' Thus he forgets that he himself created the illusion he calls 'Paris', and that this emptiness is his own, that it was he who tricked himself.

Beyond this trick, reality waits like a shadow. For these words from Wilhelm Stekel, about the sadomasochistic ritual, speak to the experience of pornography:

> The actual scene is a disillusionment because it never corresponds to the unconscious desire; and in itself it is a fiction behind which a totally different scene is hiding.

The temporary illusion of realisation which pornography gives to its audience must always turn into despair.

And whether the image has given us despair or given us hope, whether it has imprisoned us or opened a door for us, we do not stand still. Again Wittgenstein tells us: 'The proposition seems to set over us as a judge and we feel answerable to it – it seems to demand that reality match the symbol of reality which has captured our minds.' If that symbol is a lie, our experience of reality will deny the truth of that symbol. The mind which is not deluded allows the symbol to be disproved by reality. But the pornographer is not sane. He has the madman's commitment to an illusion. Even his sense of *himself* is bound up with that illusion. He imagines he is invulnerable. In his pornographic fantasy he has placed himself above nature. He has placed himself above her as culture. In his mind he imagines he *is* culture. For in his mind he has replaced his actual, material self with a cultural image of himself that denies that materiality. Now if the reality of his delusion is destroyed, he imagines he himself will be destroyed. In a world of delusion made of images, his only conscious knowledge of himself is an image. Without culture, he imagines he does not exist at all. Therefore, he must defend his imaginary existence against reality. And thus it is logical that he should imagine reality has set out to destroy *him*.

For of course, in a metaphorical sense this is true. Reality will destroy delusion. Nature will bring the mind back to whatever is the real and painful experience from which it hides. And the part of the mind which believes in this delusion will die. The delusionary self will die. This reality which the pornographer fears is a formidable enemy.

She has invaded him. She lives in his body. Even as he breathes, she attacks him. Even as he touches, desires, aches, she assaults him. He must act out against her. He must silence her, imprison her, bind her, punish her, and if necessary, even annihilate her, if he is to defend his illusion.

Thus we see an ominous movement takes place. Culture must turn into event. The pornographer imagines violence after he imagines object. Then he imagines his fantasy becomes an event. And finally, the fantasy *does* become an event. In a newspaper, for example, we read that a television drama in which a woman was set afire with gasoline was imitated by a man in Boston. There, a real woman's body was set afire with gasoline. We read that a television drama which depicted a group of girls raping another girl was imitated by two girls. Thus, in California, a nine-year-old girl was actually raped.

But the movement of the pornographic mind does not stop here. Culture has been made into event. And now event will be made into culture. Thus we read that in New Jersey, a wealthy man is tried for the rape of several women. And in the testimony we learn that he filmed himself and four other men while they raped, sodomised, and beat their victims. And we discover that when in a California desert, the bones of women's bodies are found buried along with ropes, knives, and saws, the man who is arrested for these murders is said to have hired women to pose for him, to have tied them, to have tortured and murdered them, while photographing each stage of these events.*

*Here an old pattern from history can be recognised. Even though the United States Army denied its record of atrocities against Native Americans, in fact the best record of these atrocities was kept by the Army itself. In the same way, the Soviet Union, according to Nadezhda Mandelstam, has kept roomfuls of letters, records, and descriptions attesting to its persecutions against dissidents. The best records of the burnings of witches were kept by the witch-burners themselves; for the history of slavery, we read the accounts of

But all this, and the attraction, also, that so many men have to the crime magazine which reports, in issue after issue, the details of a real murder of a real woman, become finally understandable to us when we see that the 'final solution' for the pornographic mind is to annihilate nature and replace nature with culture. Thus the document which records the death of a real woman, a woman who represents nature, reality, and the part of the self that is denied, becomes the ultimate pornographic form. For this document, which is a piece of paper and therefore a cultural artifact, *proves* the death of nature, the destruction of a woman's body, the annihilation of the denied self. Now the mind can both have and not have this denied part of the self, and reality is replaced with culture.†

But pornography gives us a lucid mirror of itself. In the film *Peeping Tom*, for instance, the pornographer has provided us with a self-portrait. The hero of the film is a pornographic photographer. And it is from this film that we learn the pornographer's secret fantasy about his own art. For in this fantasy, the hero uses a camera that conceals a deadly spear. As he photographs a woman, his camera releases a spear which simultaneously murders her. Thus he is able to murder her as he makes her into an image, and to replace her body with a record of her death agony.

And pornography also records the ultimate despair of its own final solutions. For indeed, what the pornographer would really annihilate is a part of himself, that self which is feeling, which is vulnerable. But of course, when a woman dies in fantasy or reality, that self does not die. Thus even a murder is not satisfying. Both in actuality and in fantasy, a pornographic murder must be followed by another murder, and this by another murder, each more violent and devastating. In one novel after another, the hero murders one woman after another, and each time he is more cruel and more destructive. For after each murder, his feeling of powerlessness returns. And so, too, a frenzy grows, and a desperate realization, which the mind must want to quiet, that this vulnerable self will always return and cannot be

---

slave traders and slavemasters. And the Third Reich, even while it was calling the accusation of genocide a 'Jewish fiction', made meticulous records, photographs, and even moving pictures of countless numbers of imprisonments, tortures, and deaths.

†On the back of *The Skin Flick Rapist* we find an imitation of a document, a tabloid newspaper, which records the mutilation and murder of women by a pornographic hero as if it were fact.

destroyed. Thus the pornographer's rage grows with each murder, for with each murder he fails more miserably. At the end of one pornographic novel, after his last murder, the hero stands on a fire escape, trembling and paralysed with fear. To the detective who had discovered him, he sobs, 'Please help me . . . I'm afraid of heights.'

Here pornography stands trembling before nature, afraid of falling, afraid of the power and knowledge of the body, pornography which in its fear of being ravaged has ravaged, which has attempted to reduce living beings to things, which has and must inevitably seek our death. Far from vitiating violence, culture writes a script for death, and produces and directs countless acts of violence against women, against children, even against men. And far from freeing the spirit from the idea of limitation, pornography slowly imprisons us in an illusion which replaces reality and leaves us devastated and despairing.

THE SACRIFICIAL LAMB

The Chauvinist Mind

> Among our secrecies, not to despise Jews (that is, ourselves) or our darknesses, or blacks, or in our sexuality where it takes us.
> Muriel Rukeyser, 'The Despisals'

On the leaflet are two familiar figures. A monstrous black man menaces a voluptuous white woman. Her dress is cut low, her skirt torn so that a thigh shows through; the sleeves of her dress fall off her shoulders. She looks over her shoulder in fear and runs. The man's body is huge and apelike. The expression on his face is the personification of bestiality, greed, and lust. Under the words 'Conquer and Breed', and above a text which warns the reader against intermarriage, these two figures act out an age-old drama.

At the heart of the racist imagination we discover a pornographic fantasy: the spectre of miscegenation. This image of a dark man raping a fair woman embodies all that the racist fears. This fantasy preoccupies his mind. A rational argument exists which argues that the racist simply uses pornographic images to manipulate the mind. But these images seem to belong to the racist. They are predictable in a way that suggests a more intrinsic part in the genesis of this ideology.

And when we turn to pornography, we discover that just as the racist is obsessed with a pornographic drama, the pornographer is obsessed with racism. In *Juvenal*, for example, we read about the 'trusty Jewess' who will 'tell you dreams of any kind you please for the minutest of coins', *Hustler* magazine displays a cartoon called *Chester the Molester* (part of a series depicting child molestation as humour), in which a man wearing a swastika on his arm hides behind a corner, holds a bat, and dangles a dollar bill on a wire to entice a little girl away from her parents. The child and her parents all wear yellow stars of David; each member of the family is drawn with the stereotypical hooked nose of anti-Semitic caricature. In another cartoon, a young black man dressed in a yellow polka-dot shirt and eating watermelon stands outside the bars of a cage in which a monkey dressed in the same yellow shirt eats watermelon and listens to a transistor radio. A film called *Slaves of Love* is advertised with a portrait of two black women, naked and in chains. A white man stands over them with a whip. Nazi memorabilia, helmets, SS uniforms, photographs of the atrocities of concentration camps, swords, knives, are sold as pornography along with books and films. Pornographic films bear the titles *Golden Boys of the SS, Ilse the She-Wolf of the SS, Leiben Camp.*

Writing of the twin traditions of anti-Semitism and obscenity, Lucy Dawidowicz tells us of a rock group called 'The Dictators', who declare 'we are the members of the master race', and she lists for us a mélange of articles found in the apartment of a Hell's Angel: devices of torture, a Nazi flag, a photograph of Hitler, Nazi propaganda, and of course, pornography. She writes: 'Pornography and propaganda have reinforced each other over the decades.'

Indeed, the association between pornographic thought and racist ideology is neither casual nor coincidental. As Hannah Arendt points out, both Gobineau and Houston Chamberlain (anti-Semitic ideologues who had a great influence on the philosophy of the Third Reich and on Hitler himself) were deeply influenced by the writing of the Marquis de Sade. Like de Sade, they 'elevated cruelty to a major virtue'.

We know that the sufferings women experience in a pornographic culture are different in kind and quality from the sufferings of black people in a racist society, or of Jewish people under anti-Semitism. (And we know that the hatred of homosexuality has again another effect on the lives of women and men outside of the traditional sexual roles.*) But if we look closely at the portrait which the racist draws of

---

*Homophobia is a clear mass delusional system. Yet to draw an anology between this system and racism and pornography would require another

a man or a woman of colour, or that the anti-Semite draws of the Jew, or that the pornographer draws of a woman, we begin to see that these fantasised figures resemble one another. For they are the creations of one mind. This is the chauvinist mind, a mind which projects all it fears in itself onto another: a mind which defines itself by what it hates.

The black man as stupid, as passive, as bestial; the woman as highly emotional, unthinking, a being closer to the earth. The Jews as a dark, avaricious race. The whore. The nymphomaniac. Carnal lust in a woman insatiable. The virgin. The docile slave. The effeminate Jew. The usurious Jew. The African, a 'greedy eater', lecherous, addicted to uncleanness. The black woman as lust: 'These sooty dames, well vers'd in Venus' school/Make love an art, and boast they kiss by rule.' As easy. The Jew who practises sexual orgies, who practises cannibalism. The Jewish and the black man with enormous sexual endowment.

The famous materialism of the Jew, the black, the woman. The woman who spends her husband's paycheques on hats. The black who drives a Cadillac while his children starve. The Jewish moneylender who sells his daughter. 'There is nothing more intolerable than a wealthy woman', we read in Juvenal. (And in an eighteenth-century pornographic work, the pornographer writes that his heroine had 'a nasty little bourgeois brain'. And in a contemporary pornographic novel, the hero murders a woman because she prefers 'guys who drive Cadillacs'.) The appetite which swallows. The black man who takes away the white man's job or the woman who takes a man's job.

Over and over again the chauvinist draws a portrait of the other which reminds us of that part of his own mind he would deny and which he has made dark to himself. The other has appetite and instinct. The other has a body. The other has an emotional life which is uncontrolled. And in the wake of this denied self, the chauvinist constructs a false self with which he himself identifies.

Wherever we find the racist idea of another being as evil and inferior, we also discover a racial *ideal,* a portrait of the self as superior, good, and righteous. Such was certainly the case with the white Southern slave owner. The Southern white man imagined

chapter. Suffice it to mention here that the fear of homosexuals historically accompanies racism, sexism, fascism, and all forms of totalitarian or authoritarian rule.

himself as the heir to all the best traditions of civilization. He thought of himself as the final repository of culture. In his own mind, he was an aristocrat. Thus Southern life was filled with his pretensions, his decorum, his manners, and his ceremonies of social ascension.

Just as he conferred the black men and women he enslaved with inferior qualities, so also he blessed himself with superiorities. He was 'knightly' and 'magnanimous', filled with 'honesty' which emanated from the 'flame of his strong and steady eye'. He was honourable, responsible and above all, noble.

And the anti-Semite frames himself in the same polarity. Against his portrait of the Jew, he poses himself as the ideal, the Aryan: fair, courageous, honest, physically and morally stronger.

But this is a polarity deeply familiar to us. We learn it almost at birth from our mothers and fathers. Early in our lives, the ideal of masculinity is opposed to the idea of femininity. We learn that a man is more intelligent, that he is stronger than a woman. And in pornography, the male hero possesses an intrinsic moral rightness which, like Hitler's Aryan, allows him to behave toward woman in ways outside morality. For according to this ideology, he is the more valuable member of the species. As the Marquis de Sade tells us, 'the flesh of women', like the 'flesh of all female animals', is inferior.

It is because the chauvinist has used the idea that he is superior as a justification to enslave and exploit the other, whom he describes as inferior, that certain historians of culture have imagined the ideology of chauvinism exists only to justify exploitation. But this ideology has a raison d'être intrinsic to the mind itself. Exploring this mind, one discovers that the chauvinist values his delusion for its own sake, that above all, the chauvinist mind needs to believe in the delusion it has created. For this delusion has another purpose than social exploitation. Indeed, the delusions of the chauvinist mind are born from the same condition which gives birth to all delusion, and this condition is the mind's desire to escape truth. The chauvinist cannot face the truth that the other he despises is himself.

This is why one so often discovers in chauvinist thinking a kind of hysterical denial that the other could possibly be like the self. The chauvinist insists upon an ultimate and defining difference between himself and the other. This insistence is both the starting point and the essence of all his thinking. Thus, Hitler writes on the beginnings of his own anti-Semitism:

One day, when passing through the Inner City, I suddenly came across an apparition in a long caftan and wearing black sidelocks. My first thought was: is this a Jew? . . . but the longer I gazed at this strange countenance and examined it section by section, the more the first question took another shape in my brain: is this a German? . . . For the first time in my life I bought myself some anti-Semitic pamphlets for a few coins.

In this way, by inventing a figure different from itself, the chauvinist mind constructs an allegory of self. Within this allegory, the chauvinist himself represents the soul, and the knowledge of culture. Whoever is the object of his hatred represents the denied self, and natural self, the self which contains the knowledge of the body. Therefore this other must have no soul.

From the chauvinist ideology we learn, for example, that a woman's soul is smaller than a man's. The misogynist and anti-Semite Otto Weininger tells us that a woman 'can have no part in the higher, transcendental life'. The church tells us that in order for a woman to get into heaven she must assume the shape of a man. Her body is incapable of spirituality. She is called the 'devil's gateway'. She brings evil into the world.

But 'blackness' also comes to stand for evil in this mind. In seventeenth-century theology, we discover the explanation that the real origin of the dark races can be found in the scriptures. According to this legend, a man named Ham, who was born on Noah's Ark, knew his wife, against God's will.* Ham disobeyed. Thus in punishment a son was born to him, named Chus, and God willed that all the 'posteritie after him should be so blake and loathsome that it might remain a spectacle of disobeidiance to all the worlde'.

And Adolf Hitler tells us: 'The symbol of all evil assumes the shape of a Jew.'

And now, if the other invented by the chauvinist mind is a body without a spirit, this dark self is also nature without a capacity for culture. Therefore the other has a kind of passivity that the chauvinist mind supposes nature to have. A woman is docile. A black man is lazy. Neither has the ingenuity and virtue necessary to create culture. For example, Alfred Rosenberg, the official anti-Semitic ideologist of the Third Reich, tells us that the Jew went into trade because he did not want to work.

*Another scriptural interpretation has it that Ham looked on 'the nakedness of his father'.

For the same reason, the chauvinist mind describes the despised other as lacking the intelligence for cultural achievement. A white anthropologist argues that instead of language, the black races have 'a farrago of bestial sounds resembling the chitter of apes'. A gynaecologist argues that a woman's ovaries are damaged by serious intellectual study. Another doctor argues that menstruation moves a woman's blood away from her brain and into her pelvis.

Here one might assume that the anti-Semitic portrait of the Jew diverges from the racist's idea of the black, or the pornographic idea of a woman, over this question of intelligence. But such is not the case. The anti-Semitic idea of Jewish intelligence, on a closer examination, comes to resemble the racist idea of black intelligence or the pornographic idea of female intelligence. In the chauvinist mind, all three are described as possessing what may be called an animal cunning. All three, for instance, are called liars. Schopenhauer calls women the masters of deceit. Hitler calls the Jew a master of lies. And the racist invents the figure of the black trickster, the con artist who can never be believed.

Thus, when the chauvinist is confronted with the fact of Jewish cultural achievement, he decides that the Jew uses culture for material ends only. We read in the writing of Alfred Rosenberg, for example, that the 'Jewish art dealer of today asks only for those works which could excite sensuality.' And Rosenberg goes on to declare that the Jew is incapable of thinking metaphysically.*

Thus, as the anti-Semite tells us he hates the Jewish intellectual, he speaks of the 'materialism' of his thought. But the idea of the materialistic Jewish spirit is very old. It has been part of the anti-Semite's repertoire at least since the Middle Ages. In an anti-Semitic legend from pre-Renaissance England, for example, a Jewish man converts to Christianity in order to protect his material possessions. Before this conversion, he leaves an image of St Nicholas to guard his shop and his possessions while he is away. When he returns, his belongings have been stolen, and in anger and retribution, he beats the image of the saint until 'his sydes are all bloodie'. But he is not

---

*In this sense, that he would separate the material from the spiritual, the chauvinist is often an anti-intellectual. At the heart of a certain kind of intellect, we discover self-reflection. But the chauvinist deplores this. He calls it 'effete'. For in the act of genuine self-knowledge, we know ourselves as part of nature, and we encounter the knowledge of the body as inseparable from 'culture'.

impressed by this miraculous blood. However, when the same bleeding image of the saint appears to the thief, the thief is impressed enough to return to the shopkeeper what he has stolen. And it is only then, when the shopkeeper has his goods back, that he converts to Christianity. Thus we are given a portrait of the Jew as a brutal man, without Christian compassion, whose spirituality only serves mammon.*

Similarly, and in the same historical period, women's intelligence was described as essentially devilish. Thus the *Malleus Maleficarum* tells us that when 'a woman thinks alone she thinks evil'. For during the period of the witch-burnings and the Inquisition, the chauvinist mind had constructed a portrait of both female and Jewish knowledge as an intelligence of sinfulness. Both were supposed to practice a *black* magic through which they learned the secrets of the earth and manipulated the powers of nature. In the chauvinist imagination, witches were capable of causing the plague, an earthquake, a drought, a pestilence; a witch could bring about impotence or sexual ravings. And the Jew, practising his own black magic, also caused infanticide, plague, hurricanes, earthquakes.

Significantly, the chauvinist mind of this time imagined that the Jew or the witch gained power by desecrating the religious symbols of the dominant culture. The Jew was said to steal the consecrated host in order to defile it; the witch blasphemed the cross and anointed the devil. For of course, to a mind which protects itself with a culture that denies nature, *to destroy the symbols of that culture is to invoke the powers of nature.* (And now should we be surprised to learn that both Jews and witches were burned during this period of history?)

It is essential that within its own mythology, the chauvinist mind believe that culture is more powerful than nature. Thus, over and over again, this mind invents legends in which cultural symbol vanquishes the evil forces of nature. We have the legend of a Jewish boy, for instance, thrown into the flames by his father for going to church. This boy is protected by an image of the holy virgin and passes through the flames unscathed. For as much as the chauvinist mind fears the power of nature, this mind must deny the reality of that power. It is for this same reason that the pornographer must humiliate women.

*Many other such legends exist. For example, a Jew studying to be a monk is visited by the devil, who tells him that he will one day be a bishop. The Jew then steals a horse and a cloak so that he will be a more impressive candidate for this office.

This denial reaches a fever pitch in the writings of Otto Weininger, who raves that 'the absolute female has no . . . will, no sense of worth or love.' He tells us, 'The meaning of woman is to be meaningless.' And within the allegory of the chauvinist mind this is quite literally true for in this mind the knowledge of self which woman represents has been erased. The female is 'little more than an animal', he declares, she is 'nothing'. Thus in one stroke he has told us that women and bestiality do not exist.

But the more the chauvinist mind denies the existence of the power of nature, the more he fears this power. The pornographer, the racist, the anti-Semite, begin to believe their own delusions. The chauvinist begins to believe he is endangered by the dark other he has invented.

And yet he cannot acknowledge his fear, because fear is another form of vulnerability. It is evidence of mortality. It is natural. It is bestial. It is part of what he wished to deny in himself from the beginning. Thus now the dark other must come also to represent another side of the chauvinist mind: the other must now symbolize the chauvinist's own fearfulness.

Therefore the chauvinist projects onto the other his own sense of inadequacy in the natural world. And therefore we understand a different meaning when we hear from the chauvinist that the black was supposed to be like a child 'whom somebody had to look after . . . a grateful – contented, glad, loving child.' Or we hear that a woman is a 'kind of middle-step between the child and the man'.

A monstrous black man threatens a defenceless white woman. But now we can see the meaning of this drama. Here are two aspects of the self personified. In the black man, the force of desire, of appetite, of wanting, is played out, and in the white woman, an awareness of vulnerability, weakness, mortality, fear can be lived. Through the forms of these two imaginary figures the memories of infancy and the knowledge of the body return to haunt the mind which would erase them.

In this sense, the 'purity' of the white woman is like the blank space in the chauvinist's mind, the vacuum with which he has replaced his own knowledge of himself. And the bestiality of the dark man is his own desire for that knowledge, a desire which always threatens to contaminate ignorance. Now, perhaps, we can understand the nature of Hitler's fear when he writes:

With satanic joy in his face, the black-haired Jewish youth lurks in

wait for the unsuspecting girl whom he defiles with his blood, thus
stealing her from her people.

The symbol has life of its own. A writer invents a character and
suddenly the character begins to surprise that writer with her acts or
his words. The chauvinist has invented the black or the Jew or the
woman to contain a part of himself. And now, through these invented
personae, that buried part of the self begins to speak and will not be
controlled by its author. Secretly, the chauvinist longs to be
overtaken by the dark self he has exiled. And he would have this dark
self punish the idea of purity. Therefore he imagines that women
want to be raped, because he himself does not want to remain pure.

And yet he is terrified. He does not want to *know;* he does not want
to be contaminated with knowledge. He is a man split against himself.
So he projects his secret desire to *know* the body onto a woman. He
believes that she does not want to remain pure. He tells us, in the
words of an anthropologist: 'women eager for venery prefer the
embrace of Negroes to those of other men.' But now he is like the
hero of the pornographic novel who is enraged because his doll was
unfaithful to him. He has come to believe his own fantasies. He calls
the woman – whom he had venerated for purity – a 'whore'. He
becomes terribly jealous of the prowess he has imagined the black
man to have. His fantasies torture him.

His mind is filled with contradiction. He tells us the white woman is
both licentious and vulnerable, eager and frightened, innocent and
guilty. For in the coupling which he imagines between the defenceless
white woman and the monstrous black man, the chauvinist can be
both rapist and raped, seduced and seducer, punished and punisher,
soiler and soiled.

He invents many ways to play out his ambivalence. He hates the
other and so he forces this other *away* from himself. He excludes this
other from places of power, and from social meeting places. And yet
at the same time, through complex lines of social dependence, he ties
this other to him. Fearing the actual life of the other, he makes a 'doll'
to stand for the other. In a bar which excludes women, he stirs his
drink with sticks shaped like women's bodies. In a neighbourhood
which excludes black men and women, he adorns his lawn with a
statue of a black 'boy', and his kitchen with a plastic likeness of a
'mammy'. In a book written for children, the same mind which hates
black people creates this fantasy of a black woman: 'She is a nice,
good, ole, fat, big, black Mammy.'

Fear and want construct a dilemma in his mind. And like the pornographer, he can never solve this dilemma. For he is at war with himself, and every allegory he constructs becomes a terrible cul-de-sac in which he must face this self again. He would separate himself from himself and yet still have himself. He would forget and yet remember. He both longs for and fears the knowledge of the body. Nature is a part of him. He cannot divide what cannot be divided. His mind is in his body. His body thinks; his mind feels. From his body, nature renders meaning. He is trapped inside what he fears.

We are familiar with the effect of this mind on our lives. It is not the mind of a single man or woman, or even of a few. Rather, this is a structure of mind which is woven into the very language of our culture and into all its institutions, habits, visions. The delusion shaped by this mind is a mass delusion and touches us all. In the wake of this delusion, millions of men and women and children have been kid-napped into slavery; men have been lynched; children murdered; women raped and murdered, held prisoner, beaten; men, women, and children systematically tortured and annihilated; people denied the most basic human rights, denied the dignity of language or mean-ing, denied their own names.

Whether the chauvinist mind expresses itself through racist propa-ganda or through pornography, its delusions are not innocent. For the mind which believes in a delusion must ultimately face reality. And because the chauvinist desperately needs to believe in his delu-sion, when he is faced with the real nature of the world, he must act. He must force the world to resemble his delusion.

For because his body, or the reality of the other, or the force of nature, will eventually speak to him and tell him the truth that he has buried, he is driven to reshape the world to his madness and silence the voices he fears. Ultimately, the chauvinist must face a crisis in his delusion; ultimately he must be violent.

We have a record of such a crisis inside a mass delusion and of the terrible violence that followed it in the tragic events of the Third Reich. It is during this period of history that Nazi propaganda arose from a crisis in the chauvinist mind. And like pornography, the propaganda was soon translated into events.

Hitler Becomes an Anti-Semite

When Adolf Hitler moved to Vienna as a young man, he entered, in the words of Lucy Dawidowicz, 'an anti-Semitic milieu'. Of the city in which Hitler shaped his political ideas, Dawidowicz writes: 'anti-Semitic politics flourished, anti-Semitic organizations proliferated, anti-Semitic writing and propaganda poured forth in an unending stream.' We know, for example, that Hitler followed the work of Georg Lanz von Liebenfels and read the magazine which Liebenfels published, *Ostara*. Hitler must have read Liebenfels' idea in the pages of this journal that the 'problem of racial pollution' ought to be solved with 'the castration knife'. Certainly he must have been familiar with the notion which inspired all Liebenfels' writing: that Jews, Slavs and Negroes, 'the Dark Ones', were closer to apes than Aryans and constituted a dark force against the blond Aryan race. He must also have read Liebenfels' theory that in a happy marriage, men ought to be physically and psychologically brutal to their wives. We know that later he shared Liebenfels' obsession with syphilis. And we know that if he read *Ostara* at all, he read a magazine in which anti-Semitic propaganda was freely mixed with pornography. In the pages of *Ostara*, lurid illustrations abounded which pictured Aryan women as succumbing to the powers of hairy and apelike men from the 'dark' races.

The juxtaposition of pornographic and anti-Semitic images was common in the publications available to Hitler during these years. The popular magazine *Der Stürmer*, for example, was also both racist and pornographic. And this was not a coincidental mixture. One must come to understand that just as the Third Reich did not simply exploit racism, but instead needed to believe in this ideology, the anti-Semite did not simply exploit pornographic images as a means to sell his racism. Rather, the pornographic ideology lies at the very heart of anti-Semitism.

If one explores the transformation of Adolf Hitler as he became one of many believers in the delusion of racism, one discovers that at the heart of the racist fantasy is a pornographic scene. And one also sees how perfectly this racist pornographic imagery served as an expression for the private conflicts and the private delusions of this young man who was to become a leader of a virulent anti-Semitic movement.

One can only speculate about the private genesis of trouble in Adolf Hitler's mind. We know that he was often severely beaten by his father. Some sources claim that as an adult Hitler practiced sadomasochistic rituals, that in his years in Vienna he went regularly to prostitutes, whom he paid to tie him up and beat him. Another source claims that Hitler demanded that his lovers humiliate him by urinating on his body. But whether or not these reports are true, everything in the configuration of Hitler's personality suggests that he was a sadomasochist. As Robert Waite writes in his psychoanalytic study of Hitler, 'he displayed other behaviour patterns thoroughly consistent with this kind of perversion'. (Moreover, we learn that 'he had a taste for pornography'.)

What is the essence of a mind in this condition? It is a mind in conflict with itself. A mind which both desires feeling, desires knowledge of the body, and would annihilate feeling and destroy this knowledge which is a part of itself. It would have sexuality and punish feeling. This is a mind which feels humiliated by the power of nature. In revenge, it would humiliate and ridicule the natural. But this mind projects the knowledge of the body and the natural self upon another being. It plays out its hatred and fear of a denied self upon another. Thus the mind of the sadomasochist feels endangered by feeling, and endangered by the material. And projecting feeling and the material onto the body of another, the mind defends itself and takes revenge against its enemy by humiliating, punishing, and destroying this other.

Now, supposing that Adolf Hitler suffered from this condition of the mind, one can see how perfectly the anti-Semitic ideas which Hitler encountered in Vienna and which he made his own serve to express this condition. Let us begin with a scene which is played out in the minds of all racists and especially in the minds of the anti-Semites of this period. This is the pornographic drama in which an Aryan woman is raped or seduced by a Jewish man, a scene with which the anti-Semitic mind is obsessed and to which it reacts in rage.

Adolf Hitler tells us that he began to realize he was an anti-Semite in Vienna. Vienna itself, he tells us, was filled with 'a conglomeration of races'. Of this 'racial mixture' he writes: 'To me the big city appeared as the personification of incest!' Here, in this metaphor, he reveals to us another meaning in anti-Semitism. He tells us that this image of the 'mongrel races' really stands for *incest*. He tells us this directly, but from this we can decipher an even deeper meaning. For here is the Oedipal scene again: a child gathers carnal knowledge from the body of his mother. And if we understand that a whole culture associates this mother's body with the knowledge of the body, we discover that at the root of Hitler's fear of miscegenation is the pornographer's fear of self.

This is no casual metaphor Hitler has used. We discover the same primal scene to exist within Hitler's racist idea about the purity of the blood. He believes, he tells us, that the Jew attempts to pollute and corrupt the purity of Aryan blood. And significantly, he describes this corruption to us precisely as 'the original sin'. Thus here again, in Hitler's own words, we discover a fear of the knowledge of the body, for partaking of this forbidden knowledge was the original sin.

Moreover, Hitler's words on the subject of pure blood serve to express another characteristic belief of the sadomasochistic mind. He tells us that in impurity he has found the source of all social problems. For all 'really significant symptoms of decay,' he says, 'can be reduced to racial causes.' From his jail cell he writes: 'The lost purity of the blood alone destroys inner happiness forever, plunges man into the abyss for all time, and the consequences can never more be eliminated from body and spirit.' And in these words – 'destroys . . . forever' and 'abyss for all time' – we hear the familiar cynicism of the sado-masochist and his despair as he tells us that the real cause of his unhappiness is an irrevocable nervous disorder, a physical condition, or indeed, *nature*.

But Hitler's anti-Semitic repertoire reflects the condition of sado-masochism in every way. For Hitler is also obsessed with the idea that he has been humiliated by the Jews. He tells us, in fact, that the Jews make fun of Aryan culture. The Jew ridicules religion, he says, and the Jew scoffs at German history, and the Jewish intellectual has mocked even himself. Thus his plan to annihilate the Jew is a pledge to stop this Jewish laughter. Moreover, he implies that the national humiliation which Germany suffered in the First World War and from the Treaty of Versailles was ultimately the result of a Jewish plot to degrade and defeat an otherwise invincible Germany.

We see, among other things, that this natural, cultural and military humiliation mirrors Adolf Hitler's own sense of humiliation as a young man in Vienna. For he was unrecognised as an artist. He was even denied entrance to art school, and his paintings did not sell. In addition, he was impoverished, lived under the most humble conditions, and even wore secondhand clothes. Thus his personal rise to power apotheosises Germany's rise to power. In both events, which occur simultaneously and are inseparable, a former degradation is vindicated.

It is common for a young man or woman of later consequence to have been impoverished and obscure. Yet we know that Hitler's obsession with humiliation persisted way beyond his youth, into a time when a whole nation pledged absolute allegiance to him. For a sense of having been humiliated is of course that same feeling which the sadomasochist experiences. And it has its origins not so much in the real events of an adult's life as in the mind's humiliation before the power of nature. For the mind wishes to believe that it is invincible against nature's power.

In the light of this feeling of humiliation, it is significant here to know that in one psychoanalytic study of Hitler, he is described as being afraid of women. We learn that in 1924, because a woman suddenly kissed him at a party, a look 'of astonishment and horror came over Hitler's face', which one witness never forgot. The same writer tells us that Hitler's mother could persuade him to rise from bed by threatening to kiss him.

Thus the sadomasochist is humiliated by his own fear. And this is why he asks to be beaten: so that he can simultaneously punish the body and control what he fears. But what he is afraid of *ultimately* is not a woman or a Jew. For these are only symbols for something inside himself. It is the feelings in his own body, which will vanquish him and make him lose control; his *body* is invaded by these feelings.

Therefore, as another part of the anti-Semitic doctrine which Hitler learned in Vienna, we discover the metaphor of the Jew as a disease. For as a disease, an invisible microbe, the Jew can invade the body and become part of the body. Over and over again, as he dramatizes the danger the Jew poses to the Aryan, Hitler uses the metaphor of contagion, plague, pestilence, poisoning; he speaks of microbes and tubercles and spirochetes. In 1942 he was to boast: 'The discovery of the Jewish virus is one of the greatest revolutions that has ever taken place.' He compares himself to Pasteur and Koch, and finally concludes: 'How many diseases have their origin in the Jewish virus! . . We shall only regain our own health when we eliminate the Jew.'

It is significant here, as we consider the pornographic scenario inside the mass delusion of racism, that the most common disease which Hitler named as a 'Jewish' threat was syphilis.* As Bleul writes, Hitler spoke of syphilis as a 'typical Jewish attribute', a 'quasi asset' of the Jew. And finally, his political accusation that the Weimar Republic caused Germany's humiliation in World War I takes on a pornographic imagery when he declares that syphilis caused

---

*Even the name 'syphilis' derives from the mind's conflict with nature. The shepherd Syphilus, believing the gods to have been too cruel when they inflicted a drought on the land, changed his allegiance to a mortal king, and for this he was punished with the disease that later bore his name.

Germany's defeat, that the Weimar Republic surrendered Germany to a 'syphilization' by Jews and Negroes.

But one recognizes the metaphor of disease from another story. For the existence of the plague is a significant event in the story of Oedipus. It is the plague which placed Thebes in danger, and which frightened Oedipus into forcing Tiresias to admit the identity of Oedipus' father. Because of the plague, Oedipus decided to choose the knowledge of culture over the knowledge of the body. Because of the plague, he destroyed the knowledge of the body in himself. Jocasta died. And Oedipus became culture's loyal son. Fearing the power of nature, Oedipus decided to use culture as a revenge against this power.

And the anti-Semitism of Vienna offered Hitler precisely the same choice. For in this doctrine, the Aryan was described as the 'bearer of human cultural development', as a 'culture creator'. And indeed, it was culture that had saved Hitler from the conflicts of his soul, by offering to his mind the mass delusion of racism. As Hitler entered the life of Vienna, we can imagine that the ideas of anti-Semitism almost reached out to him. For they gave to him an almost perfect expression for his private conflicts, and at the same time, a way to escape from knowledge of himself. The sexual imagery of anti-Semitism, the idea that the Jew corrupted Aryan blood, the metaphor of the Jew as a disease, the notion that Jews spread syphilis – all these ideas came from the Viennese anti-Semitic movement. Through believing in these ideas, Hitler became an acceptable member of society. If he was an outcast, he was also valued as a member of the society of outcasts, who told themselves that they owned the future. Through his delusion he was to become effective in the world. Now Hitler was to unify the various ideas of anti-Semitism and make them into a powerful political doctrine.

It is significant in this light that the moment at which Hitler himself said that he decided he had been born to lead a movement which would restore Germany to racial purity and pride was a cultural moment. He had attended the theatre, for he loved Wagnerian opera. And after a certain performance, moved to tears and near ecstasy at the sight of Teutonic warriors in all their glory, he resolved to himself that he would devote his life to regaining this glory. This culture at one and the same time told him who he was and what he must do.

Finally, the anti-Semitic movement gave to him a means of fighting 'the Jew'. Like Oedipus, he chose culture to vanquish 'the plague'. It was by culture that he had been convinced. And it was through culture that he would convince others. Thus, like the pornographer, who takes out revenge against 'woman' with his images, Hitler used culture to take out his revenge against the Jew.

In *Mein Kampf,* Hitler writes that after his entrance into the German Workers Party, he 'at once took over the management of propaganda'. In shaping the Nazi party, he tells us he regarded the department of propaganda as 'by far the most important'. But of course this is so. For this is the scenario for the pornographic mind. And in order to exert power over nature, pornography must produce a set of illusions; it must change perception by distorting reality; it must replace the real with delusion. As Hitler himself tells us, propaganda 'tries to force a doctrine on a whole people', because before the real event of a political movement can take place, propaganda 'will have to first spread the idea of the movement'.

And this is precisely what Adolf Hitler was to do. For among pornographers, he was a master.

EROS: THE MEANING OF DESIRE

> *Without warning*
> *As a whirlwind*
> *swoops on an oak*
> *love shakes my heart.*
>
> Sappho

The Child

At the beginning of this century, the painter Paula Modersohn-Becker drew a portrait of an adolescent girl. The child's eyes, shadowed and dark, at once look out to us and away from us, look downward towards her nude body, and away, as if from shame, look inward, and off into space, as if she wished to avoid the fact of herself. She is a girl just before the moment of womanhood. She has no breasts, no hair where a woman might. Her hands are clasped and raised to cover her mouth, as if she would protect and silence her own capacity to be a woman.

For a woman, to look on this simple drawing is to be moved past any pretence back to an earlier self. The simple fact of her body. The intelligence. The sexuality without a woman's sexual body. We fear for her. Our own dark memories live in her. She is intensity of feeling and shame, she is sensitivity and embarrassment. She is the creature who hides behind our masks of self-certitude, our impersonations of self. In her posture we meet again the real feeling of our bodies.

The girl who begins to be a woman. When I look on this drawing and remember myself as an adolescent child, I am reminded of Anne Frank. The girl almost a woman who has become a symbol for all the innocents who were slaughtered in the Holocaust. Whose diary was filled with the sensitivities of a young girl awakening to her sexuality, and to her life in the world. In this book of hers we have been given a sensual record of the lives of those sacrificed, and therefore we are moved.

She tells us every detail, all the small dramas of the life of the body, of which the adolescent girl is so aware. We learn what it is like to sit for three days without moving or speaking. We hear her careful description of her sufferings with a flu; she tells us all the remedies brought to heal her. She tells us how each member of her family was able to bathe, of how they were able to relieve themselves when the plumber turned off the water for the day. She gives lessons in how to peel a potato. All this detail brings us home to ourselves. Anne Frank was not a document. She was not a number or a photograph. Not simply part of an abstract idea or a madman's fantasy. She was flesh and blood.

This being – just over the edge of womanhood – was the most feeling and idealistic of creatures. It is her belief in the goodness of humanity which is able to bring a heart numbed by the horrible events of the Holocaust back to its own grief. Above all, she immerses herself and her readers in the world of feelings. She tells us she likes to see a person angry because from this anger she can read character. In her dreams, an old friend she had misjudged pleads to her, '. . . help me . . . rescue me'. She is filled with compassion, like all adolescent girls, for the mute and the weak.

That the adolescent girl becomes ashamed of this body which she begins to feel so powerfully. That a girl just turned woman should be the symbol of those who perished from the violence of a mass delusion. That it is another girl becoming woman, Iphigenia, who is sacrificed to the principles of warfare and violence, in our mythology, in our dreams. That now, in this late twentieth century, we see the faces and bodies of girls, their bodies barely showing breasts, in postures of seductiveness which suggest to us that these souls have already gone through a kind of rape. That the innocence and vulnerability of childhood has been sacrificed in these young women, as girls too young for sexuality promise their bodies to men.

The obsession of the pornographer with the unformed body of a child virgin. The girl kidnapped and sold into sexual slavery. The young woman accused of witchcraft and burned. In the Holocaust, babies torn from their mothers' hands and murdered, young women seduced, used, delivered of early pregnancies or dying in abortions, the child who is raped or abused.

There is a thread in the mind of this culture which ties together all these acts of violence to minds and bodies of children and young women. For the calculated use of a not yet grown woman's body in pornographic poses is part of culture's symbolic murder of all that is childlike in our souls. When we love a child, we love human nature before it has been reshaped by culture. This is what we mean by 'innocence' and 'naiveté'; not that the child has no sexual feeling, but that this feeling has not yet been corrupted by culture's hatred and fear of nature, and that the child's idea of self has not been reshaped to a humiliating image.

When we read the words of Anne Frank, a promise comes to us. Perhaps this is a child who might have reached adulthood with this 'innocence' intact. Through what we see as wholeness in her we touch again our own wholeness. But when we see the child's body remade into a pornographic object, we witness the death of a hope in us. Here is the child's flesh stripped of meaning and the child's body fragmented from spirit.

When we seek happiness, Freud tells us, we look for the prehistoric wishes of childhood. And in our dreams, the presence of the child is like the presence of an essential self. When a child is born to our dreams, we know this is a new part of ourselves, or a very old part of ourselves reborn to consciousness. We take the child's appearance as a sign of transformation. At one and the same time, the child brings us joy and change.

Yet daily, as part of the normal rituals of our culture, we sacrifice this child in us. Since birth, we terrorise the desires of the child. What is joyful and irrepressible in our natures lies mute and still. From our fear of natural change, we murder the hope of new life in us. In our myths, Iphigenia, the young girl, on the edge of womanhood, on the edge of erotic power, is murdered, and this event is the first act in a war in which a whole generation of young men is immolated. But it is no different in our lives; through acts of violence to the soul and body, we destroy the young.

In these acts, we attempt to destroy eros. For isn't it eros we rediscover in the child's world? The beauty of the child's body. The child's closeness to the natural world. The child's heart. Her love. Touch never divided from meaning. Her trust. Her ignorance of culture. The knowledge she has of her own body. That she eats when she is hungry. Sleeps when she is tired. Believes what she sees. That no part of her body has been forbidden to her. No part of this body is shamed, numbed, or denied. That anger, fear, love, and desire pass freely through this body. And for her, meaning is never separate from feeling.

But all this is erotic and erotic feeling brings one back to this state of innocence before culture teaches us to forget the knowledge of the body. To make love is to become like this infant again. We grope with our mouths toward the body of another being, whom we trust, who takes us in her arms. We rock together with this loved one. We move beyond speech. Our bodies move past all the controls we have learned. We cry out in ecstasy, in feeling. We are back in a natural world before culture tried to erase our experience of nature. In this world, to touch another is to express love; there is no idea apart from feeling, and no feeling which does not ring through our bodies and our souls at once.

This is eros. Our own wholeness. Not the sensation of pleasure alone, nor the idea of love alone, but the whole experience of human love. The whole range of human capacity exists in this love. Here is the capacity for speech and meaning, for culture, for memory, for imagination, the capacity for touch and expression, and sensation and joy.

This is why the child in the pornographic mind must be sacrificed. She must be degraded, objectified, defiled, raped, and even murdered. For the child reminds us of our own wholeness. In our minds, she stands for physical and spiritual transformation, birth and death. She is the part of nature beyond control. But she is also meaning and culture bound up with nature. In her, nature is filled with meaning and culture expresses nature. And the child's crime is that she reminds us of eros.

The Way of All Ideology

And it was then I knew that the healing
of all wounds
is forgiveness
that permits a promise
of our return
at the end.

Alice Walker,
'Good Night, Willie Lee/I'll See You In The Morning'

I

I began thinking about political theory by thinking about the way we think. I speculate about ideology. About form. And then about dialogue. The three phenomena occur to me at once. Forms: the forms of hierarchies, of institutions, of habits, the way things are done; the forms of language, gesture, art, of thought, and equally, of emotion. What we say to one another being often what it is predictable that we will say; what I will say, if you say that: Dialogue.

But a speculation about dialogue is also a speculation about ideology. For so often we speak as if my questions and your answers, my statements and your responses, were all written down somewhere in a great codicil of conversations. As if, in the same code, who 'I' believe myself to be, and who I believe 'you' to be, were also written; as if it were recorded that there must be an 'I' and a 'you', the 'you' corresponding to the inevitable 'other': the enemy.

And now I sit up straighter and glare in the eye of an imaginary 'you' who forbids me to have such thoughts as the one I am about to utter, and I ask this 'you': What if all our efforts toward liberation are determined by an ideology which despite our desire for a better world leads us inevitably back to the old paradigm of suffering?

This is not a question filled with dread, I tell this 'you'. For now this other half of a continual dialogue in my mind has become the censor. *She* reduces, maligns, misinterprets my thoughts. *She* challenges, troubles, and unsettles me. And I argue with her. I tell her, this is a question filled with hope. It is filled with the implication that our dialogues can be transformed into real speech, to a liberating conversation; it is a question imbued with the suggestion that we might free ourselves from the old paradigm of warfare, that I may not need an enemy.

Who are these two in me? The 'I' with whom I identify, the 'you' whom I define as the not 'I'. They always shift; they are never the same two. One day 'you' is the nag, the dictator, the time and motion expert, the boss, the destroyer. And on that day 'I' am the dreamer, the seeker, the poet, the visionary thinker, the daring questioner nevertheless terrified by this other, who looks over my shoulder, nevertheless afraid of her judgments, even falling silent when I sense her disapproval.

At other times 'I' am the authority, the good girl, the stable and predictable one, whereas 'you' are a secret thought, a hidden memory, a long-buried desire. When I was a married woman, this 'you' remembered all along that I had been in love with women, remembered the passion I felt in my woman's body for another woman, disrupted the comfortable, acceptable image I had of myself.

But now, in my recent thought about thinking, this 'you' is the commissar of knowledge. She is politically correct. She is moral. Her ears are pitched for heresy. She hears me, for instance, think about psychology, about the structure of the mind, the structures of emotions, and she whispers to me words to the effect that I am being apolitical, that I am being one of *them*. In my mind, I have become exhausted arguing with her.

Yet in and through this exhausting argument I know I am split from myself. I watch the phenomenon in myself. What I think of as myself is actually split in two. A new thought, a new way of seeing – which is at its heart the articulation of a new feeling, and hence a new experience in the world – wishes to be born. In the effort to exist, this thought thrusts away all doubt, all second thoughts. But these second thoughts are thoughts of alarm. They are afraid of change. They would remain the same.

Slowly I begin to identify myself with the new thought. I split away from my doubts, calling this doubting self 'you'. Now I project the doubting half of my own inner conversation upon another. I supply her with her missing part of the dialogue. As I argue with myself, I imagine I am arguing with her. I have created a figment of my denied self whom *she* has now come to represent.

I have encountered the idea of a denied self before. Writing of racism in the 1960s, James Baldwin spoke in *The Fire Next Time* of the creation of the 'nigger' in the white mind. The idea of the nigger, he observed, said nothing about black character and everything about white racist character. The nigger is the denied part of the white idea of self, a fantasy of another's being created out of a purposeful ignorance of the self. And I discovered the same delusion, the same denied self, in the pornographer's idea of a woman.

Moreover, as I wrote about the pornographer's mind I discovered that pornography itself was not so much an art form as it was an ideology and an ideology which, like the ideology of racism, *requires* the creation of another, a not-I, an enemy. This is a world view in which the self is irrevocably split so that it does not recognize its other half, and in which all phenomena, experience, and human qualities are also split into the superior and the inferior, the righteous and the evil, the above and the below. What is superior, according to this ideology, is by rights above all that is inferior. For the righteous must have authority over and control of the evil.

And the other, the not-I, bears all those qualities which are lesser and bad; thus the other is the enemy who must be controlled or annihilated.

The one and the other. Now, as I think about my own thought, I ask myself if racism and pornography and the unholy warfare in my own mind can have a common origin? For if this were true, I reason, it would bear on my own efforts to liberate myself from the ideologies which oppress me and to free myself from the imprisoning conditions of a society hostile to female being.

Images, gestures, facts of history, whole patterns of culture begin to assemble in my mind, and I am reminded once more of the traditional association, in the mind of this civilization, between the other and nature; and between the 'one' (the identified self, the white, anglicized man) and culture. How women are said to be closer to nature, more emotional, lacking in intellect or spiritual calling, needing the authority of a man, a man's cool reason, the spiritual control of a male voice, a male God. Peoples of colour envisioned as bestial, and superhumanly sexual, as sensual, and over-emotional, even dangerous, with natural cunning, needing to be mastered, counselled, told how to live, to speak, to work.

In this ideology the denied self, projected onto the other, embodies all that is part of the natural, sensate life of the body and all of the natural emotions which so often cause one to feel out of control, even frightened of oneself. Through this ideology's fantasy that the other is dangerous, one sees above all a mind which *fears natural life*. The desire to hide from nature is the secret raison d'être of this ideology. Through this ideology the mind imagines that to wish is to command, or that feeling can be replaced by concept.

Because we are natural beings we do not have power over nature; we face physical death, the possibility of injury, the certainty of ageing, the continual vulnerability of flesh to pain, the experience of separation, loss, and grief. And our feelings too have a life beyond our conscious control. We want what we are not supposed to want. Remember what it is painful to know. Become overwhelmed with ecstasy or rage or pain and lose our bearings.

The mind would control natural life by denying natural power and by keeping a knowledge of that power apart from itself. Yet knowledge of natural power and the life of natural feeling cannot die; this knowledge, this life persists even with our own hunger, our own breathing. Because of the very persistence of feeling, the mind which wants to deny this life must give it some mode of existence. Thus the mind creates a fantasy of another being, the other, who embodies all the qualities of the denied self.

But now, alongside my thought about this pattern of our culture to deny nature and to associate nature with the other, I consider another cultural pattern. And this is the preponderant hostility within culture to creativity.

In an essay called 'Poems Are Not Luxuries', the poet Audre Lorde has made an illuminating connection between this civilization's fear of the associative and musical language of poetry (a language which comes from the depths of reason beneath rational consciousness, from dark, unknown regions of mind) and the same civilization's fear of black skin, of the female, of darkness, the dark other, Africa, signifying an older, secret knowledge.[1]

For, of course, it is not simply inventiveness which is feared. The new machine, the new gadget is worshipped. What is really feared is an open door into a consciousness which leads us back to the old, ancient, infant and mother knowledge of the body, in whose depths lies another form of culture not opposed to nature but instead expressing the full power of nature and of our natures.

This fear of the knowledge of the body has created a dualism between culture and nature, intellect and emotion, spirit and matter. And the same fear has made of women – as it has of peoples of colour and of Jews – symbols of feeling, carnality, nature, all that is in civilization's 'unconscious' and that it would deny. This is why it is so terrifying to the traditional mind of our culture to confront a woman who is scholarly, or a black political philosopher.

I remember that in Germany the period before the Holocaust was remarkable both for the assimilation of Jews into German culture and for an extraordinary burst of creativity among Jewish people. The anti-Semite had regarded Yiddish culture as inferior, and through this denigration he spared himself the recognition of what for him would be an impossible formula. Because within his symbolic reasoning, the existence of a Jew who was 'cultured' would mean that nature and culture are not forever separate. Now the anti-Semite had to confront a Jew who could not only speak German but write great poetry in German, write great German music, and expand the boundaries of German science. These accomplishments must have created a terror in the anti-Semite's mind; each of them represented a union between nature and culture. And in this metaphorical system, such a union could only mean that unconscious knowledge – our physical knowledge of the power of nature and the memory of the power of our mothers – would become conscious. The anti-Semite is afraid to know himself.

Should it be a surprise then that this period of history was also remarkable for the breaking of many other separating paradigms – the breakdown of traditional forms of art, of traditional family structures, of the old Newtonian idea of the structure of the universe which separated matter and energy, of the separation between mind and body? And finally, that the burst of extraordinary creativity in every kind of field was not experienced exclusively by Jews; it was a phenomenon for which later this period as a whole was to be thought remarkable.

If before I failed to see that a fear of nature and a fear of creativity must be inextricably associated, it is only because, schooled in my own culture and its paradigms, I have failed to see that nature and creativity share the same origin, are born in the same breath. For I have come to age in a culture which opposes spirit to the flesh and which uses culture as a way to deny the power of the natural.

And now I begin to suspect that all ideology must share a hidden tendency. For beyond a just description of the truth, an ideology holds the promise that one may control reality with the mind, assert the ideal as more real than reality, or place idea as an authority above nature, and even above our sensual experience of nature: what we see, what we hear, what we feel, taste, smell.

And with this promise, always, inevitably, no matter what the ideology, the idea of the other is born. For another must become a symbol and a scapegoat for the ideologist's own denied knowledge that this ideology is not more real than reality and must bow to contradictory natural evidence.

The list is long. The persecution of the Christians. The persecution of the heretics. The Inquisition. The Pogroms. The persecution of Socialists and Communists. The Stalinist purges. (And into this fabric is woven the continual persecution of peoples of colour, of women, of Jews, the fear of lesbians, the silencing of our creativity.)

Ideology. Ideology, form, and dialogue. One begins as a socialist arguing that matter comes before spirit. One wins a revolution and vanquishes the enemy. But then one discovers the enemy is not yet dead. She is a poet whose words are vaguely unsettling. Who doubts. And then there are the prisons again, the police again, the old terror again. The war is still waging.

And there is still a war waging within me. I have been schooled in the ways of this culture. In my own mind unknowingly I choose the same solution to emotional dilemma that my culture has chosen and has taught me to choose. Though I argue against pornography and racism, my own mind splits against itself, creates a 'you'. Now this 'you' is the ideologist, a part of myself I hide from myself. She is afraid of my own creativity. She asks old questions which exclude the possibility of new insights. She has categorical ideas of thought or expression from which she will not deviate. She dismisses my ideas with labels, epithets, catch phrases. She purposely misinterprets me and seizes on small mistakes to humiliate me.

And she is a martinet. She wants me to produce a comprehensive world view so that nothing in the world is unexplained. She is a Prussian soldier in the world of the intellect. She is not interested in unanswered questions, in uncertainties, intuitions, barely grasped insights, hunches. Moreover she wishes every idea to be consistent, to conform to one ideal. She is not familiar with Freud's notion that in the unconscious what seems contradictory to the conscious mind is resolved.[2] She is impatient for resolution.

Moreover, she argues to me that I should not cite Freud. She is given to categorizing everyone as either enemy or not an enemy. To her way of thinking, one cannot agree with some ideas belonging to one thinker and disagree with others. A thinker is either good or bad and one must not quote bad ideas. Indeed, she censors not only my imagination and my thinking but my reading.

And, predictably, she is obtuse to musical, to associative language. Though she lives in my mind alongside a poet, claiming to have respect for poetry, every time a line of poetry begins to be formed, she silences it. It does not fit her idea of what is moral or useful.

And, above all, she values production. She cannot understand a poetry without clear purpose. Before each line is written, it must, to pass her censorship, clearly relate to some moral cause. It must argue for liberation. That a new expression at its birth may have no obvious relationship to liberation, but may, in the end, be more liberating than all her expectations, has not occurred to her. And cannot occur to her. For above all she labours in defence of ideology, in defence of the desire to control reality with the idea and to describe reality as always *predictable*. Thus, it is contrary to her real purpose to let herself know that from the darker, unknown part of my mind great riches might come. She is ashamed of such riches, for such riches speak of a larger reality than she is willing to admit exists.

This is the way of all ideology. It is mind over body. Safety over risk. The predictable over the surprise. Control over emotion. But the history of ideologies is also a tragedy. For in the beginning a political theory is born of genuine feeling, of a sense of reality. But in a state of feeling alone, the knowledge of oppression remains mute, and the reality of oppression is explained away by oppressive theories; it is said, for instance, that members of the working class have failed to raise themselves by their own bootstraps or that poverty is a sign of having sinned against God; of lacking God's grace. A theory of liberation must be created to articulate the feeling of oppression, to describe this oppression as real, as unjust, and to point to a cause. In this way the idea is liberating. It restores to the oppressed a belief in the self and in the authority of the self to determine what is real.

But when a theory is transformed into an ideology, it begins to destroy the self and self-knowledge. Originally born of feeling, it pretends to float above and around feeling. Above sensation. It organizes experience according to itself, without touching experience. By virtue of being itself, it is supposed to know. To invoke the name of this ideology is to confer truthfulness. No one can tell it anything new. Experience ceases to surprise it, inform it, transform it. It is annoyed by any detail which does not fit into its world view. Begun as a cry against the denial of truth, now it denies any truth which does not fit into its scheme. Begun as a way to restore one's sense of reality, now it attempts to discipline real people, to remake natural beings after its own image. All that it fails to explain it records as dangerous. All that makes it question, it regards as its enemy. Begun as a theory of liberation, it is threatened by new theories of liberation; slowly, it builds a prison for the mind.

As I sit to write, the ideological part of my mind dictates that an essay about political philosophy should not be invaded by emotion. This objection partakes of the duality of literary forms. It rests on the claim that truth is more truthful when it emanates from a disembodied voice. This part of my mind has accepted the illusory possibility of objectivity.

And like the racist or the pornographer, this part of my mind schooled in ideology projects whatever is unacceptable in myself onto others.

As I was composing the notes towards this writing, I was forced to confront my own self-denial and projection. Waiting in line to be served in a restaurant, I began to notice an older woman who was sitting at a table alone. She was not eating, and she seemed to be miserable. I assumed she was waiting to be met. Her expression, the paleness of her skin, something in her posture all indicated to me that she might be ill, perhaps even seriously ill, perhaps dying. I imagined then that she was nauseous. I was hungry. Yet as I looked at her I felt my appetite begin to ebb, a nausea seemed about to invade me by virtue of her presence. I was afraid that I might be seated at a table next to her, so that I might become more nauseous, or be contaminated. Slowly, despite another voice in me that urged reason and compassion, I felt an anger toward her. Why was she sick in this restaurant? Why force people who are eating to participate in her misery? I wanted to shout at her that she should go home, but of course, I did not. I was deeply ashamed of my feelings. And because of this shame I hid them away.

Later, seated at a table across the room, after I had eaten breakfast and forgotten the woman, my friend left the table. Then idly I glanced in the woman's direction again. And I saw that she had been joined by an older man, whom I felt was her husband, and by a younger man, whom I presumed to be her son. Now I imagined the cause of her waiting. In my mind, I saw the older man going to pick up his son; the son being terribly late, leaving his sick mother to wait for him. And I was indignant on his mother's behalf. Not knowing for certain whether he was her son, whether she was ill, or whether he indeed had been late, I began composing a speech in my mind. I felt justified in my anger at him. After all, was he not a man and she a woman? Were not women always waiting for men, being taken for granted, being caused misery? Were not sons as a lot ungrateful and unkind and disrespectful to their mothers? Someone ought to speak to him. *I* ought to. I ought to tell him how ashamed he should be for making his poor mother wait.

But, at last, fortunately, I began to laugh at myself. For, of course, it was I who had been ashamed, ashamed of my own responses to this woman, I who had been unkind in my thoughts toward her. And now I who could assuage my own guilt by being angry at someone else, whom I imagined responsible for her pain. From her persecutor, I had turned myself into her champion. And in all this, I avoided confronting or knowing myself.

And now as I looked at my imagined portrait of her son I saw myself. For according to my ideological explanation of male hostility toward women, men are afraid of women, and most particularly of their mothers, because they fear death. And was not that precisely what I had projected on her, my own fear of my own death, of the possibility that my body might fail me, and instead of giving me hunger, give me nausea?

Because I was ashamed of my feeling in myself, because of the ideologist in me who censored my own feeling and did not let it live long enough to be explored and understood, I was in danger from the most dangerous brand of ignorance, ignorance of myself.

This is one of the ways ideology hides the truth. One is only allowed, through the justifying framework of ideas, to acknowledge certain emotions toward certain people. A woman can hate a man for oppressing her. Black can hate white. Working class can feel rage at the ruling class. All of these are made acceptable by theories of liberation. And as such they are liberating angers. But another whole range of emotions exists which ideology defines as unacceptable. Suppose, for instance, one feels a love for the enemy, or a particular member of the enemy class. Suppose one feels anger and hatred toward another of the same oppressed group? Suppose a woman hates a woman? These emotions are defined as 'incorrect'. And they become hidden. Thus, I become blind toward my own anger and fear of another woman, because this feeling is not correct. In this way, by its own denials and blindnesses, each new ideology creates its own forbidden, subterranean world of reality.

But now another set of questions begins to arise in my mind. Without ideology, someone in me asks, how can one argue for liberation? How can one even think, or see deeper cause, make that analysis which opens out to social change? Is not this writing itself ideological? For I have interpreted conflict as a conflict between idea and nature, culture and nature. Am I arguing that thought itself is dangerous? Am I making an intellectual case against the intellect? Or, in a different light, am I not invalidating all that political theory makes evident?

II

In my mind now another couple is forming, another split between two parts of myself. And this is not the old pair, the visionary and the censor. Rather, both of these are ideologists. One of these is my political self. She has always seen things in terms of divisions of power. She knows that there are those who have the power to shape the lives of others. She knows the forms of that power, both visible and subtle: money, social position, language, education, simple physical force.

But now another is born, and she is a psychological thinker. She loves to gossip. She loves to try to understand her own deeper motives and the meanings of the lives of those around her. She is fascinated by the mind itself and by the shape of feelings. The political thinker is suspicious of psychology for, so often, psychologists have obfuscated or denied real political oppression. And yet, the psychological thinker is also suspicious of purely political thinking. For she has begun to notice how often the political mind will disguise and deny personal feelings with correct political rhetoric. I call these two thinkers Rachel and Agnes. The quality of their dialogue has not been illuminating.

Rachel the political theorist says: 'I'm more worried about being raped than about the danger of ideological thinking. Somehow it seems to be more relevant to my everyday urgent life.' Agnes the psychologist says: 'Don't you know that your own mind shapes your everyday life?' Rachel says: 'Don't you know male, white, capitalist power shapes my life?' Agnes says: 'And you have no power to change this?' Rachel says: 'I will take the power.' Agnes says: 'Don't you know your own mind shapes the way you take this power, determines whether you succeed or fail?'

They go on like this. The result is boredom. Agnes wins, then Rachel wins, then Agnes wins. But slowly each has reduced her ideas to the ridiculous. All the subtleties of both, all their perceptions, have been erased in an attempt to erase the truths which they offer each other. Their arguments become sadly predictable.

Here there is another aspect of ideological structure. Dialogue – which is finally perhaps the form of all thought – must become a war. One must lose and the other win. There must be a clear victor. One must be shown to be wrong. And therefore, each kind of thought is pitted against the other. The listener must choose between one and the other, either a truth or a falsity.

And yet Agnes has much insight to offer Rachel, and without Rachel's questions, Agnes's thought is curiously out of touch with reality, even as she argues for a knowledge of reality. For instance, Rachel tells Agnes that to have no political theory is impossible. For having no theory simply implies that one agrees with the political structures that exist, with the status quo. And moreover, Rachel explains, one must be able to name and locate oppression if one is to argue and struggle against oppression. Otherwise, she says, one begins to believe that oppression is simply a state of nature.

On the other hand, Agnes has wisdom to give to Rachel. She says that there are two kinds of anger. The first is accurate and appropriate; it is *known*. But the second is not accurately placed. It is displaced and therefore *unknown*. The first anger, she says, liberates one, both in mind and in body. But the second anger, she warns, imprisons. It becomes obsessive; it turns into bitterness; it leads to self-defeat; it turns us against ourselves. Because this second anger hides another deeper anger, the true anger, of which one is ashamed.

Therefore, she tells Rachel, a political theorist who does not explore her own emotions is in danger of turning against herself.

As I write I realize that this question of two kinds of anger is essential. For me, it is the missing link between political and psychological understanding. I recall an episode from a case history of a child so severely abused by her parents that for years she never spoke. Finally a therapist broke through her veil of silence, and she began to trust the world again. Just as she was doing well her father, who had almost murdered her by trying to burn her alive, came to visit her. He promised to call her nightly, and to return in a week, to be a kind and loving parent. However he did not call, nor did he come. And the child was angry at him. Yet she could not admit her rage to herself. She was ashamed to admit that she might be abandoned in this way by her father, unwilling to admit her anger. Thus she displaced her anger on those who were close to her, on her friends, on those who had nursed her back to health, whom she had just recently learned to trust. Slowly she became alienated from everyone around her and began to retreat once more into herself, rejecting the world. But finally, she discovered and admitted the real source of her anger. She spoke out her rage against her father and acknowledged that he had left her, failed her, and that he was not capable of loving her. Only when she acknowledged her real anger could she trust herself and the world again.

To escape from genuine sources of anger is to escape from the self. And this escape is shaped and coloured by shame, for one hides a feeling only if one is ashamed of that feeling. But ironically, to hide feeling does not get rid of shame; rather it increases one's inner feeling of humiliation, or of dishonour. For the very act of hiding *proves* to the self that what is hidden is terrible. Living in such a deceit, one lives with the constant and inarticulate feeling that one's inner self is evil, wrong, or even repulsive. And moreover, since one is hiding, one is actually lying, and this lie compounds one's feeling of wrongness. It is thus inevitable that displaced anger will lead to self-hatred and even to a desire for self-punishment. (The oppressed attack one another not only because it is safe but also because such an attack is an expression of self-hatred.)

But of course this self-hatred must be veiled, too: it is given another name. Thus the abused child complained of real irritations and difficulties, but these took on momentous proportions.

Ideology is capable of masking many different kinds of appropriate angers. For years I have noticed that male anger at women is often expressed in the name of 'revolution'. Although it has been almost always women and not men of the upper class who showed any concern for suffering of the poor, it was a woman, Marie Antoinette, who became the symbol in male revolutionary culture for aristocratic callousness. Patricia Hearst and not her father was kidnapped. And similarly white women became the symbol for Southern race privilege. (Though white women are not by any means without blame, one must be suspicious when a woman is chosen to symbolize a predominantly male power system.)[3]

But one is capable of many displaced angers. In the name of female liberation, we attack another woman because she is 'incorrect'. We say she is identified with males and then associate our anger at her with our anger at male power. Yet through this accusation we can express our anger at women, at our mother perhaps, or at ourselves. On the surface our attacks may be perfectly justified by fact. But this does not belie the other fact that these accusations serve to hide us from our real feelings. These feelings give a certain tone, an inappropriate rage or finality to our expressions. And in the end it is only when feelings are accurately named and explored that we cease ultimately to destroy ourselves, in body and mind, with our anger.

But here is another essential link between psychology and political theory. The secret existence of a hidden anger creates a false anger. And because ideas are intermingled with and even proceed from feeling, this false anger leads to the distortion of political theory. Thus there are two uses for theory. The first purpose of an idea is to explain reality. But a second purpose is to escape or deny reality. The same political theory can be used to arrive at truth or delusion.

I can find no better description of theory as madness than in Isaac Deutscher's portrait of Stalin. Speaking of Stalin's behaviour during the period of Soviet industrialization and agricultural collectivization after 1929, Deutscher writes: 'He was now completely possessed by the idea that he could achieve a miraculous transformation of the whole of Russia by a single *tour de force*. He seemed to live in a half-real and half-dreamy world of statistical figures and indices of industrial orders and instructions, a world in which no target and no objective seemed to be beyond his and the party's grasp.'[4] When Stalin insisted that 17 million tons of pig iron could be produced, certain economists and managers voiced fears that this was impossible. Enraged by their opposition, Stalin labelled these men and women 'right-wing' opportunists and 'wreckers'.

Similarly, Stalin's collectivization of farms turned into a war on the peasants, and the old way of farming was destroyed before the new way of farming was functioning. Again, Deutscher writes vividly of this cast of mind: 'The whole experiment seemed to be a piece of prodigious insanity, in which all the rules of logic and principles of economics were turned upside down. It was as if a whole nation had suddenly abandoned and destroyed its houses and huts, which, though obsolete and decaying, existed in reality, and moved, lock, stock and barrel, into some illusory buildings.'[5] Since the hidden motive behind such ideology is to escape reality and deny real thoughts and feelings, it is predictable that this ideology would destroy the real for 'illusory buildings'.

And precisely because it exists to disguise hidden thoughts and feelings, such an ideology must be fanatical. It must insist that no other truth than its own is possible. The very idea of an alternative suggests a search. But any search might disclose the original lie. In this atmosphere, anyone who deviates from the correct position is suspect. Now, ironically, ideology creates an atmosphere hostile to ideas. And fanatical ideologists, claiming that they possess the only description of reality possible, become anti-intellectual. Creativity is a threat to those in this frame of mind.

Of course the political theory inspired by delusion must be hostile to knowledge. In place of the development of the soul, self-knowledge, and education, such an ideology substitutes indoctrination. Before Stalinism took hold, the poet Osip Mandelstam accepted the end of democratic forms of education. Of this, Nadezhda Mandelstam writes, 'Isn't this the basic error of our times and of each one of us? What do the people need to be indoctrinated for? What satanic arrogance you need to impose your views like this! It was only in Russia that the idea of popular education was replaced by the political concept of indoctrination. When M. himself became a target for it, he was one of the first to revolt.'[6] In the same way, movements have been known to turn against their most creative and ingenious members. For example, speaking the correct line of the day, which held that all portraits of black people had to be tragic, Richard Wright accused Zora Neale Hurston of creating 'minstrel' characters. 'But I am not tragically coloured', she responded.[7]

But who or what one really *is*, ceases to matter to ideology. For ideology gives birth to still another deceit: the enemy. The poet Osip Mandelstam, the writer Nadezhda Mandelstam, both once socialists, become enemies. Zora Neale Hurston is an enemy.

And moreover ideology makes over the real, material enemy – one who has actual power over our lives, or who actually poses a danger – into an inhuman entity. Suddenly this enemy ceases to possess any human qualities. No explanation can be offered, psychologically or materially, for his behaviour. He is evil incarnate, sprung unborn and whole from hell. We refuse to understand him except as a kind of thing, a force. To consider that he may have a soul or that he may have been born innocent becomes a heresy.

And this enemy is oddly generalized. Now everyone male, everyone female, everyone white, everyone black, everyone Chinese, or Jewish is by virtue of biological identification the enemy.

At times the genuine anger of the oppressed also becomes generalized, from the force of experience and time, and for self-protection. But hatred for a delusory enemy has a different quality. It is final and relentless; it renders an irreversible judgment in the form of an idea. This is the idea of a natural, or inborn badness: the enemy becomes a monstrosity by virtue of characteristics acquired at birth. Andrea Dworkin has written of this kind of thinking: 'It was this very ideology of biological determinism that had licensed the slaughter and/or enslavement of virtually any group one could name, including women by men. Anywhere one looked, it was this philosophy which justified atrocity. *This one faith which destroyed life with a momentum of its own.*'[8] Moreover, because the enemy serves as a mask for hidden thoughts and feelings, new enemies must always be created. If, for instance, men are the enemy, women who associate with men soon also become enemies.[9] One understands why this idea of an inhuman enemy must lead to violent atrocity. For such an enemy represents an original lie. A lie that is part of the self, always present, always threatening, powerful.

We live in a society which is built upon a prejudice toward women and peoples of colour, homosexuals, Jewish people, the disabled. In that society we are the other. If we make those who are not oppressed as we are oppressed into enemies, we do not have the power to make them suffer as we do. What has been called 'reverse sexism' or 'reverse racism' is impossible, since racism and sexism are institutions which by definition include social, political, and economic sanctions.[10] And yet, if we produce a delusionary enemy in our minds, we do damage ourselves; we sacrifice a part of ourselves to that delusion; we lose part of our own power, the power of consciousness.

> But he fears the inner city of his soul
> Wilhelm Stekel, *Sadism and Masochism*

Agnes and Rachel have tried to banish each other from consciousness. But it is the very association of their thoughts and the confrontation between their two visions that is illuminating.

One cannot kill off a part of the self. If I silence my doubts, they grow larger. If I forget an earlier self, this self haunts me in my dreams and tries over and over to break through my ordinary consciousness, even with violence. If I deny my own emotions, I begin to imagine they exist in another, and this other becomes my enemy. But if I own my feelings and trace them to their origins, they lead me to a self-knowledge that is liberating and healing.

Every time I deny myself I commit a kind of suicide. And it is, in this light, interesting to know that Hitler, the prototype of the fascist man, committed suicide. For his hatred and fear of 'the Jew' – and then the Slavs, and black people, the gay, the disabled – was ultimately a denied self-hatred. Of this one story comes to mind. When he wrote *Mein Kampf* Hitler recorded that he became an anti-Semite one day when he saw an old man dressed in a caftan walking through Vienna. 'Is this a Jew?' he asked, and then said to himself, 'Is this a German?' deciding forever that this Jew could not have been a German and was eternally separate and different from himself. His biographers reveal that when he was a young art student he bought his clothes from a Jewish man who sold second-hand apparel, and the piece of clothing he wore most often was a caftan purchased from this man. Moreover, what Hitler did not know is that the Jewish caftan was really German dress from the Middle Ages, preserved by the Jewish people who were exiled from Germany at that time.

Indeed, the part of myself that I have exiled is essential to me especially because she asks troublesome questions. There is a reason Rachel exists. Her abstract ideas, her feeling of righteousness, originated in my own experience. She is a part of what I have lived and felt; she is ingrained into my very being. And so too Agnes is a part of my seeing, my own sense that I know, my ability to perceive. If they disagree, it is, as Freud suggests, perhaps a fault only of our limited knowledge. For they are both expressions of myself and somewhere they must meet.

And what matters above all, in any dialogue, I begin to see, is intent.

Rachel may see what Agnes is forgetting, or Agnes may know what Rachel does not know, yet if either one intends to make the other into an enemy, what they say to one another is distorted. It is not only that a certain intention behind words will make me defensive and thus deaf to reason. This is true. But it is also true that a false intention will distort the speaker's words.

I can be angry. I can hate. I can rage. But the moment I have defined another being as my enemy, I lose part of myself, the complexity and subtlety of my vision. I begin to exist in a closed system. When anything goes wrong, I blame my enemy. If I wake troubled, my enemy had led me to this feeling. If I cannot sleep, it is because of my enemy. Slowly all the power in my life begins to be located outside, and my whole being is defined in relation to this outside force, which becomes daily more monstrous, more evil, more laden with all the qualities in myself I no longer wish to own. The quality of my thought then is diminished. My imagination grows small. My self seems meagre. For my enemy has stolen all these.

III

> My whole outlook upon social life is determined by the question: How can we recognize the shackles that tradition has laid upon us? For when we recognize them we are also able to break them.
>
> Franz Boas

Difference. Conflict. Trouble. Separation. These exist in and out of our minds. But we need not experience these through the old paradigm of warfare. What I know from the political theory of liberation is that where an old paradigm exists, a new paradigm can come into being.

I think, for example, of the paradigm of diversity instead of the paradigm of struggle. Along with his discovery of the struggle for survival, Darwin discovered that an environment tends to be richer and more sustaining to all the life in its boundaries when many different varieties of life forms exist within that environment. Or I think, for example, of the fact that any art form flourishes when many different artists are creating through that form. I think of an example from modern physics, in which science itself has had to accept two contradictory descriptions of reality as true. For light has been proven equally to be a particle and to be a wave. And modern physics must accept both these theories at the same time, hoping that at some time this paradox will answer a riddle, or that the answer to a riddle will solve this paradox. For the seeming existence of contradiction can be a gift of knowledge in a disguised form. So often in the history of thought a paradox has led to the discovery of a larger and more fundamental truth, even a new paradigm, in the attempt to reconcile two apparently contradictory phenomena. And we may fail to see this more fundamental truth precisely because we have been blinded by our belief in an old paradigm, an ideology.

This is the state my mind is in now: contradiction. At one and the same time, I agree with a political description of reality and with a psychological description of reality. At one and the same time, I see that social and economic forces shape human behaviour and that human behaviour is shaped by the life of the child. At one and the same time, I believe that we are shaped by circumstance and that we shape the circumstances around us. In my own mind I experience the same dualism which haunts civilization between psychological thinking and political thinking. Yet, I cannot give up either vision, because both to me are equally true and experienced as such every day, every moment.

Thus I begin to learn to live with questions. With uncertainty. With an unknowingness. At times frightening, at other times this state of suspension makes me fall in love with the world. I find myself laughing. I am surprised, delighted. The universe holds a secret larger than me. I listen.

And then it occurs to me that it is a coincidence of perhaps some significance that science should have to hold in its canon two contradictory notions in any age in which modern physics has challenged the old dualities between subjective and objective truth, matter and energy, time and space, in a time in which it is known that nothing in the universe is solid, that everything is mortal, changing, continuing to move, and that the line between one entity and another, myself, for instance, and the air around me, does not exist.[11]

Everywhere the old either-or begins to break down. The personal is political, the political psychological. Anger and love are part of one another. Hatred becomes compassion. The old idea of who the self is and who the world is becomes too small.

And this bears directly on our condition as women. For the 'idea' of a woman is born, of a duality, out of the false concepts of masculine and feminine. The very word 'woman' signifies all those qualities which the masculine mind splits off from itself, declaring that one is either male or female. And in the female live all those qualities the male has decided are inferior or suspect.

And this bears on our condition as those who would liberate ourselves. For we who struggle for liberation begin to make enemies of each other. In the struggle we create mutually exclusive categories of being, moral orders, and judge each other righteous or not righteous. We create saints and sinners. And wars.

And in all this, do we forget that we have swallowed the old paradigms, been raised in the same woman-hating culture? We ourselves have learned to associate women with nature, dark skin with dangerous knowledge. In a part of us, we are afraid of all that masculine society fears. We fear female power, in ourselves and in others. And we fear separation. We do not like another woman to think differently than we do. We confuse ourselves and our own integrity with that of other women, whom we confuse with our mothers, whom we confuse with nature. That which in society has created conditions which imprison us also determines the shape of the dialogue we have between us, the shape of our efforts toward liberation. Just as society has separated the idea of 'woman' from the idea of 'knowledge', we cease to be able to accept our own thoughts, feelings, and sensations as a source of authority. We, too, long for an ideology which will erase our own experience.

Thus, we may have to relearn thinking. We have to learn to tolerate questions. Like Jane Goodall, who waited interminably for the trust of the primates she observed, we may have to cultivate patience. We may even have to learn to cultivate paradox; welcome contradiction or a troublesome question. We may have to learn to love knowledge for its own sake, not as a means to power. This is not to argue that one cannot argue. This is not to argue against thought. But rather to argue against the old dualities. Against ideology. And for the intellect. For the clear intellect which explores the self and the world with a genuine desire to know.

After all, the two ways of seeing which pose a contradiction in my mind do have a common ground. Both perceive the world as damaged.

Both hope to change the world for the better. Both have a passionate desire to heal suffering. And finally, both of these ways of seeing the world, in their most profound visions, are forgiving.

For a deeply political knowledge of the world does not lead to a creation of an enemy. Indeed, to create monsters unexplained by circumstance is to forget the political vision which above all explains behaviour as emanating from circumstance, a vision which believes in a capacity born to all human beings for creation, joy, and kindness, in a human nature which, under the right circumstances, can bloom.

When a movement for liberation inspires itself chiefly by a hatred for an enemy rather than from this vision of possibility, it begins to defeat itself. Its very motions cease to be healing. Despite the fact that it declares itself in favour of liberation, its language is no longer liberating. It begins to require a censorship within itself. Its ideas of truth become more and more narrow. And this movement that began with a moving evocation of truth, begins to appear fraudulent from the outside, begins to mirror all that it says it opposed, for now it, too, is an oppressor of certain truths, and speakers, and begins, like the old oppressors, to hide from itself.

And finally, as I think about thinking, I begin to know that all original thought – political, scientific, poetic – shares one quality. That is the desire to know the whole truth, to understand and to know what is obscured or what has been forgotten, to take in the unknown. And this desire to know is perhaps finally a way of loving. It is intimately connected to an attitude which honours all that is living. For the desire to know deeply all that is, as part of our outrage over injustice and suffering, accepts the truth, the whole and compassionate being.

Notes:

1. Audre Lorde, 'Poems Are Not Luxuries', *Chrysalis: A Magazine of Female Culture*, no 3 (1977), pp 7–9. See also Audre Lorde and Adrienne Rich, 'An Interview with Audre Lorde', *Signs: Journal of Women in Culture and Society* VI, no 4 (Summer 1981): pp 713–36, esp. pp 728–29.
2. Sigmund Freud, *Collected Papers*, ed. Ernest Jones, trans. Joan Riviere, 5 vols. (New York, Basic Books, 1959), 5: p 184.
3. Similarly, to picture a black man as the symbol of the rapist is a covert expression of racism, not because black men do not commit rape, but because this is a predominantly white society and because the image of a black man as a rapist has a history in the racist imagination of this white society. In the same

way, a supposedly leftist censure of Zionism often reveals beneath its surface an anti-Semitism. For the same objections to nationalism (or military power, defence, and aggression) are not leveled at the Arab states, or at the Soviet Union, or indeed at France, or at Canada, or any nation that remains sovereign. Moreover an exaggerated fear and censure of Jewish power belongs to the history of anti-Semitism as does the choice of the Jew as the scapegoat for anger at bankers, capitalism, communism, anarchy, racism, and imperialism.

4. Issac Deutscher, *Stalin: A Political Biography* (London, Oxford University Press, 1961), p 321.

5. Ibid, p 326.

6. Nadezhda Mandelstam, *Hope against Hope* (New York, Atheneum, 1979), p 114.

7. Cited by Mary Helen Washington in her introduction to 'How It Feels to Be Colored Me', in *I Love Myself When I Am Laughing: A Zora Neale Hurston Reader*, ed. Alice Walker (Old Westbury, NY, Feminist Press, 1979), p 17.

8. Andrea Dworkin, 'Biological Superiority: The World's Most Dangerous and Deadly Idea', *Heresies* no 6 (1978), pp 47–51, esp. p 48. Emphasis mine.

9. Andrea Dworkin describes an incident which took place on a public panel in 1977 on lesbianism as a personal politic. Members of the audience shouted at her, 'Slut, bisexual, she sleeps with men.' Andrea answered their accusations by saying that she did not sleep with men. Of this answer she writes, 'All my life I have hated the prescribers, those who enforce sexual conformity. In answering, I had given in to the inquisitors, and I felt ashamed. It humiliated me to see myself then: one who resists the enforcers out there with militancy, but gives in without resistance to the enforcers among us' (ibid, p 46).

10. I owe this description of racism to Ricky Sherover-Marcuse.

11. It is a significant part of these synchronous events that Einsteinian physics should have aroused a 'pitch of fury' in the fascist mind. Einstein, with his self-described 'distrust of every form of authority', had unnerved the fascist mind with his suggestion that time is not a fixed and immutable dimension. Bruno Thuring wrote in alarm that now instead of one geometry there might be as many geometries 'as one likes!' He described Einstein's theories as a Jewish plot to 'relativize all concepts' which must lead to 'chaos' (Bruno Thuring, *Albert Einstein's Umsturzversuch der Physik*, cited in Frederick V Grunfeld, *Prophets without Honour* [New York, McGraw-Hill Book Co, 1979], p 152). And the Nazi ideologist Alfred Rosenberg used the term 'the Albert Einsteins' to refer to Jewish intellectuals and artists (cited in Grunfeld, p 149).

Part II

Every woman who writes is a survivor

Introduction

In the last two decades, a significant change has taken place in literature. More women have written; more books by women have been published and read and reflected upon than ever before. And this change in quantity has been accompanied by a qualitative shift in the way we think about writing by women. Many of we women who write think of ourselves as part of a literary and social movement. It is a collective movement that has altered consciousness, both by its substance, and through the experience of collectivity itself.

When Tillie Olsen said that 'We who write are survivors, "onlys",'* she meant that, among other things, the woman who writes has found a voice; she has spoken. In my early twenties when I read her now

---

*Tillie Olsen, *Silences*, New York, 1978; London, Virago, 1981; p. 39. In *Silences* Tillie Olsen has written an extended footnote for the word '*only's*', and I feel this essential to include here also:

'For myself "survivor" contains all its other meanings: one who must bear witness for those who foundered; try to tell how and why it was that they, also worthy of life, did *not* survive. And pass on ways of surviving; and tell our chancy luck, our special circumstances.

' "*Only's*" is an expression out of the 1950s Civil Rights time: the young Ralph Abernathy reporting to his Birmingham Church congregation on his trip up north for support:

I go to Seattle and they tell me, "Brother, you got to meet so-and-so, why he's the only Negro Federal Circuit Judge in the Northwest"; I go to Chicago and they tell me, "Brother, you've got to meet so-and-so, why he's the only full black professor of Sociology there is"; I go to Albany and they tell me, "Brother, you *got* to meet so-and-so, why he's the only black senator in the state legislature. . ." long dramatic pause ". . .WE DON'T WANT NO ONLY'S".

' "*Only's*" are used to rebuke ('to be models'); to imply the unrealistic, "see it can be done, all you need is capacity and will." Accepting a situation of "only's" means: "let inequality of circumstance continue to prevail." '

classic essay, 'Silences in Literature', I had not yet found my voice. Even though I wrote, I could not write about my own life, a woman's life. Instead, I kept my own kind of silence by writing in what I thought was an acceptable way, about the world in which men live.

Human beings imitate the behaviour of others, and learn from this imitation. This is a method of learning, the way infants learn to speak or use utensils, fundamental to our natures. We act as others do out of the desire to be included, and because we love. Thus the paucity of contemporary writing by women has a significant effect on the young woman who may want to write. She must act as if in a vacuum, without example. Silence leads to more silence.

I do not believe that a clever group of conspirators knowingly created this silence. But there is a set of rules and circumstances and attitudes which has caused this silence and it has a pattern which has the effect of a plot against women. Moreover, this pattern has an intent. It is an unspoken intent, carried by the culture we share, to exclude the speech of women from consciousness. The culture which educated me and whose language I speak wants to silence women.

I have argued that women have come to symbolize the natural in this culture. And I believe it is because women symbolize nature to a culture which denies natural power, that what we have to say is feared. This fear stretches throughout written history. It was there in the nineteenth century at the genesis of the woman's suffrage movement. The leaders of the abolitionist movement did not want women to speak out for the abolition of slavery in public. Female abolitionists rose to protest this prohibition. It was there when the Christian Church was founded, and St Paul suffered women to be silent. Later, the witch-burners, Sprenger and Kramer, likened the speech of women to the sound of a hissing serpent. And Hegel only refined this view when he said that though women are intelligent, we are not fitted for science or 'certain forms of artistic creativity'.

But these opinions are simply symptoms of a deeper condition. Circumstance creates the illusion that women do not have a proclivity for the 'higher arts'. Girls are conditioned from birth to be submissive and ingratiating, to be modest and to place the needs of others before themselves. These are not the qualities a writer needs. Traditionally a woman's life is arranged so that she has no time to create art. She is responsible for children 12 hours a day. She does not have a room of her own. She lacks the support of patrons, grants, admirers, recognition; tradition itself is against her from the start. Though she was wealthy and more educated than most women, George Sand had to deny convention and raise a scandal in order to live the life of a writer.

Moreover, should a woman finally be published and her work become recognized or celebrated, she is liable to be forgotten by later generations. Those literary scholars who preserve books and write literary history hold the same prejudice against writing by women that makes it difficult for women to write in the first place. Hence a great many fine books by women have been lost to us.

We know from the history of art that many artists are neglected in their own time, and that great works fall into unjust neglect. We know of the poverty and ignominy that have caused an unnatural silence in many writers, men and women. It is a hard task in our society for anyone, male or female, to hold life and limb together while being an artist. But for women, the task of survival is even harder, for we must add to the conditions which all artists face, the special abuse which women who are artists meet.

In her book *Silences*, Tillie Olsen has documented a special prejudice against women as writers. I quote from her figures: in Twentieth-Century Literature courses, six percent of books written by women, 94 percent written by men; in critical surveys of fiction, a range of one female out of 13 male writers surveyed, to one female out of 30 male; in critical reference works, 91 percent male writers; the Nobel prize for literature granted to 49 writers, only five women; the Pulitzer Prize for poetry granted to 50 recipients, only 11 of them women; the Guggenheim Grant given to 419 recipients, only 79 women. Her list continues. These conditions continue.

The feminist movement has not been able, except for a few exceptions, to change these conditions. And yet, my life as a writer has been deeply affected, and perhaps even made possible, by this movement. For me, the discovery of my own voice as a writer occurred simultaneously with my own entrance into the feminist movement. Neither one can be said to have preceded or caused the other. But because of the feminist movement my own voice grew strong inside me.

In my life as a writer I have encountered both great difficulty and great good fortune. I have suffered all of the traditional difficulties that women writers experience: poverty, neglect, a paucity of time for my writing, a mind overburdened with domestic care, the cares of raising a child, and a literary establishment hostile to my efforts. The feminist movement has not yet changed the way we live: we live in a society in which men hold power over women, and this is also true for the literary world. And yet, I was very lucky to have found my voice just as the feminist movement began. For this movement has given me the connectedness to other human beings which writing, of its nature, seeks.

The feminist movement created a listening atmosphere for writing by women. Of the conversations between women that have gone on in this last decade, the theologian, Nelle Morton, writes that we 'heard each other into speech'. My work has been heard into existence by other women. And as I heard each new utterance, each new poem or story or thought from other women, a braver, and more daring, authentic speech grew up in me. In this way, our listening atmosphere spread to larger and larger realms of meaning.

I do not believe that biological differences in men and women make that much difference in our aesthetic judgements, nor in the way we think, nor in the content of our art. Moreover, men and women do share a grammar and a history of poetics. However, our different social experience has made a significant difference in the form and content of our art. A woman can write and think like a man, and some women do, especially women who have had an exceptional experience for a woman, that is to say, the experience of a man. But a woman can also think and write like a woman.

In this last decade, alongside the feminist movement, a women's culture has come into being. And this culture, we have discovered, has a tradition. Women have always had distinctive art forms: journals and letters, lullabyes and gossip and bedtime stories, quilts and embroidery, china-painting. As part of a woman's cultural movement, we have revived an interest in these forms, and look on them with a new respect. And because we have experienced ourselves as a sometimes forgotten, sometimes silenced culture within another dominant culture, we have learned to question the word 'universality' and to recognize that this word in its current usage refers only to a narrow stream of human culture: white, male and European.

When a whole culture is silenced or forgotten a particular kind of knowledge is also lost. For example, as the number of Yiddish speakers vanishes, the language, in its vital form, also dies. Yiddish is a language of the home, of the kitchen, of childrearing, of the intimate relations between members of a family, of the life of the body.

And one can repeat this story of loss many times for many languages and cultures. The words and forms and ways of remembering which belong to women are not preserved. When one reads a history of England, one does not learn of the history of domestic life, but of the life of courts and Parliaments. When one studies the history of art, one does not read about the evolution of the quilt, as a form, nor does one hear the life stories of any quiltmakers.

And what do we lose when we lose these languages and stories and forms? The word *challah* means a twisted loaf of bread. A *quilt* is a blanket or a bed covering sewn together from discarded bits of fabric. But they are both more, they contain worlds of meaning. They transmit a feeling for old ways of being, old wisdoms. The lives of women and children. The work our great-grandmothers did, and what they knew.

And there is something more in this history of loss which bears on what it is to be human. When we preserve a culture, we acknowledge its value; we acknowledge the value of those who made that culture, and most important, we give to the daily acts and thoughts and lives of that people signification. A people who preserve their own culture, preserve in this act their human right to be self-reflective, to wonder about and seek to know who they are, why they live. To preserve a culture is to assert the right to culture at all. The novelist and anthropologist, Zora Neale Hurston (whose own works have been shamefully neglected), knew this when she wrote down and saved the stories of the voodoo cults of Jamaica and Haiti. And she knew also what an important dimension of humanity lives in the tale, the song, the image: the spirit in us wanting to tell.

Wanting to tell and connect and see oneself among the many, and the many reflected in oneself. To commune with others in this truth telling. Hungering for an image of one's life that corresponds to what one feels. Hungering for a resonance. Knowing that without this resonance a range of knowing and feeling seems to die. Gets buried inside oneself, like an old grief, and tears away at one's insides, until all that is left is an old tired bitterness, and an unspoken complaint; *no one will hear, it is of no use,* no use to seek an authentic bond with the rest of humankind.

A certain kind of tiredness and bitterness has been endemic to women. Not only to the silenced writers. But to all of us. For writers and artists give to the whole community its speech. And the absence of a writing by, for and of women sends a whole community of women into a despair of speech. Or if not into apparent despair, still a giving up, a bored complacency, into a falseness, a limitedness, or a continual state of mourning. Just in this way oppression leads to more oppression. The poor get poorer. For despair and giving up, and bitter tiredness and bored complacency, make it hard for a woman to fight. But fight a woman must if she is to write.

There is the child at home, needing more time than you can give her if you are to write. The demand, in many women's lives, of a relationship with a man who says he must be put first. The prejudice of universities or publishing houses, not only against women, but against the subject matter of women's lives. The job outside the home, domestic work and writing, itself hard work, added on to that. All this requires a strength and a spirit that despair steals away. And this makes for a downward spiral, a worsening of conditions and then spirit and then conditions over and over again.

But that spiral can move in the opposite direction. Any effort towards liberation that succeeds, no matter how exhausting, gives one energy. The feminist movement was not able to change the conditions of most of our lives. But it did interrupt our silence among ourselves. And this I know gave me the strength to keep on, to write and speak and hear.

In these last decades, I have witnessed the birth and growth of a women's culture, a phenomenon, a fact, which made to me, in the deepest parts of my soul, an inarguable testament to the worth of my woman's life. There was no grand plan. As with other cultural movements, writers and artists and musicians sprang up spontaneously with the same ideas in mind. All over the country, women who had participated as the secretaries or assistants to editors of magazines or small book companies began to demand that more writing by women be published. Special issues of magazines appeared devoted to work by women. Anthologies of women's works were collected.

In Berkeley, California, which is where I live, the poet Alta, assisting the editor of a small press, had learned the trade. Now she established her own small publishing company. She called it the Shameless Hussy Press. And she published my first book of poetry, *Dear Sky*, along with Ntoszake Shange's play *For Colored Girls*. All over the country in the next years presses owned and operated by women proliferated. The Women's Press Collective, Diana Press, Persephone Press, Olive Press, Kitchen Table Press, Effie's Press, New Woman's Press are a few of the presses which were established to publish books by women. Countless feminist magazines and newspapers also came into being – *Amazon Quarterly, Aphra, Feminary, Heresies, Sinister Wisdom, Chrysalis, Black Maria, Chomo-Uri, Quest, Plexus, Lavender Woman, Azalea, The Lesbian*

Tide, The Second Wave, Country Women – with an amazing range, and large and small circulation from California to Illinois, from Wisconsin to Connecticut, from Florida to New York.

Within and without universities and colleges women began to study the works of other women, for the first time reading Kate Chopin, Anzia Yezerskaya, Gwendolyn Brooks, H.D., Agnes Smedley, Harriet Arnow, and reevaluating the work of Elizabeth Barrett Browning, Emily Bronte, Emily Dickinson, Virginia Woolf. And the teaching and learning of this literature, like the act of writing itself, became an act of survival. Women felt an urgent need for this knowledge, demanded courses about women be included in the curriculum, and finally fought for and won the establishment of several departments of women's studies.

Over the past years I have taught many classes in both literature by women and creative writing for women. In one class, as I prepared a lecture on the poetry of Sylvia Plath, I felt a chill spread over my ability to think or create. I was editing away my own responses to her poetry. I felt I needed to present my students with what 'the critics' had said of Plath's poetry. What the critics wrote of her poetry was shot through with a subtle misogyny. One critic wrote that her 'capacity for intellectual objectivity' and her 'range of technical resources' were narrower than another male poet. As I read these words I felt my own objectivity narrow. I wrote this poem.

Waiting for Truth

Their bodies lined up against the walls
waiting for truth, my
words thread the room
like fishing line,
'She put
she put her head in an oven
she put her head in an
oven,'
I stutter,
my words enter space and I
slide down the line
terrified, where are we
going?
Their bodies wait for information.
'There are places I have been,' I

want to tell them.
The book behind me reads:
    'Sylvia Plath's range of technical resources. . .'
'There are places I have been,' I
want to say, my body
all night sleeping,
did I dream
running in Harlem
dream the markets of the
poor,
was someone diseased, was the disease
spreading? Did I dream
an escape? Was I safe in a
classroom, sitting close
to a friend, sighing relief,
writing the movie script,
telling where I had been,
was I singing?
Did they say my name?
That I was supposed to write words
on the chalkboard, I
was supposed to address and I
stuttered,
'What I have seen
the places I have been and I
promised everyone there
I would speak only of them:
the one who sat in a corner for a week,
the one whose breasts ran dry,'
And the book read,
    'Sylvia Plath
    Sylvia Plath's range of
    technical resources was narrower
    than Robert Lowell's,' and I*
stuttered:

---

*The line 'Sylvia Plath's range of technical resources was narrower than Robert Lowell's and so, apparently, was her capacity for intellectual objectivity' is from the essay 'Sylvia Plath and Confessional Poetry', by M.L. Rosenthal, which appears in *The Art of Sylvia Plath*, Charles Newman, ed. Indiana University Press, 1971.

'The one whose lovers
were frightened by her
children, the one who
wished her children,'
   'Narrower than Robert Lowell's and so,
   apparently, was her capacity'
her children would be
     'for intellectual objectivity.'
would be still.
Sylvia Plath's range of
technical resources
she put her
was narrower
head in an
there are places I have been
Everyone on the street was diseased.
There are places you have been.
Trying to speak
the script
claiming my mind, was it
a dream
or did I live, 'range of
technical.'
Their bodies in transformation.
She put her head in an
repetition
repetition
is no longer
no longer
interesting in
poetry
he said
but goes on
which one put
her head in an
in life, in
autobiographical detail, gas,
milk, a pair of kids, technical resources, a bottle
of chicken fat, two dinner guests, a box of books,
Achoo Ido Achoo Ido Achoo   *I*   *do*
and an interesting sense of rhyme

> *range of*
> *chattering, 'There are places*
> *we have,' suddenly the whole*
> *been, there are places, bodies*
> *lined up, the walls, the whole world*
> *suddenly the whole world is making*
> *terrific sense I am chattering,*
> *'Yes,' I say to the bus driver, taking me home,*
> *'I am afraid of freeways.'*
> *'Yes,' I lecture a tree*
> *near the sidewalk, 'I am free.'*
> *Yes, I am afraid of rats, knives, bullets,*
> *I am, there is, I am there is,*
> *I sing, walking the street,*
> *a fish on the line,*
> *shouting to my feet,*
> *'But I will not be afraid*
> *of voices nor of,'*
> *There are places we*
> *'nor of pieces of paper.'*
> *have been.*

If today it seems obvious that a woman teaching literature by women ought to bring her own experience as a woman into the classroom, it was not then. What silenced us as writers censored our vision as readers, and as teachers. One must remember that women were not even allowed to enter universities until the beginning of this century.

In one sense, to teach women's studies is to break the taboo against the serious study of women's lives. In women's studies classes, as in the poetry of Sylvia Plath, diapering and cutting onions, the dreams of little girls, marriage quarrels, menstrual cycles became no longer trivial, or invisible details, but rather significant clues to meaning. And the study of literature by women from this widened understanding went hand in hand with the creation of a new literature by women.

There was an astonishing quantity of written words. Countless poems, plays, essays, stories, novels were written, read, reviewed, answered. Bookstores were established which sold only women's books. Libraries were set up. And along with the proliferation of the written word, there were the readings. Women gathered, filling rooms or auditoriums, or cafes or bars, to hear these words spoken, read out loud, sung.

In the beginning all poetry was oral. And it did feel, as we spoke and listened, that we were reaching far back into human history, and into a deep part of the human psyche to find an earlier, vivid poetry. I had had the same experience of what poetry could be once before, when watching a film made of a group of black poets reading their poetry out loud. I had never forgotten that film. In it I witnessed a poetry I had always wanted but never seen take a real shape.

I read my poems aloud with Alta, with Judy Grahn, with Pat Parker, with Nellie Wong and Deena Metzger, and Kathleen Fraser and Joanna Griffin and Frances Jaffer, and Beverly Dahlen and Alice Walker and Adrienne Rich and Willyce Kim. I heard the poetry of Honor Moore and Luise Bernikow and Audre Lorde and Diane di Prima and Margaret Atwood and June Jordan and Marilyn Hacker. The audience was not polite and still and reverent, not deciphering or bored. There was laughter and crying and shouting and some noise and a kind of quiet that is stillness instead of just absence of sound, centrifugal. We were touched to the core by what we heard. Amazed. Released. There were arguments and disagreements and resolutions and there was love. There was a 'yes' being said to us, a 'yes' we were saying, yes I know, yes, tell me, yes, I hear, oh yes, oh yes, that is how it is.

I remember the first time I heard Judy Grahn read 'The Psychoanalysis of Edward the Dyke'. Women had rented an old house, painted the walls, set it up as a centre, and this reading inaugurated the place. The two Victorian rooms were filled to the breaking with women pressed against each other and flowing out into the hall, through the door and on the stairs leading to the door. Judy sat on the floor surrounded with candles and declared that this was the last night of a certain kind of poetry and the first night of a new kind. Now there would be poetry, she said, that belonged to us all. When she read her story about a tall lesbian woman who is told by her analyst to have her legs sawed off I began to laugh. It was at first an awful and painful laughing. I had denied that I was a lesbian. It was that old laugh of despair, of embittered silence, and then it was a weeping laugh and then angry, and finally wild, even frightening, with a heady kind of joy, because oh, the laughter had done something to my lungs, and oh, I was breathing so deeply now, I would never be the same, after taking in this air.

Intimate, close, and privately shared love, woman to woman or man to man or woman to man is one of the miracles of this life. But this precious intimacy, as needed in its own right as it is, is not enough for me. For I have found in my self, beyond the wish for approval or to please the crowd, an authentic desire for a wider communion, a sharing of meaning, a connectedness.

I think I cannot tell here, without writing a novel that would evoke sight and sound and texture and feeling, what it has meant to be part of a community of women and of writers. The speech of that community let me know myself, and a listening there let me speak. And beyond these things, I partook of more. How is it we have travelled so far away from each other and ourselves? How is it we forget? I think of the deaths, the losses, and I recall these lines from the poetry of Muriel Rukeyser, 'Speak for sing for pray for/everyone in solitary/every living life.'

Women and the Creative Process: Lighting the Dark

The following article is a transcript made from remarks I made as a member of a panel that met at Stanford University in 1973, as part of a symposium on the creative process. In this talk I weave together several of my own poems which speak to the subject of women and the creative process.

Something that Virginia Woolf mentioned about lighting up places that have been dark before is a thought that I have on my mind all the time when I'm writing, and when I'm teaching literature too. I'm aware of how little of women's daily lives is reflected in literature, how little of our *real* daily lives. There's a lot of mythology that we see about ourselves around us all the time, particularly on the television and in the popular media, but also in our 'great literature', which is great in other aspects until it comes to women; and often we see in women a two-dimensionality which is not evident in the rest of the work. Or we see a strange flaw in the story. *Alcestes* is the tale of a woman who gives up her life so that her husband can live. It has beautiful dramatic movement which moves one to tears and rage. Yet finally the story becomes ludicrous, because Alcestes is brought back from death by Heracles. In the Greek mythos, a woman who made such a virtuous sacrifice for her husband could not be made to die. But in the same mythic tradition Antigone dies. The woman who is determining her own life and standing up to a man and refusing to give in to his power has to die – she really dies. The stories of Alcestes and Antigone for me bear upon Virginia Woolf's 'Angel in the House'; that is, I don't think that strong women *have* to die. There are circumstances in society – real ones – which make the likelihood of

our strength diminishing very high. But there is also the literature –
the kind of message that comes across to us in *Alcestes* and in
Antigone we learn, we internalize. And the woman writer internalizes
that as much as any other woman, but it reflects itself in the process of
her writing. So that I find for myself a constant struggle not to feel
guilty for my strengths or my anger. And that reflects itself, I think,
sometimes in a split, myself against myself, which is a theme, if you
study the literature that exists by women, that runs through the
work of Emily Dickinson, Emily Brontë, and Virginia Woolf. I think
the other thing that happens is that our real experience is not
reflected, is not talked about, and so we don't ever see it ourselves.
This bears on what Wittgenstein says about a child needing language
to perceive a sunset. We don't have the language to perceive and
recognize our own experience.

This is a poem that I wrote about an experience that is very rarely
written about or even spoken about: it happened to me, and it's about
a woman who is recently divorced and whose child is visiting the
child's father and she happens to run into both of them on the street.
It's called 'Chance Meeting'.

> *This is how it happens.*
> *I am walking away*
> *from the bookstore,*
> *my head reeling with*
> *images of bear cubs their*
> *fur glistening*
> *with dew (disappearing*
> *from the poet's glance*
> *into forests) and my mouth full*
> *of the poet's words against the*
> *rich who*
> *DO NOT HEAR WEEPING.*
> *I wonder at the strangers*
> *walking the pavement and*
> *want to go deep*
> *into foreign country*
> *where poverty is visible*
> *and no bones are made*
> *about pain,*
> *when I see*
> *(in the window of a shop)*

*a sign reading 'closed' and
know I am late,
move swiftly thinking of
dinner and zucchini plants
and a dog that
needs to run free and you
I want to be with, then
suddenly
there is a mistake,
    my car
appears
in the middle of the block,
it carries my daughter
with her father
and his new woman
they are going
to a restaurant.*

*I slip quickly
down
the street
so she won't see
me, my daughter, there should be
no tears, a
pleasant dinner.*

*My daughter, my heart cleaves
at this, when I see
you, I want to
touch your face, window, glass
SIDEWALK, STRANGERS,
CARS, DO YOU KNOW,
I fed this child
through the night
whom now
I run from.*

There is another struggle that goes on in the life of a woman writer which was pointed out by Tillie Olsen in her extremely important essay 'Silences in Literature'. It's about the silences in the life of writers, ones that are unnatural interruptions. Very few women who have achieved great work in writing have been mothers, and she points this out in that essay. Those who have been mothers have been in an economic class allowing them to have constant help with their children. This is changing now, there are a lot of women who are mothers and are writing, but it's a process of attrition. I want to read you something about that, rather than speaking about it. And after I read this, let me talk a little bit about the form of it, which is to me also interesting. And I hope it is to you.

This is the story of the day in the life of a woman trying to be a writer and her child got sick. And in the midst of writing this story someone called her on the telephone. And of course, despite her original hostile reaction to the ring of the telephone, she got interested in the conversation which was about teaching writing in a woman's prison, for no pay of course, and she would have done if it weren't for the babysitting and the lack of money for a plane fare, and then she hung up the phone and looked at her type-writer, and for an instant swore her original sentence was not there. But after a while she found it. Then she began again, but in the midst of the second sentence, a man telephoned wanting to speak to the woman she shares the house with who was not available to speak on the telephone and by the time she got back to her typewriter she began to worry about her sick daughter down-stairs. And why hadn't the agency for babysitters called back and why hadn't the department for health called back because she was looking for a day sitter and a night sitter, one so she could teach the next day and one so she could read her poetry. And she was hoping that the people who had asked her to read poetry would pay for the babysitter since the next evening after that would be a meeting of teachers whom she wanted to meet and she could not afford two nights of babysitters let alone one, actually. This was the second day her child was sick and the second day she tried to write (she had been trying to be a writer for years) but she failed entirely the first day because of going to the market to buy Vitamin C and to the toy store to buy cut outs and crayons, and making soup from the chicken carcass that had been picked nearly clean to make sandwiches for lunch, and watering the plants, sending in the mortgage cheque and other cheques to cover that cheque to the bank, and feeling tired, wishing she had a job, talking on the telephone, and putting out newspaper and glue and scissors on the kitchen table for her tired, bored child and squinting her eyes at the clock waiting for *Sesame Street* to begin again. Suddenly, after she went upstairs to her bedroom with a book having given up writing as impossible, it was time to cook dinner. But she woke up on the second day with the day before as a lesson in her mind. Then an old friend called who had come to town who she was eager to see and she said, 'Yes, I'm home with a sick child', and they spent the morning talking. She was writing poetry and teaching she said. He had written four books he said. Her daughter showed him her red and blue and orange coloured pictures. She wished he didn't have to leave so early she thought but she didn't say, and went back to pick up tissue paper off the floor and fix lunch for her and her child and begin telephoning for babysitters because she knew she had to teach the next day. And the truth was, if she did not have a sick child to care for, she was not sure she could write anyway because the kitchen was still there needing cleaning, the garden there needing weeding and watering, the living room needing curtains, the couch needing pillows, a stack of mail needing answers (for instance, if she didn't call the woman who had lived in her house the month before about the phone bill soon, she would lose a lot of money). And besides, she had nothing to write. She had had fine thoughts for writing the night before but in the morning they took on a sickly complexion. And anyway, she had begun to think her life trivial and so it was, and she was tired writing the same words, or different words about the same situation, the situation or situations being that she was tired, tired of trying to write, tired of poverty or almost poverty or fear of poverty, tired of the kitchen being dirty, tired of having no lover. She was amazed that she had gotten herself dressed, actually, with thoughts like these, and caught herself saying maybe I should take a trip when she realized she had just come back from a trip and had wanted to be home so much she came back early. And even in the writing of this she thought I have written all this before and went downstairs to find her daughter had still not eaten a peanut butter sandwich and she wondered to herself what keeps that child alive?

Two things I want to say about the form of that. First, I wrote it to free myself. It all happened, and I wrote it on the day that it happened, and I had all this garbage in my head that had to be removed before anything else could be written. I was in a state of total anxiety. Secondly, though, the language is intentionally very simple, and when I think of this kind of language I always think of Gertrude Stein. I feel that I can go back and find experiences that have been lost, through using the most simple language that I can manage. That the more complex language is, the more difficult the imagery or metaphor, the more that it's dependent on a certain way of thought, a whole structure of civilization, that's already alienated me from what's there. And one of the ways that I have for myself of understanding what is really happening is to speak as simply as possible. I retyped it today to read to you and I found myself wanting to correct it. There are places where it's very rough. And I decided to leave it the way it is because I think that one of the ways that it expresses the state of reality that I was describing is in the kind of impact that occurs in the language: there is phrase after phrase after phrase, and you can't quite figure them out. Well, that's what the experience is, of being with a sick child at home; there's implacable interruption, your life *is* an interruption; there is the formlessness, which is what's very upsetting about the experience. Upsetting if one is trying to use one's mind in a creative form.

After I wrote this piece I wrote a second poem. I had been in a discussion with a group of women who write about the conditions that an artist needs to work. Half of us felt that the artist has always to suffer, has to endure suffering. I wasn't in that half. When I spoke earlier about not underestimating the difficulties of carrying off the juggling act of both writing and raising a child, it reminded me of Virginia Woolf's statement that she did not want to ever underestimate what sacrifices she had made for her writing, that is, not to have a child. I think that women have a difficult situation either way. This is a poem that deals again with any artist and the circumstances of life.

> This is a piece of writing about the parts that die.
> Which parts have died or will die I cannot clearly name.
> Their deaths occur before
> the shapes of their identities
> still infantile, still motionless and curled
> become clear.
> One feels only a vague lack and remembers
> the causes of death more than
> what actually died.
> One of the causes certainly is death
> itself, the deaths say for instance

the death of the father (or it might have
been a mother) and with this dies
the lack of awareness of death that
makes the child's life
youthful.
But some of the parts die
a slower death;
a certain eagerness of
mind for instance seems to be subject to
a permanent sleep
and the causes of this moribund process
are woven into every minute during
which circumstances appear to be
overwhelming and the subject perhaps
turns her back and
says, 'All this is making me tired.'
And some of the parts struggle and
refuse to die but weaken,
the voice becoming hoarse
and even a bit cynical
for instance
considering one human
being's compatibility for another.
And some
one is glad to see buried and done
with as when the subject learns
for the final time
that expectations are dangerous
that opening one's mouth
is foolish
that going forwards or backwards
is a reciprocal process;
And some
one forgets ever existed
except as perceived
in the eloquence or grace of others
and that may be perceived with anger or even
jealousy for
the question is, is it true
that one is either born to jump high
or one is not,

that one holds genius in her hands
at birth, or
one does not,
that birth
and not
the lack of presence
of food and mother and father
and grants-in-aid or
state supported schools
or central heating
or books on shelves or curtains or windows
or laudatory remarks
or degrees in frames
or accidental falls from carriages or private
rooms, or paint brushes or
ink or a reading public or space or time or
folded laundry or letters in boxes
but birth alone is the spark
that determines every baby
every child, every youthful or aged
step towards a destiny
written only for geniuses and that true genius
evades every accidental, fortuitous or
systematic detail of life?
Or is genius instead
like all the other
parts that can die
before naming
a substance
variable in shape and colour
altered by circumstances and
perishable.

That poem is part of a group of poems I'm writing called 'The Tiredness Cycle'. And that is a whole area of women's knowledge, of a certain particular kind of tiredness, where one goes on. There is I think a danger in a woman's life of a kind of lack of connection with the rest of the world, which is really not her fault. Emily Dickinson lived during the years of the Civil War and had a correspondence with several famous abolitionists, and wrote not a single word in her poetry about the war. But look at Emily Dickinson's life, look at the possibilities in her life – they were not great for having any knowledge of that war beyond pure sentimentality. This is a poem that I wrote about times of feeling that separation.

My daughter pleads with me
for the life of our goldfish
souring in a tank
of ancient water,
'I want them
to
live,' she
says. Late at night
I pass the green tank
still full of guilt.
I have chosen
in the hierarchy of my life
to go to work
to shop, to cook dinner, to
write these words
before saving the fish;
choices surround me.
Nothing is ever right.
Every breathing space
asks for help;
dust multiplies in the
    hallway;
lecture notes fly away
through windows which
need glass and paint
and in the back of my mind
somewhere
is a woman
who weeps
for Chile
and shudders at the
executions.
All along she
has been
pondering the social order
and her
worried thoughts

> *slow*
> *my*
> *every movement.*

Let me go to the other side of this experience. I've been talking about
the attrition and the difficulties. There is also a kind of joy that
women are feeling slaughtering the angel in the house – the angel in
the house is the one who flies up behind you when you're typing and
says, 'Don't say anything nasty. Don't say anything mean about
anybody, don't be angry. Go and help everybody else, give your life
for your husband or your children or your neighbour before you write
these words.' This is an angel-slaughtering poem which I had fun
writing and it's called 'The Song of the Woman with Her Parts Coming
Out'.

> *I am bleeding*
> *the blood seeps in red*
> *circles on the white*
> *white of my sheet,*
> *my vagina*
> *is opening, opening*
> *closing and opening;*
> *wet, wet,*
> *my nipples turn rose and hard*
> *my breasts swell against my arms*
> *my arms float out*
> *like anemones*
> *my feet slide on the wooden*
> *floor,*
> *dancing, they are dancing, I sing,*
> *my tongue slips from my mouth*
> *and my mind*
> *imagines a*
> *clitoris*
> *I am the woman*
> *I am the woman*
> *with her parts coming out.*
> *with her parts coming out.*
>
> *The song of the woman with*
> *the top of her head ripping off, with*

the top of her head ripping off
and she flies out
and she flies out
and her flesh flies out
and her nose rubs against her ass,
and her eyes love ass
and her cunt
swells and sucks the waves.
and the words spring from her mind
like fourth of July rockets,
and the words too come out,
lesbian, lesbian, lesbian, pee, pee, pee, pee, cunt, vagina,
dyke, sex, sex, sex, sex, sweat, tongue, lick, suck, sweet,
sweet, sweet, suck
and the other words march out too,
the words,
P's and Q's
the word
nice
the word
virginity,
the word
mother,
mother goodness mother nice good goodness good good should
should be good be mother be nice good
the word
pure
the word
lascivious
the word
modest
the word
no
the word
no
the word
no
and the woman
the woman
the woman
with her

parts coming out
never stopped
never stopped
even to
say yes,
but only
flew with
her words
with her words
with her words
with her parts
with her parts
coming
with her parts
   coming
   coming
   coming
   out.

The Journals of Sylvia Plath:
A Review

In 1966 I was handed an extraordinary book of poems called *Ariel*, written by a poet I did not know. I read these poems hungrily for they astonished my ear and amazed my sense of the truth. I wanted more. But there were to be no more such poems. On 11 February, 1963, when she was 30 years of age, Sylvia Plath had taken her own life.

A legend is made from the simple outline of events. This was the eve of the feminist movement. Plath's poetry crackled with a particular rage known only to women. She used metaphors of the female body and domesticity; she revealed for the first time private realms of feeling. The brilliant achievements of her last years and her premature death became, for a whole generation of women, an emblem of their struggle against silence.

In was not feminism in her poetry that lured the reader, it was honesty. There was none of the traditional sentimentality about women's lives left in her voice. In her poetry, 'cow-heavy' women stumbled from bed to feed infants; kittens were seen to 'crap and puke'. We were laid bare to ourselves.

One longed to know more about the life of this poet as if, in the details of her existence, one might find a clue leading to a secret or truer knowledge. Seven years ago her letters to her mother appeared, giving some substance and even hinting at feelings beneath the surface. But 'Dame kindness . . . is so nice'; the old honesty was not there.

Now, with the publication of her journals, we have that familiar, thrilling voice again, the blood-jet, truth-telling voice of her poetry. And they are here at last on the page, stories to ponder, to try to understand. In one place she writes, 'I dislike being a girl, because as such I must come to realise that I cannot be a man. In other words, I must pour my energies through . . . my mate.' Later she will become an 'old maid', living at the periphery of life, having sacrificed love and children for her art. She worries that she will never meet a man who can match her brilliance. And finally, once married, she finds that she is losing herself in her husband. She cooks for him, gladly types his poems and begins to look to him for definition, to tell her what to do.

Only once does she mention the political events of her time when – as she does in *The Bell Jar* – she refers to the execution of the Rosenbergs. Yet, on every page of her journal one can feel the heavy atmosphere of the fifties with its witch-hunts, its sexual repressions, its reactionary ideas about women. Over and over one feels the author suffocates in this atmosphere.

Plath suffers all the difficulties of any young writer: The feeling that her work is not valid unless it is published; that she has no right to write otherwise. And hence there's a vulnerability before editors. In relation to her husband's work she can see that often those who edit magazines are too frightened to accept daring work. But she cannot see this for her own work. And she is distressed by the remarks of academic colleagues, professors of literature who look askance at writers.

Yet the most violent struggle she endures is with herself. During her second year of college, Plath attempted suicide. Throughout her remaining life she fought against depression. In these journals she describes her experience of depression with such evocative precision that one is brought to an altogether new compassion for this kind of suffering in oneself and others.

Two tendencies in her mind defeated her. She scrupulously applied a rigid standard of perfection to herself in all things and she tried too hard to be 'nice'. She suppressed her hatred and her anger, and she directed all her rage at herself. In one passage she dissects her face with an attitude that is close to cruelty. She expected herself to be the perfect scholar, teacher, wife, daughter.

She hectors herself unendingly, addressing herself as 'you', about her writing, admonishing herself that she has not written enough poetry, or, if she has written poetry, prose. She is obsessed with writing for publication, yet no publication, no matter how prestigious, really satisfies her. And every rejection damages grievously. She calls herself spoiled, failed. 'Time to take myself in hand', she writes. She finds fault with herself because she does not know the names of all the stars, the flowers. She takes random hostility to heart. When a few small boys throw snowballs at her, she decides they must have sensed something rotten in her.

Plath's journals give us a record of her continual labour toward sanity and survival. With a therapist, she discovers her hidden angers, and begins to transform self-destruction into self-knowledge. She fights her 'demon of negation' valiantly. The sometimes rasping, sharp, outrageous mad voice of *Ariel* must have been healing. Here she expressed her human imperfections almost with triumph; she is no longer 'nice'. (That her husband, who acted as co-editor on this book, destroyed the last two volumes of her journal, written during the time she wrote these poems, is an inestimable loss.) This is a great work, intensely revealing, moving. Reading it should shake you to the core.

212

Making the Park: A Foreword

Making the Park is an anthology of poetry by women published by the Kelsey Street Press. This book was edited, handset and distributed by a collective of women who are themselves all poets. Many such presses exist now. They are run cooperatively or singly by women and they publish many fine books, beautifully made. The existence of these presses is an astonishing phenomenon which has, for the most part, been ignored by the literary establishment. I was asked to write the foreword for this book in 1976.

This is a collection of poetry by five women, designed by a woman, edited and printed by women, and that all this labour was done by women was no accident. When the first few anthologies of poetry by women, past and contemporary, were issued, it was generally agreed that such was a necessary solution to make up for centuries of imbalance, of book after book and journal after journal in which the work of only one (or perhaps two or three) women were published. But the anthologies and collections of women's work continue to appear, and we who are writers are beginning to understand that it is no longer balance that is sought; it is community.

It is not only that a wave has propelled through our lives which has moved us to speech where before there was silence; it is that in addition to seizing the right to speak, to be writers (painters, architects, athletes), we have taken upon ourselves the right to name our own experience in our own manner, with our own literary standards, and our own shape of line, plot, and sentence.

We are not the first women to declare that in our makings is the embryo of a distinct culture. Virginia Woolf, in *A Room of One's Own*, approached the question of what she hoped would be one day a peculiarly female sentence, a future shape, free perhaps of the male need for peroration. A more open form. And before her, Elizabeth

Barrett Browning was most clear about the dangers proceeding from the judgements of the male literary establishment, whether they be for or against. In a letter addressed to Arabel, dated 10 July, 1851, she wrote of the publication the *Guardian*:

> So the Guardian has attacked 'Casa Guidi'. No wonder. . . The curious thing is. . . that the self-same Guardian praised me to the skies last spring. . .said that I had a glorious career before me. . .that I wasn't weak like women in general. . . Oh, I assure you my Guardian took me graciously under his protection. . . But Guardians prove faithless, it appears, and I am a ward betrayed.

More succinctly, in writing to John Kenyon of a dedication in which Poe had called her 'the noblest of her sex', Browning wrote, 'What is to be said, I wonder, when a man calls you "the noblest of your sex?" "Sir, you are the most discerning of yours." '

Because in fact, concerning the question of male guardianship over writing by women, it is difficult to say which is more harmful, misunderstanding praise (so often by comparison to and at the expense of other women) or misunderstanding condemnation. Or simply misunderstanding, fatally so, as in the many interpretations of the poetry of Sylvia Plath which mistook the liberating honesty of *Ariel* to be a nihilism preceding suicide. In fact, Plath herself assessed these poems as very strong, and from her letters one realises she was beginning to reassess her work, to be no longer the girl who wrote home that her husband's work must always come first, and that her ambition was to be a good minor poet.

Where the shadowy corpus of males who decide, among other questions, who is and who is not a major writer found in Plath a death urge, we find a confirmation; we recognise a language electric with rage, with the anger of a being who, wanting to survive, refuses lies.

For if we are to have our new sentence, our community, a renaming of the female experience after our own image, we must refuse all lies, not only the ones that say women cannot write, but those that have defined our experience other than we've lived it, so that we have become a material reshaped by a psyche foreign to ours into the witch, the bitch, the whore, the all-loving mother, the goddess of male sexual pleasure.

In this collection of poems, the pronoun for human experience is changed – the ever oppressive 'he' is not generic here. In these pages we read: 'The poet is a fool/*she* is happy without solution [emphasis mine].' Or again, 'In the swimmer/is some genius and this/ persistence; *she* bends her head [my emphasis].' And in this collection the female is not material but shaper. In the poem 'Thirst' it is now the male who is object, like Alice in Wonderland, diminished and reshaped in the surreal and subjective vision of the author, 'he seems very small.' In these poems, realizing the plea of Virginia Woolf *(A Room)* who asked when someone would write that 'Chloe likes Olivia', the stereotype which says that women hate women is absent; here women direct their deepest feelings to other women ('Inside and Out', 'Exchange').

And in some of these poems human experience is stretched with naming into a realm never recognised before. Now, as we are beginning to write honestly about motherhood, everywhere the same cry is heard. Adrienne Rich, writing of her research into 'the past realities of motherhood', after finding, in books mostly by men, so little of woman's experience told, wanted to ask, *'But what was it like for women?'* Jane Lazarre wrote of this same research, 'I lived in an exile whose inner turmoil and outer dullness threatened to shatter my sanity and keep me wandering over barren deserts, beating all the while on the slammed doors of kinship.' I remember with a painful clarity my own exhaustion and disorientation after a day of isolation from adult voices, wishing desperately for words, for the conversation which would unlock my experience for me. 'Making the Park' was not written then, but it is the poem I longed to read.

The form is one immediately recognizable to a mother, the cadence that of thought which is not only interrupted but, as Tillie Olsen has said of the lives of mothers, is interruption:

> *she remembers*
>   *there's a park   dark*
>   *park   she was there   green*
> *park   the children ran   there was a park and*
>   *maybe people*

I recognize so many of the lines in this collection – could claim them as parts of my psyche. 'I know how to wear hand-me-downs', 'Walls soften to cloth', 'who wraps the bright foil of a sentence round her wrist and then wonders where to deliver it'. The terror of immobility, 'and fear is the alibi', the feeling that our bodies despite us force us to truth, 'Something I cannot name which passes through me like lightning.'

These poems that were written by a group of women who have worked together over several years are part of our reality. The doors of kinship open. *Suddenly we find we are no longer straining against all the old conclusions; we are no longer pleading for the right to speak: we have spoken; space has changed; we are living in a matrix of our own sounds; our words resonate, by our echoes we chart a new geography; we recognize this new landscape as our birthplace, where we invented names for ourselves, here language does not contradict what we know; by what we hear, we are moved again and again to speech.*

216

Lesbians and Literature

'Lesbians and Literature' was the title of a panel at the Modern Language Association convention held in San Francisco in December 1975, at which I made these remarks. It was first published from a transcript in Sinister Wisdom, *Fall, 1976.*

I want to talk about silences and how they affect a writer's life. Of course many of us have read Tillie Olsen's book on silences in which she talks about the effects of material conditions on writers' lives and especially on women's lives, but I want to talk today about psychological silences – silences that occur because of psychic conditions and particularly that silence which affects us as lesbians.

I feel in fact that the whole concept of the muse, or of inspiration, is one that is kind of a cop-out concept. There is something very fascinating going on in the writer's psyche when there is a silence, an inability to write, and it can't very well be explained by 'well, today I was inspired', or 'it's flowing now'.

But in fact, each silence and each eruption into speech constitutes a kind of event and a kind of struggle in the life of the writer. To me the largest struggles in my life around silence had to do with the fact that I am a woman and a lesbian.

When I first recognized my anger as a woman, my feelings as a feminist, suddenly my writing was transformed. Suddenly I had material, I had subject matter, I had something to write about. And then a few years after that I found another great silence in my life. I found myself unhappy with my writing, unhappy with the way I expressed myself, unable to speak. I wrote in a poem – 'words do not come to my mouth anymore.' I happened also in my personal life to be censoring the fact that I was a lesbian and I thought I was doing that because of the issue of child custody. That was and is a serious issue in my life, but I wasn't acknowledging how important it was to

me both as a writer and a human being, to be open and to write about
my feelings as a lesbian. In fact, I think that writers are always dealing
with one sort of taboo or another. If these taboos are not general to
society, you may experience in your private life a fear of perceiving
some truth because of its implications, and this fear can stop you from
writing. I think this is why poetry and dreams have so much in
common – because the source of both poetry and dreams is the kind
of perception similar to that of the child who thought the emperor had
no clothes. The dangerous perception. Dangerous to the current
order of things.

But when we come to the taboo of lesbianism, I think that this is
one that is most loaded for everyone, even for those who are not
lesbians. Because the fact of love between women, the fact that two
women are able to be tender, to be sexual with each other, is one
that affects every event in this society – psychic and political and
sociological.

For a writer the most savage censor is oneself. If in the first place,
you have not admitted to yourself that you are a lesbian, or to put it in
simpler language – that you love women or are capable of wanting to
kiss a woman or hold her – this one fact, this little perception, is
capable of radiating out and silencing a million other perceptions. It's
capable, in fact, of distorting what you see as truth at all.

To give you one example, there have been numbers and numbers
of psychoanalytic papers, poems and articles written on the Oedipal
relationship. Everyone seems to recognize that the son can love the
mother and that then there is the conflict with the father. This is
supposed to be a big taboo and yet everyone can talk about it easily.
And yet, who of us really, even lesbians, can talk about the love of the
daughter for the mother? Yet all human beings learn love from their
mother whether they are male or female. Everyone who's ever been a
mother knows that for a fact, a child learns to smile from the mother,
learns to enjoy being held. The first love-affair, male or female, is
with the mother.

I feel that the mother/daughter relationship is one that is central to
all women's lives, whether they have made the decision to be heterosexual or homosexual. In fact, when you come to a relationship
between the mother and the daughter, you come to a relationship
inevitably about the daughter and her own self. If she cannot accept
the love she's felt for her mother, if she cannot accept that identification, she cannot accept also the love that she's felt for herself. We
get back here to what I think is the central problem with women's

writing: that is self-hatred, hatred of the body, hatred of one's own voice, hatred of one's own perceptions. In fact, the female voice is characterised as ugly in this society – especially our mothers' voices. Our mothers' voices are characterized on TV as loud, as harassing, as bitchy, as fish-wifey. Many women, whatever our sexual identification, try to move away from the mother rather than to go back and look at this important relationship. This is only one way in which, as a writer, censoring your feelings of love for women can affect your perceptions.

In fact, I want to tell you the story of a poem that I wrote. I wrote the first line of it a year before the rest of the poem was written. This was a case in which the muse came back a year later, and a real process occurred while she was gone. The poem is called 'The Song of a Woman with Her Parts Coming Out'. The title occurred to me and the first few lines, but I just simply could not go any further and it was a mystery to me why. It was during a period in which I was in a relationship with a woman whom I loved, but I was not writing about anything in that relationship because I was worried about child custody and because she also was not really willing to call herself a lesbian. And so therefore I couldn't really call myself a lesbian. I couldn't use that word to myself and words are magic. Shakespeare understood word magic. In *King Lear* just the simple 'nothing' changed everyone's life in that play. Words have a tremendous power and I believe that it is extremely important to use that word, to be able to say: I am a lesbian.

The rest of this poem did come out when I re-examined this in myself and decided that indeed I had to use that word. I had to be open about my sexuality in my writing. 'The Song of a Woman with Her Parts Coming Out' came to me.

Transformations

I wrote this piece in response to a request by Beth Hodges, who was editing an issue of Sinister Wisdom, *and wanted to present the ideas of several different feminist writers on the transformative effect of convergences and connections in our work. I was in the process of writing* Woman and Nature *and within this piece I quote a passage from that manuscript. I refer to the work of Carroll Smith-Rosenberg in this article. She is an historian, author of 'The Female World of Love and Ritual: Relations Between Women in Nineteenth Century America' (*Signs, Vol I no 1*). This piece was written in 1976 and published in the same year.*

I want to send you something rough – not unworked, unthought, but rough, showing, as Eva Hesse once wrote, 'the mark of the hand'. First, it seems to me that the convergences we notice, the ones that excite us, *are* transformations, and that transformations are transformational. We are a community of those coming to speech from silence. This is an elementary fact we share – a history of illiteracy, suffocations, spiritual and literal, burnings of body and work, the weight of the inutterable surrounding all of our lives. And in no way can this shared history be separated from what we write today, nor from our love of each others' voices. Tillie Olsen has written two pieces of work transformational to me on the subject of silence: 'Silence, When Writers Don't Write' and 'Tell Me a Riddle'. (The one about the silences of writers and literature, the other, the story of a life robbed of speech, singing at its end.) And today, I read, with recognition, in Ellen Moers' *Literary Women,* this sentence: 'Nevertheless, in their shared commitment to voicing the unheard, Sand and Gaskell appear to stand together as women writers. They shared that heightened feminine sense of the preciousness of language to those who are self-taught, who only yesterday, in the case of women and *le peuple* both, had no voice.' And on the same page, Moers quoting Sand: 'oblivion is a stupid monster that has devoured too many generations. . .Escape oblivion. . .Write your own history, all of you who have understood your life and sounded your heart. To that end alone I am writing my own. . .'

This week I have been reading and writing about the humus, and about all the delicate cycles which keep the soil alive – the passage of nitrogen through air, plant, soil, micro-organism, the exchange of oxygen and carbon dioxide, the intricacy of the relations of living things. (And of course, there was a theory in nineteenth-century patriarchy that the soil was dead. A fixed, stable reliability.) And I have been thinking that indeed thought, too, especially in the twentieth century, and most specifically the study of literature, and even literature itself has been treated as dead. The universal. The classic. The major writer. The standard. The eternal form. And like all dead things, this version of literature has been separated from all that sustains the living, from intricate relations with other living forms. So, for instance, in this old patriarchal study of writing, we never encounter the question (let alone the answer) why does this writer write? Yet, this question is central to all our writing now.

Why we write, as feminists, is not separable from our lives. We have woven together a kind of textured echo chamber, a flexible moving acoustical system, the new sounds we utter changing the space even before we hear each syllable. Our writing, our talking, our living, our images have created another world than the man-made one we were born to, and continuously in this weaving we move, at one and the same time, towards each other, and outward, expanding the limits of the possible. (But this paradox of the nature of movement is reflected in the universe.) And whatever faith I have in existence, I feel most acutely in my writing and in my love for other women, and it is out of these reasons that I write: How I love clarity and how I love women who are thinking clearly about *our condition*.

From the beginning this movement involved personal transformation as part of a recognition of political circumstance: And yes, this was for me too a starting point of terrible transformation, meeting with a group of women, not raising our consciousness so much as piercing through the language we had been given to find hidden realities, testimonies, each utterance allowing all of us more vision, until finally we found ourselves using the power of our minds, turning this inward vision outward. From the shared experience to the vision of how things are.

But this is not an easy movement: the pure terror, for instance, of recognizing how deeply ingrained is rape in the male concept of male sexuality. How far flung and far back the practice. How our daily lives are salted with threats of violence. To live with this insight. (Even after my own work on rape several years ago, reading Susan Brownmiller's book kept me in a continual state of shock for days.) One cannot keep such a vision to herself. One could not even visualize it fully alone; we first began to speak of the reality of rape together, we saw the signs of woman-hating together, almost holding hands, like children in a dark house. And now we live with the ghosts we have routed. The old punishments and the old lessons we force into consciousness. Mother-hatred, self-hatred, fear and awe of the fathers. And we do battle, not only with the ghosts of patriarchy within us, but with reality again: we see men are still in power, and to survive we transform, re-tell old stories, listen, hear again.

This is a kind of bravery, and I am in love with this quality, and this affirmation, *Do you see what I see?* And there is joy in these shared perceptions and a kind of healing.

Listening to the work of Carroll Smith-Rosenberg, I am made aware of the redemptive quality of history, how deep the need to restore our past, how deep the need to *transform* our past. I had written (in *Woman and Nature: The Roaring Inside Her*) a piece called 'Her Body', a recounting of tortures (in the name of cure or cosmetics) to the female body in patriarchy. Now, as a curative response to that section, I write a piece called *The Years*, naming parts of the body as our history, our resistances to torture. 'History' is the hair of this body of resistance:

History

> We begin to see that so far from being inscrutable problems, requiring another life to explain, these sorrows and perplexities of our lives are but the natural results of natural causes, and that, as soon as we ascertain the causes, we can do much to remove them.
>
> Charlotte Perkins Gilman, *Women and Economics*

> The history of mankind is a history of repeated injuries and usurpations on the part of man toward woman, having in direct object the establishment of an absolute tyranny over her. To prove this, let facts be submitted to a candid world.
>
> *Declaration of Sentiments and Resolutions*, Seneca Falls, 1848

222   *Every woman who writes is a survivor*

Fine light hairs down our backbones. Soft hair over our forearms. Our upper lips. Each hair a precise fact. *(He has never permitted her to exercise her inalienable right to franchise. He has compelled her to submit to laws, in the formation of which she had no choice.)* **Hair tickling our legs.** The fact of hair against skin. The hand stroking the hair, the skin. Each hair. Each cell. *(He has made her, if married, in the eye of the law, civilly dead.)* **Our hair lying against our cheeks.** The assemblage of facts in a tangle of hair. *(He has taken from her all right in property, even to the wages she earns. He has denied her the facilities for obtaining a thorough education, all colleges being closed against her.)* **Hair rounding our vulvas.** How continual are the signs of growth. How from every complexity single strands can be named. *(He has created a false public sentiment by giving to the world a different code of morals for men and women.)* **Hair curling from under our arms.** How tangles are combed out and the mysterious laid bare. *(He has usurped the prerogative of Jehovah himself. . .)* **Hair which surprises us.** Each hair traces its existence in feeling. *(. . .claiming it his right to assign for her a sphere of action, when that belongs to her conscience and to her God.)* **Which betrays our secrets.** The mysterious becomes the commonplace. Each hair in the profusion has its own root. *(He has endeavoured in every way he could, to destroy her confidence in her own powers. . .)* **Hairs grow all over our bodies.** Profusion is cherished. Profusion is unravelled. Each moment acquires identity. Each fact traces its existence in feeling. *(. . .to lessen her self-respect. . .)* **We are covered with hair.** The past reveals itself as a story we might have lived. The past is cherished. *(. . .and to make her willing to lead a dependent and abject life.)* **We stroke our bodies: we remark to each other how we have always loved the softness of hair.**

Transformational works, conversations, acts, lives, the list could go on. Mary Daly writing of process. Virginia Woolf of Shakespeare's sister (but even more of her own mother). Judy Grahn writing, speaking these lines, 'I will not shut my mouth against you./do you not turn away your shoulder./we who grew in the same bitters/that boil us away/we both need stronger water./we're touched by a similar nerve.' Adrienne Rich, 'A dream of tenderness/wrestles with all I know of history/I cannot now lie down/with a man who fears my power/or reaches for me as for death/or with a love who imagines/we are not in danger.' This list could continue indefinitely.

I remember a scene from a film (taken from a novel by Bertolt Brecht) called *The Shameless Old Lady*. In this film, an old woman, after the death of her husband, changes her life completely, sells all her kitchenware, refuses to live with her children, befriends a young prostitute, stays up nights with a group of men and women drinking and talking, and finally, just before her death, takes off in a new automobile to tour the south of France with her young woman friend. Two scenes in this film are, for me, unforgettable. In one, a man, a shoe repairman and the intellectual of this nightly drinking group, holds a book before his assembled friends and reads from it a passage about the collective nature of thought. That no one really ever conceives an idea alone, that thought has a social genesis. One of the men in the group challenges him, protesting that he is not reading this but is making up the passage from his own mind. The shameless old lady looks on approvingly at the dialogue, delighted by all this talk, such an isolation has her life been before.

The other scene I love is a brief silent moment during which one of the women (the younger or the older, I can't remember which) brushes the other's hair.

And one other scene. This from a film I want to see. It is a film made by a woman about two women who live together. This is a scene from their daily lives. It is a film about the small daily transformations which women experience, allow, tend to, and which have been invisible in this male culture. In this film two women touch. In all ways possible they show knowledge of what they have lived through and what they will yet do, and one sees in their movements how they have survived. I am certain that one day this film will exist.

Notes on the Writing of Poetry

Both of the following pieces are on the process of writing.
'Notes on the Writing of Poetry', 1977, was written for an unpublished
anthology edited by Lynda Koolish. 'Thoughts on Writing', 1979, has
been published in The Writer on Her Work, *edited by Janet Sternberg.*
Now, I use this idea of the two parts of the self, which I talk about in the
second essay, in teaching.

Distrust of words. Words as inadequate. Especially social forms.
Finding social forms painful. The issue of honesty. Does this spring
from the heart? 'Nice to meet you'. The word 'nice' grating. Feeling
inarticulate. *Dumb.*

Or taking words exactly as they are spoken. What is said, the
language, as accurate. The echoes of words. Their unintended
ironies.

Loving the usages 'she' and 'woman' after years of being unable to
use these. As if they were cordoned off, walled away, tainted. Now
using 'girl' again in a new cherished way because my daughter is
turning from a child to a girl and the word has rich meaning for me.

Earning. Truly earning the meanings of words, so that a word never
suggests more than one knows deeply.

Yet, not allowing words to limit or reduce knowledge, but rather to
make the depths visible – just there, in half light, half shadow, barely
decipherable outlines of whole ages.

And the music as inseparable from this. Music of words. And if the
rhythm is too predictable , conventional (contrived) , this is the same
as a cliché, in my ear, making the sense *not true.*

Thus changing the beat from the expected rhythm just slightly. (As
in Thelonius Monk or Billie Holiday.) So the music bends back on
itself, letting you catch the ironies, making you listen hard.

And the off beat like a second thought. The speaker interrupting

herself. The image behind the image. Doors slightly askew, *ajar.* To be jarred. Did I hear that? What
>   did I
>   hear?
Or putting two things together. *Things.* I say things instead of metaphors (interrupting myself). Because metaphors have become so literary. Something to invent rather than given. Therefore not true. A plastic piece of language. Not metaphors but THINGS, REAL THINGS, THOSE WERE REAL THINGS I DREAMED. Not equivalents of reality. I *did* dance on the tables, I *did* fly. Wonderful exhilaration of realness. 'To touch the real.' And I put the two things together the way they *really* occur in my mind. Not the taught, and learned associations, but the wild, outlaw (extra-patriarchal) associations. The natural and often shocking alliances we discover in sleep.

The form of these notes themselves allowing this kind of association and the formal essay as a kind of violence, a kind of mutilating plastic surgery to the real process of thought. Actual subjective thought being then disguised as objective – springing from no particular being.

But actually all my writing springs from passion. I work, live out of passionate attractions, love, of things, friends, existences. The more articulate my love, the more precisely I detect this in myself, the more informed is my language. I need to speak.

And my love for women threads through all my poetry. And I find myself passionately in love with honesty and clarity in women. Women speaking truth.

And my passion leaning toward the difficult, the painful arrival. Therefore distrusting the easy and the comfortable. Not because difficulty is a virtue but because ease is ease is comfort. Yet again one does not so much make an effort against this ease. Because underneath the appearance of ease and comfort (the expected, the conventional) I always find a great effort to keep up appearances. So that the effort against this must be a kind of letting go. The effort against fear. Against the fear of falling into the unknown. And therefore allowing failure. Rawness. Temporary lack of skills. (Loss of balance.)

I once had a teacher who praised my skilful poems and did not like a series I brought in that were raw, simple and honest. But this series was a breakthrough for me, and took several years to come again. I was speaking in those failed poems of what most concerned me, troubled me, made me feel leaden. Struggling against muteness.

And then out of muteness the words appear in a simple order. And they usually do not make immediate logic, but they do make sense. In an inviolable arrangement. Like a bar of music, a series of notes, without which there is no poem. So that if I mis-remember and write the words 'the woman swimming in tears' instead of what I heard 'the woman who swims in her tears' I have lost the poem.

The exhilaration of finding the right words, as with a tuning fork, what sounds right, not the prettiness of the sound, what it does, what they do, those sounds when spoken, along the spine.

And a dogged faithfulness to that sense being necessary. The best teachers able to hear false notes – those I tried to 'get away' with – that movement away. (Jo Miles has this kind of ear.)

And the other kind of getting away. The poem which works, which pleases, but which is not all. Which exists in place of the true poem. And that poem is underneath. Has not yet been exposed. So that next to the poem wanting to be written it is like a shallow breath. (Of all the poets I know, Adrienne Rich always drawing the deepest breaths, the poems we long for.)

The necessary feeling of ignorance which must come before one can approach these depths either as speaker or listener. To wipe out what has been heard before. The silence on which the music is grounded. (And the inside voice always coming in music. Only music. Like words learned in initiation and repeated over and over until their meaning comes clear. Craft only serving this tone, only attempting to preserve, make shine.) This ignorance being a kind of rebellion. A refusal to accept that what one thinks one knows is all there is. So that 'somewhere else' the soul knows more, and finding that inner voice in the silence, out of ignorance, is finally like finding what one, in this other sense, *knew*, all along, so that we say we recognize.

So much defiance needed for the possible. All the labour of feminism. Casting away all the denials of female experience. The denial of what we *know* to be true. Unwrapping yards of bandages. Like the bandages wrapped around the dead. From our eyes. Ears. Hands. Skin. All we are complicit in hiding.

Poetics? (Says this voice we lean in to hear) What? Poetics? What is that?

It is more that on hearing one leaps. When I first heard poetry read out loud the way it can be, by black American poets. And the joy I felt at that possibility. As if poetry had suddenly broken out of incarceration. And I break out of incarceration. This *thing* frees me.

This is the essential act of art. The beauty, for me, this ritual through which my feelings become real. (And where 'audience' can become a foreign concept. Where Artaud burns down the theatre. Where no one in the place is not a singer.) Because in this moment, we all sing.

Thoughts on Writing: A Diary

7 August, 1979

Last night I dreamed that I wrote the beginning of this diary in Sanskrit. The night before in a lecture (not in a dream) Sanskrit was explained to me as 'the mother of all language'. And perhaps poetry is also the mother of language. And thought. And once again, I have solved a problem in writing by falling asleep and dreaming. So here I pose another principle which after all is not irrelevant. Above all the act of writing calls on faith.

Here, a voice in my head, with whom I am always having a dialogue, asks, 'Faith in what?'

But I tell the voice, 'Wait, that will come. Stay with the experience because this experience renders a precise meaning.'

For instance, when I was writing *Woman and Nature: The Roaring Inside Her*, which is a kind of extended, long prose poem, after several months of writing little paragraphs and doing research and making plans I came across what I thought was a terrible problem. There were sides to reality that this voice could not utter. Now the idea of creating another voice, of an entirely different tone, seems obvious. But it was not then, although even then there were two other voices in me. One was the voice of despair, which said, 'This will not work.' And another, that calm writer of poetry, said simply, 'Wait.'

A few nights later I dreamed the solution: I woke with a clear idea that I needed two voices posing conflicted visions of reality.

Now in fact (and this, in retrospect, is what I find most interesting about writing that book, which took me four years), the voice of despair and the calm voice of poetry correspond exactly to those two different world views which, roughly speaking, in my book I designated as the voice of patriarchy and the voice of woman and nature, and which came to me first in a dream.

Woman and Nature: In the chapter called 'Terror' a man tells a woman of the meaninglessness of the heavens. He speaks of the void. He quantifies the vastness and the void. He tells her the human body would perish in that space, and that, in that magnitude, all human meaning becomes insignificant. 'He tells her how perishable she is and how little there is to perish.' The voice of woman and nature answers in that chapter that the stars 'are unmerciful witnesses' to his delusions, and later sings, '. . . we know these meanings reach you . . . the stars and their light we hold in our hands . . .' Because this voice does not despair. And does not despair because it sees the physical universe as embodying meaning.

When I wrote this chapter I had in mind a poem whose first lines ('You if you were sensible/When I tell you the stars flash signals, each one dreadful,') have admonished me for years. The poem is 'Under the Oak' by D.H. Lawrence. In the poem, a man speaks in an intense and anguished voice to a woman whose silliness is implied when the speaker must ask her to refrain from turning and saying to him, 'The night is wonderful', after he has described his terror of the stars to her.

In the last verse of this poem Lawrence creates out of this same woman an inhuman being ('What thing better are you, what worse?'), and, linking her to the dreadful signals of the stars, he asks what she has to do with 'the mysteries' of this earth, or with his 'ancient curse'. Finally, in words that reverberate to woman, the stars, and what we know as chance, Lawrence asks, 'What place have you in my histories?'

Lawrence's words are much more complex than my voice of the patriarch in *Woman and Nature*. Still, what the stars give him is dread, and as a being in the universe he feels cursed. The woman with whom he speaks is variously insensitive and foolish ('twittering to and fro/Beneath the oak. . .') or part of the mystery that has cursed him. As all these, she is either better than him or worse, but no kindred.

This emotional tone, a kind of ambivalent bitterness toward the universe and woman, informs much of modern poetry, such that there is a range from the anguished and ambivalent despair of Lawrence to the almost scientific usage of words, as sound units without sense, that is called concrete poetry. It is more or less the official artistic dogma of our age against which feminism, as an influence on poetry, is in rebellion.

But this split view of the universe and of woman is not new. Someone/thing better or worse than myself. Nature as divine or devilish. The muse, who is feminine, as cruel or benevolent.

And now the words 'mother tongue', language, widen out for me, as I see that our relationship to the one who has given us birth, and to that universe which engendered our being, might be the same as our relationship to language: we must trust words and the coming of words.

And how the conflict between these two attitudes (or voices) – that of despair towards language, the muse and the universe; and that of love of language, of faith in the universe to render meaning – how this has raged in myself. And how it is played out daily in my work.

The voice of despair arrives as a kind of terror (just as I called it in *Woman and Nature*). I am certain before I begin writing a piece that I will not be able to put sentences together, or worse, that all I have to say has been said before, that there is no purpose, that there is no intrinsic authority to my own words. And that is where the struggle begins. Because I must then find the place in myself where my words have authority, some true and untouched place that does not mutter what has been said before, that speaks feelingly, enough to electrify the rhythms of speech, and make in the very telling a proof of authenticity.

This process can take days, and during those days one looks as though one is doing nothing. Here is where despair enters.

I, for instance, clean off my desk. I make telephone calls. I know I am avoiding the typewriter. I know that in my mind, where there might be words, there is simply a blankness. I may try to write and then my words bore me. At such times the whole world of words seems to be irrelevant, as if my faith in language itself had gone. And my faith cannot be restored by any sort of reasoning or logic. Now, I am in another world and I am deaf to singing.

9 August, 1979

I come back to this problem of despair in writing, myself caught up in it today, feeling a dullness about all language. In the morning I am irritable. I feel as if my sleep had been disturbed, as if a dream were intruded upon, and I am not quite certain how to proceed. This is a profound disorientation. When I am not giving forth words, I am not certain any longer who I am. But it is not like the adolescent searching for an identity; no, this state of mind has an entirely different quality, because in it there is a feeling of loss, as if my old identity, which had worked so well, which seemed to be the whole structure of the universe, were now slipping away, and all my attempts to retrieve it seem graceless, or angry, or blaming. And the old voice of protection and order in me whispers like an Iago that I betray myself.

And now I remember the substance of a revelation about faith I had a few months ago. I was walking in the woods and became aware suddenly of a knowledge that enters me in that kind of silence, especially in the presence of an organic life that is not controlled by man. This is a knowledge of a deeply peaceful kinship with all that is alive, a state of mind that language struggles to render, and yet that, paradoxically, makes me want to sing. And at the same time I became aware that the whole impulse to science in western civilization must have been born of doubt. Indeed, all the great questions of science (what is the nature of matter, what is the origin of life, what is the cause of all motion in the universe, what is light) all these began as religious questions, and remained essentially religious until the nineteenth century. So one doubts the feeling of presence, the feeling of unity with all beings, in oneself; one seeks instead of proof, 'scientific', quantifiable. Sense data. So perhaps this accounts for the poetic quality of many scientific truths, and yet, also, the fact that the scientific method abolishes intuition (although indeed intuition has solved many 'scientific' problems).

In *Woman and Nature* I made the voice of science, the voice of patriarchy, hostile to intuition, and all the time I wrote that book, the patriarchal voice was in me, whispering to me (the way the voice of order whispers to me now) that I had no proof for any of my writing, that I was wildly in error, that the vision I had of the whole work was absurd.

And what is this state of mind that the voice of order brings about in myself, and that is akin to scientific doubt, and to patriarchal disapproval? I want to draw a portrait of this creature of despair who inhabits me, capture her, name her. Write a phenomenology of her.

She is, for one thing, concerned with the question of efficiency. She would not have me 'waste' any time. And so, to that end, she would have me know what I am going to write during any day's work before I write it.

And now seeing these words here, I see again how similar this creature is in every way to the patriarchal voice of science, which defends its very existence with arguments of efficiency, saving labour, use, production. But underneath this rationale, is fear of the loss of control, and fear of death.

Because each time I write, each time the authentic words break through, I am changed. The older order that I was collapses and dies. I lose control. I do not know exactly what words will appear on the page. I follow language. I follow the sound of the words, and I am surprised and transformed by what I record.

And so perhaps despair hides a refusal and perhaps in this refusal is that terror born of faithlessness, which keeps a guard over my thoughts, will not let dreams reach the surface of my mind.

When I had written the first draft of *Woman and Nature* the book had a disorganized quality. I had several small chapters, some a paragraph, some a few pages, and no final sequence for them. And so I put the little pieces all in a logical order, by topic, or chronology or whatever seemed most reasonable. But this order did not 'work'. It was like a well-built bench that had no grace, and so one did not want to sit on it.

So I began again putting the pieces together, but this time I simply followed the words intuitively, putting pieces next to one another where the transition seemed wonderful, and that was when the shape of the book began to seem beautiful to me.

I read this in a book on Jewish mysticism: 'Language in its purest form, Hebrew, according to the Kabbalists, reflects the fundamental spiritual nature of the world.'

Before I wrote *Woman and Nature* I knew I wanted a kind of symmetry and a kind of repetition built into the structure. At first I began to create these purposefully. But very soon they began to occur in the work quite unbidden. So, as more and more in the work I began to oppose science with a mystical view of the universe, my work took on a life of its own, and began to resemble the patterns of the universe that it envisioned.

There is a meditation that is also an old Shamanistic practice in which one concentrates on the body of an animal, or a shell, or a tree, or a mountain, until one becomes that mountain. (This going into and becoming the other is the way of knowledge directly opposite to scientific objectification.) And when one writes *about* a phenomenon, one's words begin to mimic that phenomenon, to become that which they describe.

I remember here the Buddhist formulation: you are what you see.

The phenomenology of despair. She tells me words cannot change the world. She says there is not enough time. She wants to know a purpose for every act. She is impressed only by the quantifiable material phenomenon. She is like a scale. Or a weighing machine. How many pages have been written? She is a judge without vision. She cannot play. She above all cannot *be*. She shares with the voice of patriarchy in *Woman and Nature* this idea that forests ought to grow near sawmills, that trees are good for lumber. As I write about her, large spaces of white ought to appear on the page indicating silence.

So much is sacrificed, in this civilization in which I write, to the engine God of despair. But still, the other voice, the intuitive, returns, like grass forcing its way through concrete.

> *So much gladness, mother*
> *I am afraid I will break, oh,*
> *why was it*
> *You never spoke to me of this?*

This poem that entered my mind a few nights ago and until now I have not written down and suddenly, for no reason I can see, wants to be written on this page here.

Too much an imitation of Sappho, the voice of despair says. Because she is also wholly absorbed with ideas of authorship, and who said what, and one's reputation, and respectability. She is prideful and out of her mouth speaks a whole chorus of social disapproval which ranges all the way from professors, male doctors of law, and male authorities with awards on their breasts, such as those Virginia Woolf envisioned, to feminists, different factions of the movement, to a friend I know who disapproves of a word I find I want to use.

Too much an imitation of Sappho, she says, and no one, she says, will understand what you are saying. And this, she says, has been said over and over again. What you wanted to say is expressible.

That moment (last week), watching the film, when I knew the filmmaker had captured a certain shape to life, which I had seen too, felt, and then tears in my eyes, crying both for the heroine in the film and that my soul was touched this way, by this film, and that also, this feeling, which perhaps has become too rare, is, nevertheless, not unique, but old, very, very old. And no, there is no logical train of words, no scientific proof, formulating what this film is saying. No, instead, the faltering words of a young boy, which on repetition seem almost sentimental – 'We cannot live without love' – these evoke in us this deep, old, old knowledge which we know, suddenly, must belong to every creature.

11 August, 1979

Now I begin the day wondering if the voice of the 'other' in society (the lesbian, the black, the Jew) takes on, both in herself and as a characteristic projected by the dominant ones, the meaning of the voice of poetry (or woman, or nature, or wildness, or darkness). Thus it is we in the class of the rejected who, it is argued, must be controlled. We *are* the problem, the scapegoat for all impulses that might change the accepted order.

The voice of despair, similarly, sees the voice of poetry (joy, playfulness, rebellious vision) as the problem. I encounter this particular kind of drama almost every day I write. I may hour after hour put off going into my study, or perhaps only for a few minutes, but the dialogue is the same. The voice of protection and order shouts at me 'necessity', as if I must go to my desk and record reason's preordained words. But if I can listen past this voice, inside is another voice – accused of laziness and childishness and too many emotions – who wants to speak, who is overflowing with language, and whose words, in some unpredictable ways, always afterwards, *after* they have been spoken, seem necessary to reason.

(Similarly, if women, blacks, lesbians, Jews were given 'what they want', enormous social problems might be solved.)

This correlation might explain why the most interesting creative work is being done at the moment by those who are excluded and have departed from the dominant culture – women, people of colour, homosexuals. And this work, unlike the decadent, and abstract, and dadaist, and concrete, and mechanist work of the dominant culture, is not despairing. This work is radiant with will, with the desire to speak; it sings with the clear tones of long-suppressed utterance, is brilliant with light, with powerful and graceful forms, with forms that embody feeling and enlarge the capacity of the beholder, of the listener, to feel.

I find myself staying away, on the whole, unless they have been recommended to me as an exception, from work by white men, because this work seems to need to blunt or even bludgeon the sensibilities of its audience. This is also true of work by women or blacks who imitate that white male contemporary tradition. And there are of course abundant examples of art by white men that depart from this tradition.

The voice of departure from protection and order is what I value most in myself. She is the one who loves, and loves fiercely (and perhaps that is why so much of poetry is love poetry). She has a sense of the largest meanings of life and can find these in the smallest actualities. If there is a tragedy, a weeping in her, this is always a grief for the loss of herself, her burial, her muteness.

Silences. Not the silences between notes of music, or the silences of a sleeping animal, or the calm of a glassy surfaced river witnessing the outstretched wings of a heron. Not the silence of an emptied mind. But this other silence. That silence which can feel like a scream, in which there is no peace. The grim silence between two lovers who are quarrelling. The painful silence of the one with tears in her eyes who will not cry. The silence of the child who knows she will not be heard. The silence of a whole people who have been massacred. Of a whole sex made mute, or not educated to speech. The silence of a mind afraid to admit truth to itself. This is the silence the poet dreads.

And now I think of the wonderful laughter of a room full of women, the excited talking. The joy. Or the almost blistering crackle of energy in a room full of women when one is singing or reading her work to the others. Every word counts.

Think of the difference between these two phrases, that 'things count' or to 'count things'.

And what of rigour, or discipline, or training? Do these belong to the voice of protection or to the voice of departure? To both now, I think, sitting here, having forced myself to come to my study before going out on errands. Because I know I will have more energy now. But perhaps the key to the difference here is intent. I speak now of the kind of joyful rigour – and now perhaps is the time to make a distinction between pleasure and joy. When one is working very hard, it may at any moment be more pleasurable to go from the work and sleep, or eat or lie in the sun. But joy, which is a different, deeper, more thrilling kind of pleasure, joy which is an experience of embodied meaning, joy may be had from working on. Even when the body complains, or the mind aches and claims it cannot go on. To find joy, even in the erotic, one must push past resistances, both in the psyche and the physical, and above all this is significant to the process of writing. But one does not intend to push past a resistance to punish oneself. Rather, one has a hunger for this joy, for this meaning that will pierce experience, and make one suddenly close to all being.

So in writing *Woman and Nature* I moved toward joy but often with great weariness and full of fear and even sometimes anguish. Because indeed the voice of protection and order *is* a resistance, and it takes great strength (courage, rigour, discipline, decisiveness) to struggle with this voice. But finally the joy was in the writing itself, to witness and be part of this process whereby the words and shape of the book began to embody its meaning, so that the very process of writing seemed a proof and to illuminate existence.

And finally I was changed by the writing of the book.

Synchronicities, the voices of trees, rivers, the wind, coincidental openings of books, a large knowledge that seemed available to me only through 'intuition' (a mode of listening to the universe) all these in my writing of the book changed me so that in my acts, in my daily acts, I was no longer a child of the age of science and rational thought. Now, writing this diary even, I still live in a profound state of disorientation. I know I find my power only when I trust language and follow words, moving with them musically, but I cannot always do this. I find myself stopping. Looking about to see where I am. Who I am. And what I am doing.

Faith is what? Only in what I know most certainly and in what can never be proved except through joy. But in this sense a diary about writing is not about writing at all. Or at least, not uniquely about writing. And if this were not so, poets would have no readers.

So all that I ask of my writing I ask of the rest of my life too. *Here (I say) the words are too thin. I have heard this before, I say, and there is more to this than is being revealed. I have said the obvious and expected. But beyond this must be something shocking, something satisfying.* And so I mark out these old words and write again. I cross out all the words except those that affect me deeply, those for which I have some 'irrational' love. I keep those and build again. And again. All the while knowing that deeper meaning will rise to the surface like the form in a piece of stone, or the grain of a polished wood, if I have faith in this knowledge inside me. If I keep working. And over and over the words do not fail me. Over and over I come to a clarifying end. A circle is made. A pattern of sense is given to those words I loved for no apparent reason. I trust my own heart again. *This experience renders a precise meaning.*

Part III

Poetry as a Way of Knowledge

Introduction

The relationship between art and politics is rich and dangerous. In America it has been popular to say that art and politics do not mix well. I do not agree with this way of thinking. A poem cannot be apolitical. All human utterance can be understood as political theory.

That which is political is that which is 'of or pertaining to a body of people'. Poetry, even in its most intimate expression, is of a body of people, for language is shared by that body. In her notebooks Simone Weil writes that 'all art is collective'. She despairs that in her time the absence of a 'real collectivity', and a 'rupture of the true pact between body and soul', had given art no immediate future.

I have written about the coming to life of a collective women's culture, and how essential that collective movement was to my own creative process. Now, from the understanding that art itself is part of a social movement, I wish to discuss how poetry, as a way of knowledge, affects political thought. For poetry, by making a pact between the body and soul, gives to the political imagination a dimension of meaning without which it loses its way.

When I say that the mixture of art and politics is dangerous, I am thinking especially of all the disastrous attempts we know from history to make art conform to political theory. In 1911 Anna Akhmatova wrote a poem 'I Wrung My Hands . . .' depicting an intimate moment between a man and woman. Such a poem, judged by the standards of Soviet Realism, was considered apolitical, and even counter-revolutionary. (The poet suffered contempt, censorship, economic deprivation, fear and harassment.)

Akhmatova's poem is thrilling because it passes beyond assumption, and the expected way of seeing, to go to the actual heart of a specific human experience, the passage of intense feeling between a man and a woman. Thus her poem could record what the political theory of her time could not see: some facts of sexual politics, some of the essence of the politics of intimacy. I am not saying that Akhmatova wrote this poem from an intellectual understanding of feminism which preceded our movement by 60 years. Rather, her poem yielded an actual phenomenon. With her intellect, she made a record of sensual fact, or her own feeling, and of the actual timbre of the human voice. In her poem she forged a pact between body and soul.

Paradoxically it is the demand that poetry express an obvious political meaning which is profoundly counter-revolutionary. A poem should not have to justify its existence. As Simone Weil wrote in the margin of her journal, close to the passage quoted above, 'works of art . . . help us by the simple fact that they exist.' The poem is like a rose, or the scent of a rose. It has no obvious use to us, but that does not mean it is useless. It is rather that poetry answers a need cried out for from an unknown part of our souls. We cannot command the use of poetry, the way we might command the use of an axe. If, as Kafka says, 'A book should be like an axe to break the frozen sea inside,' even when we ourselves are wielders of the axe, we are also the frozen sea. The use of poetry can only be had by surrender.

When I say that no poem is apolitical, I am not implying that poetry *ought* to be political, but that it *is* political. Political theory cannot possibly teach a poet to be political, because poetry precedes formal political theory in the imagination, and because poetry is closer to the original form of all thinking. For this reason, poetry teaches political theory imagination.

The political theorist who judged Akhmatova's poem 'counter-revolutionary' did not predict the insights of feminism into sexual politics. Which is the more significant failure, to fail to know the meaning of poetry, or to fail to know the meaning of sexual love? To this question I answer that an ignorance of poetry is like an ignorance of sexual love, and to fear a knowledge of one is like fearing a knowledge of the other.

Certainly I often find poetry frightening. I will go to lengths to avoid writing down lines that are forming in my mind. And when I am developing a poem, I must prevent one part of myself from finishing the poem in a quite conventional, predictable way before it is ready to be finished. Like human intimacy, poetry can overturn our ideas of who we are, so that when we begin to speak the language of poetry, we feel the same risk one feels in closeness. But with poetry one risks closeness to oneself. As Nadezhda Mandelstam writes, the process of poetry is a process of 'listening into oneself'. And one is apt to find a strange voice there that, later, one will recognise as familiar.

Buried feeling. Buried perception. Lost knowledge. The poem is like a dream that while I dream reveals me to myself. My body becomes a chamber of resonance whose sounds I record.

The poet returns to the knowledge of the body as a source of truth. I am not speaking here of a mute and mystified flesh as our culture sees the body. I am speaking of the body as the seat and author of intellect, of perception, of imagination and vision. There are forms of intellect and imagination which try to be separate from the knowledge of the body. But poetry cannot deny this knowledge because sensuality is the very medium of poetry.

One cannot, for example, ever successfully paraphrase a line of poetry and still retain all the meaning of that line. The act of writing poetry is a very concrete art, and very precisely sensual. Particular words, like particular notes of music, must be recorded. Each particular word carries a particular rhythm, or rhyme, or tonality, or relation to another set of words, and a range of meaning, and a history of social usage, and in all these is the meaning of each line.

Poetry is musical. And music originates in the body, from the rhythm of the heartbeat, shaped by what the human ear can perceive as beautiful. It moves directly through the body, resonating with the physical heart and the metaphorical heart at once. The poetic image is also physical. It speaks through precise sensual detail: the taste of a madeleine. The face of a particular woman or child. Geese flying in formation. White, even teeth. The glimmer of light on a leaf. Through the eyes, the mouth, the nose, the ears, the feeling body, the poem enters consciousness.

'The fear that goes with the writing of verse,' Nadezhda Mandelstam writes, of Stalinism, 'has nothing in common with the fear one experiences in the presence of the secret police.' In the one case, we confront the fear of creation, of change, of the unknown. We are *moved*. But in the other case, we fear the prohibition against feeling, against upsetting the order of things, and always, at the back of such a fear, lies the threat of punishment to the body.

The fear of poetry is the fear of sexual knowledge is the fear of women is the fear of the knowledge of the body, of darkness. In our culture, women, the darker-skinned ones, Jews, all the 'others', have become symbols for a natural, lost self. When we speak in the language of poetry, that forgotten self threatens to return to consciousness. In the censorious mind, poetry speaks the language of wilderness and danger.

Listen to the associations. Poetry is female. Effeminate. A kind of witchery. Voodoo. A black art. Sentimental. Mysterious. Silly. Unreasonable. Romantic. Uncanny. *No serious decisions can be made with poetry.* It is an 'inferior', childish form of thought.

Of the significance of poetry, Audre Lorde writes: 'The white fathers told us "I think therefore I am" and the black mothers in each of – the poets – whisper in our ears – "I feel therefore I can be free." ' Writing that in each of us there is 'a dark place' from which 'our true spirit rises', she says, 'For women, then, poetry is not a luxury. It is a vital necessity of our existence.'*

When I was a girl growing into womanhood, two of my closest friends invited me to go once a week to the public library in the city with their father, Henry Steinberg. Henry Steinberg was a communist, one of those who was tried under the Smith Act in the United States. On the drive into the city, he would often discuss ideas with me. He introduced me to socialism, gave me my first copy of Edward Bellamy's *Looking Backward*, gave me my first radical education. For me, those were astonishing Saturdays. I was discovering worlds and myself. And not the least part of those days were the times when we listened to chamber music or operas or symphonies through the library's earphones, or when together we leafed through books of art. When I look back to discover what brought me to see my own suffering as part of human suffering, and to consider that, together, we all might change our lives for the better, I see that those days were transforming. The whole day. The talk. The new ideas. The respect with which Henry spoke to us, his own curiosity about the world, the drive to the city, the music, the beauty, were all of a piece.

I had not encountered such a wide world of sense and feeling in my family. I believe that quietly, unknowingly, all of us had suffered the loss of this world. I drank it in as a world which had all along belonged to me, a world for which I was made and outside of which I had always before been alien. I believed that I felt happy in this world because I was an intellectual and my family had not been so. But I was wrong. Later, I was not happy in the atmosphere of the university. It was not intellect I had been longing for, it was freedom.

Those Saturdays took place near the end of the 1950s, the decade of McCarthyism. One could not discuss the idea of socialism freely in

*'Poems are Not Luxuries,' *Chrysalis* No 3.

the school I attended. And on those Saturdays my curiosity could live. That feeling of freedom was expressed in every part of those days, not only in our theoretical discussions, but also through the music we listened to, the reproductions of paintings we saw and the fact that we had come into a strange neighbourhood, the inner city, where people of different colours and histories lived.

For me the process of art and the idea of political freedom have always been inextricably mixed, not always theoretically, but since I can remember, in *feeling*. When I entertain a new and previously forbidden political insight, I feel exactly as I do when I begin with a new, unheard-before line of poetry. There is a sense of outrage, of danger and risk, and yet a joy that carries one past fear. For inside, one feels as if a door is opening onto a view, which, even if one never suspected it was there, was a needed view, and filled with a bright clear air.

In those moments a self previously buried in propriety and convention, or in the habits of others, or in the fear born to repression, a self not allowed to breathe, whose questions and feeling never reach consciousness, is suddenly revealed. I know these moments to be profoundly healing. And if there has been any consistent shape to my life, it would be that again and again I seek ways to find this authentic self.

Children love secret paths. They trace private ways into a plot of ground sanctified by its separation from the scrutiny of the adult world, and the rules invented by adults. Secrecy leads the child into a place of freedom where she may commit the outrageous act the soul needs to survive. Within the human psyche, which at one and the same time contain the brave child and the censorious parent, poetry is a secret way through which we can restore authenticity to ourselves.

This is perhaps why poetry has been so important to feminism and to the feminist movement. Language itself had made us invisible to ourselves. The very vocabulary we inherited locked us into a diminished state of being. We were wives, girls, ladies; we were women, she, female. We were virgins, whores, lesbians. We were frigid, nymphomaniac. Housewives. Hired 'girls'.

The very structure of the mind is determined by language. Language enforces conventional thinking more effectively than any prison, for, before we even articulate what we feel, language censors us, not only through the meanings of words but by the conventions of speech, of normal usage, and by the structures and forms of written language.

Poetry is no respecter of convention. But there are poetic conventions which can be as rigid and suffocating as any others. I am not speaking here of the form of the sonnet or the sestina, which have, in other times, prevented authentic expression. The current convention has been for free verse, and to write a sonnet or a sestina is now, therefore, a departure from convention. I am speaking of a convention which is less formal, and thus more subtle, more invidious. That is the idea that certain words are not 'poetic' and certain subjects not fit for poetry.

Because of this conventional notion, before feminist poetry began to appear (and short stories and novels) a certain kind of experience, shared by most women, was rarely written down. No frame was put around our lives. We could not and did not reflect on them, through literature. We did speak about our lives. But that speech, that vocabulary, and the intonation, the context of that speech, was not acceptable literature.

And just as there were things said among women which could not be written, so also there were things unsaid which had to be written first before they could be spoken. And so out of the old language we made new poems, and stories and plays. We recorded a speech commonly uttered in women's lives, yet never before used in literature. And the very act of making this record brought us to the edge of the unspeakable. For once literature reflects on the evident, one begins to see what is not evident.

In short stories, novels and poems, women began to record the daily speech of women, and to give voice to the unimaginable. Now, for us, language had a new kind of sound. It was not that this sound was formally new. It could be produced through the oldest forms. Rather, it was new to us because it brought us to recognition. This was the forceful and shocking effect of the poetry of Sylvia Plath. *Ariel* was filled with onions, napkins, baby crap, menstrual blood, and these not kept in a safe domestic realm, but threaded in with the history of Auschwitz, the idea of faith, of suicide, of salvation. And all filled with a particular unique kind of rage, a rage duplicated exactly by no other circumstances than by a woman's circumstance.

Critics have suggested that feminists have made a martyr of Sylvia Plath, and that by this martyrdom, we worship self-immolation. This is to misunderstand, along the lines of old misunderstandings, the meaning of Plath's work and her life and death to a whole generation of women. Her work became known to us, in the United States, after her death. Now, for the first time, we found a rage we ourselves knew

articulated and framed on the page. Someone had been brave enough
to cross a line, a line which existed socially *and* in poetry. She had
broken the silence. And now we could speak too. She had given us
language. And that she was dead? This seemed to us not so much the
price she had to pay for the intensity of her voice as a fact of history:
that this voice of women had been destroyed in a multitude of ways
for so long. Many feminists believe, and I among them, that Sylvia
Plath would have had a better chance to survive in the decades that
followed her death. One who suffers as she suffered needs not only to
be heard but to be understood.

In my poem, 'The Song of a Woman with Her Parts Coming Out',
I experienced for myself the sense in which words are magic and can
affect the world. For to fear the use of such words as lesbian, dyke,
cunt, vagina, was to give these words the power to shame me. When I
sang them out in a poem, this power to shame became something else:
my power to be, free of definition, to see that the emperor has no
clothes.

Language contains so much more meaning that we suppose it to
have. When a poet diverges from the old forms, even older meanings
surface. One may not, for example, understand that the grammatical
use of 'he' as a generic term meaning 'human' has a large effect on our
thinking. Yet the continuous use of 'he' as a persona for the human
limits our imagination. And one knows this immediately when one
encounters 'she' used as the centre and reference point for all action
in a literary work. This is the magic of a group of poems written by
Judy Grahn called the 'She Who' poems. In these poems, she not only
created a new form, she made a kind of radical thought possible for
the listener.

> *She Who*
> *she, she, SHE, she, SHE, she WHO?*

or

> *She Who continues*
> *She Who has a being*
> *named She Who is a being*
> *named She Who carries her own name.*

To resonate to the music of 'She Who' is to open the mind to the
possibility that perhaps a woman is the subject and not the object.

And then perhaps to consider that in some time past history's recording, this was evidently true, and that past one's own conscious memory, this was evident to oneself.

Language itself contains a memory of past and original meanings. If we have believed that culture can be separated from nature, language tells us otherwise. For the word 'culture' itself is built upon a metaphor for our connection to the earth: to cultivate, to cultivate the soil. Again and again I have entered the process of making a poem only to be led to older meanings, deeper meanings, in myself, and in culture through this language which we share with history.

I began to write poetry at an early age, and by the age of fourteen felt that this would be my work. Many who write poetry begin to understand the process of poetry immediately. I did not. It took me years to understand that a poem is not simply a description of a state of feeling, or an idea. The poem does not happen after the fact. The poem is an event which is at the same time a record of an event. The poet is like a walker. She walks in the sand, and while she walks, she leaves her footprints. In the process of writing a poem, one is moved and is moving, and moves. The words one writes find feelings in oneself, and these feelings find words of their own, which in turn locate other feelings. In this way, slowly, step by step, a knowledge buried in the body comes to consciousness.

This is a healing process. We cannot live without reason, but reason can become too muscular and thus insensitive and incapable of knowing. So many times have I felt that beginning a poem I am abandoning and entering a madness within myself. But, even through the feeling of madness, I have felt a relief. I have felt that, as Deena Metzger writes, 'I have let the horses of the sun lead too often, have followed Apollo and his reason, instead of running with the Dionysian dark.'

Recently, while I was walking in San Francisco, I saw a very old, mad looking man wandering the streets talking to himself. He looked as if he had been wandering that way for years. Suddenly, he stopped in the middle of the sidewalk, put his hands to his face and cried out, 'I think I'm going crazy.' But what I witnessed was that, for a brief moment, he became sane.

Simply to speak the truth heals. The blood of the wound heals the wound. To speak to a receiving ear, to be understood, even if only by one another, or by oneself, heals. And for every part of ourselves that we hide in darkness, for every lie that we tell ourselves, we suffer. It is this deceit which causes madness, and often, illness in the body, too. Can we be said to exist at all outside of this darkness? Separated from our authentic cries, we become weak imitations of who it is we think we should be. We build our lives after a diminished image of humanness. And this diminishment is part of any image, no matter how humane, which does not treasure darkness.

What does the poem do? Does it point to a solution? Does it rally for the cause? Does it provide a moral lesson? Does it prove theory? Though it may by chance do any of these, it should not be bent to these purposes. For its most radical purpose is to remind us of ourselves.

And is it not fundamental to any radical thought, to trust this human self, body and soul, heart and mind, larger than we imagine, in whom we all partake, whom we all share? We are the miracles by which we can survive.

The Sink

I wrote The Sink *in 1969, while my daughter was an infant. (I read the story into a tape-recorder while I walked with her in my arms.) These three stories were published in a collection called* The Sink *in 1974 by* The Shameless Hussy Press, *one of the first feminist presses, established by the poet Alta.*

THE SINK

It was dark out; she was 40 years old, and she was sitting under the sink. Forty. Married 20 years. She dreamt the marriage, and it happened that way, down to the colour of the dresses of her bridesmaids, the colour of her husband's hair, and their children's. Red. Red like carrots. Like carrots before they are cooked. Like the carrots she cut into four pieces every evening at eight o'clock and wrapped in cellophane to go in their lunch bags. Three lunch bags. Folded over with a name on each bag. And then she would close the refrigerator and clear the drain, clear the sink and the drain of carrot peelings, because they stick in the pipes and clog the sink if they are not removed, the same as coffee grounds. She had lost interest in coffee, though. That's what he said, the man she had married, with red hair. Just like a woman, he said, flighty. You have an interest, like soap or coffee, and then one day you just let it drop.

She had started with Italian coffee, the time he took her to an Italian restaurant and the waiter insisted they drink after-dinner coffee and the cups were small and the coffee very sweet and thick. She bought an espresso pot. She had to send away. She looked every day in the mail. It came packed in confetti with instructions in Italian, and she put the water where the coffee grounds were supposed to be. But she finally mastered it, and open-pot coffee, and drip and steam and Turkish coffee. Finally, she even bought her own grinder. And she learned that the coffee shrub grew wild in Abyssinia, that the Dutch drank Java in the eighteenth century.

But she lost interest. Pots gathered dust on the shelf. She finally took to buying pre-ground percolator coffee in huge tins in the supermarket.

The same thing had happened to her as a young girl with soap. Her favourite aunt went on a trip around the world and sent a bar of soap from every country. Myrurgia soap from Spain. Sandalwood from India. Lilac from England. She began to take long baths. She stored bars of soap with her sweaters and her lingerie so they would be perfumed. And once, on a date with her husband, the man she finally married, a bar of soap fell out of the sleeve of her sweater.

But that was twenty years ago. And now it was pipes. The house was old. The pipes were no good. She started with crystals of drain cleaner every week. The pipes were cleared, but a small amount of water always floated to the bottom of the sink, taking five or ten minutes to gurgle itself downward. So she could never keep the sink clean. The cycle got interrupted. The cycle of rinsing and draining after washing the dishes, because there was always this last bit of water sitting in the sink, preventing her from laying her hand on a clean dry sink at the end of the day in the kitchen.

She found a book on plumbing. She took the pipes apart and discovered the catch in the first joint, filled with collected refuse. So she cleared it out. And the sink worked perfectly. Every last drop of water flowed down and out the drain, so smoothly she never even saw it collect.

But the catch jammed up again. Within a week it was full and she did not know why. The trouble might be under the house; she might have to dig up the foundations.

Her husband did not understand the importance of the drain pipe. He mentioned the large cost of major plumbing and the disruption it might cause in their lives, and so they did nothing.

She began to clean the catch out every week. And it was then that she noticed the catch would start to get full in the middle of the week, and water would start to collect in the sink. A small amount of water, but it angered her, so she began to clean the catch twice a week.

Now she heard footsteps. Perhaps the man she had married was coming to the kitchen. He might eat. He might wash the remains of his plate down the drain. She waited.

She wondered if there might be a leak in the drain. She could feel the pipe on the back of her neck. Water might drip on her hair. But she did not want to wash her hair that night. She began to pick at her nails. She calculated when it was that she had last washed her hair, because she liked to wash her hair twice a week, not more often or it would get dry – and not less, because her hair got stringy. It got dirty in three or four days. And when her hair got stringy her face looked pasty. So she liked to plan the washings for days when she went out, only she never knew when she might go out. She was worried. She had just washed her hair yesterday, so she put her hands on top of her head and held them there, even though her back began to ache.

In fact it all began to ache. There was not much room for her under the sink. She was doubled up; her feet under her had gone to sleep. Her chin was bent into her chest and had begun to feel as if it were growing longer. She folded her hands over her breasts and felt each movement of her ribs as she breathed. She perspired.

But it was not his footsteps she heard. No one came to dump their uneaten breadcrumbs, or their bits of lettuce with mayonnaise down the pipe. She waited, as she had waited the night before, and the night before, and every night since she first realized that someone had been putting garbage in the drain in the middle of the night.

At first she lay awake night after night listening for any sound in the kitchen. But at close to five in the morning she would somehow fall asleep. By 10 o'clock, when she usually wakened, they had all gone, the man she was married to and the two children, and their lunch bags were gone from the refrigerator. She would go and stare at the sink, where she found bits of cold cereal, egg and banana floating in a pool of coffee, the remains of their morning.

Now the house was retired. She could visualize its order from her hiding place. Everything was smoothed out. All the wrinkles were out of all the clothes that hung empty in closets. Everything was in its place. The lumps beneath the blankets breathed in and out. And the wet was wet and the dry was dry. All the dust was outside the windows with the earth. Food was cool and glistening behind the white door of the refrigerator; and garbage was wrapped in black plastic cans by the backyard fence, or was on its way through the floor of the house, through the floor of the earth, by pipes and rivers, out to the sea.

Everything save the catch in the drain was ready. She longed sometimes, staring at it all, thinking of the order and the multitude of ways she kept it, she longed to join the garbage in the waste can and become part of the air – the way that objects slowly carbonize, turn into compost, or bits of particles, vapours.

Or she longed, when everyone had gone off to sleep, to put on her coat and leave as if she had never been there. To go some place under a different name and make messes. Some place where she could make the dry wet and the wet dry. Where she could wrinkle her clothes, where she could spread the contents of the refrigerator over the furniture, like cheese over crackers.

And afterwards she dreamt that she would throw herself down some drain and plummet out to the sea and swim along with the waste and the garbage in one great bath.

Tears rolled over her face. She didn't move to clean them off. She sighed and she had a great urge to let her head rest against the drainpipe, but she didn't. She held on. The house waited for her. Her head began to hurt listening for the sound of the drain.

Everything she knew was ready, except the drain. When that was clear, her life could begin.

THE PLAIN ONE

When I saw my face, large blue eyes in a small white face like a baby's face, I knew this was no longer my face. The three white hairs on my chin had always been cut, I always cut them, and the white hair on my head was brown, light brown, with increasing strands of grey, as the years went on, more grey, around my face that was pink, or ruddy, or flushed and large with large jowls, a large jaw, a double chin, and a high broad, shiny forehead. I was the plain one. Sister got married. Andy married. Bill eventually married too, and the twins lay next to each other in the back yard with twin stones. Only I stayed on, to comb his white hair. Sister, I said, do you remember his white hair and how he liked us to brush it? And she nodded and smiled that smile we would all do anything for, like a gift amongst all her meanness. Because she was given the doll. Mother gave her my doll after she had broken her own. Katherine, my sister, took my doll and then she was married to Charles and they left for California while I stayed and took care of mother and father. I was never married. 'Look who I've brought to see you,' the nurse said to me as if I were a child, and she brought in my niece's children. Katherine's daughter whom we called little Katherine. Her children had come, and one was my child. I took her from the railway station, her mouth red with lipstick, wearing blue jeans and a blouse from Mexico and we took the lipstick off and bought her wool dresses. They lived, little Katherine and her young husband and their children, Jane and Anne, in the big city, and Jane had come to live with me now, in a small town, and we took the lipstick off. 'Look who. . .' the nurse said, her hair blond as straw, bottle blond, while the other washed my feet. 'This was my child, my sister Katherine's grandchild,' I would have said, but in my mouth was only silence. She sat one Christmas on my porch and poured out tea on her tea table, 'Tank u Bom Bom, Tank Nu Nu,' and we took her to see the ducks, Katherine and I and Charles while little Katherine and her young husband talked and talked and decided to try again, to stay together, to keep their family together and have another child. 'Look who I've brought. . .' and then Jane's voice said, 'Anne, Anne is here.' Annie whose hair was blown about her head the way mine always was, but still, no one seemed to mind, and the wind blew over the field of weeds that look like chard outside my window. And the young woman finished wrapping my feet, and she turned me round in my chair so I could see them. 'The snow. . .' Anne said and I nodded and then I shook my head to make her finish her sentence again because I only heard her say 'the snow', and there was no snow I could see. There was never any snow here, where I came, after mother and father died, he lasting longer, in the big walnut bed overlooking the barn, while I brought him trays and took away pans and then I went to teacher's college. While Katherine and Charles were married and had little Katherine to raise and Charles sold cars in California where there is no snow, I went to teacher's college and then I went to teach the children of Indians in Idaho. Sister could never understand, she could not understand when I told her about the little wooden building they gave me and the bed with bedbugs and the hiking shoes why I loved that place but I was different and finally I came to the place where there was a college in the fields, right in the centre of the fields, so at least I could be close to them, Katherine and Charles and little Katherine and later Annie born after Jane who was my child after she came to live with me when little Katherine divorced and we took the children. I had never known. I had known it had to be done, that Katherine and I had to take the children, but I had never known why because little Katherine was always so sweet, so shy, so sweet, smiling up at me from brown eyes, her chin tilted down to her chest the way that man took her picture, that wonderful picture when she hid behind the velvet curtain. But when she came to help me gather Sister's things, after Sister died, she got so wild, and said such things I will carry with me to my grave. I never drank even a taste of what she drank to make her that way. But Katherine would drink now and then, though she took

the pledge the same year I did, she was never one for church, and
Charles quite the opposite, always had his glass, though they had to
limit him at the end. And Sister so lonely when he died. How we miss
the dead! One would never guess. Where do they go, the dead?
Where will I go? 'They are all gone into the world of light.' But, do I
cast a light? Well, let's find your glasses she said to me. In the drawer,
in the drawer someone said, and Anne held my hand as they wheeled
me to the window. And there in front of the fields, in a red jacket,
squirming in Jane's arms, was Anne's baby. And I myself have held
that child. I held her on a chill Thanksgiving day when Anne came
from the city with her new husband. 'Was it because he was Jewish?'
Katherine had asked when Anne told her what we had all known and
kept from her while she was ill, that they had divorced, gone their
separate ways. Like her mother, but not like her mother at all. And
Katherine was taking the picture while I held the baby our faces
together in front of the blazing red berry bush, the bush I had grown.
'A garden enclosed is my sister my spouse; a spring shut up, a
fountain sealed.' And Katherine had said to me, 'Be careful', and
then loud and clear in that voice I will always remember, sang out,
'She doesn't know how to hold a baby.' But I held them all. Even
Katherine herself. Katherine I held you! I was here first, and I will
leave last, with the memory on my hands of the baby limbs of you all,
Katherine, little Katherine, Jane who was mine, Anne and the
littlest, Carson, who Jane held for me, in the window, and I waved,
and she waved and wiggled and it seems, tears came to her brown
eyes, a little fear, and they wheeled me away. My hands had shaken
that day because of the arthritis and the pain in my right hip made me
unsteady. But Katherine always talked like that, and what did she
know? She'd not made her own way. She never got to Hawaii.
Though I have been to Europe and to Asia and ridden a camel past
the Sphinx. And I have slept in a bed with bedbugs and kept valuable
Japanese wood blocks in my closet, and I have had friends who came
to my house year in and year out to play canasta, and admire my lilies,
my rose bushes, my wild onions, my succulents, my gourds, my plum
trees, my cyclamen, my daffodils, my oranges, my persimmons, and
now all I have is a field of chard. Who would have known? Who
would have known we could miss the dead so? All I have of Katherine
is the telephone number of a cemetery. There was not even a service,
only an urn. But they all came back to me. I tell you when she died,
when Charles died, when we started to die, the edge came off all their
voices. And I was too harsh. I knew it, they knew it, but who else was

there, to raise Jane. I who had never loved a man. I who held only babies, babies from other flesh, other wombs, I was to raise my own child, and I knew then that the look on my face was not right. I know now what I did not know then, but still. 'The soul's dark cottage, batter'd and decay'd, lets in light through chinks that time has made,' that's what they say. And the earth was without form and void, and darkness was on the face . . . that's what they say. I might have held her then. Some say they get too old for holding, but I know now, one is never too old. But still. But still. I did not do wrong. I did what I could. I nursed them all. Mother and father and brushed father's long white hair. Katherine remembers how I did, and made my own way then and taught many children and raised my sister's grand-daughter, and nursed Katherine till her death. I did what I could. Until there was no voice in my mouth anymore, nor motion in my limbs, then what could I do? I looked. My eyes spoke. My eyes grew like lakes. I could not prevent it. I could prevent it no longer. My eyes spoke clearly and they, one by one, came to me. Jane, my Jane, sat by me night and day, holding my hand and stroking my head; my oldest friend came and put her face to mine, we had never touched before, never before, and then Anne, Annie who Katherine raised, with her hair blowing over the fields of chard like mine, held my head to her breast and ran her fingers in my white hair. I never would have guessed that this was the end, that this was what would be at the last. I did what I could, what was right. I who have never known a man. I stood in my garden, a large woman, I was, in a large hat, at dawn, tending my flowers, my rose bushes, my lilies (I was known for my lilies) my pomegranate tree. And my jaw was large, too large for a woman, and always set squarely. They told me I looked fierce when I thought. But I was shy. I never lay in bed with a man; I never was married, but I raised a child. I plucked turkeys every Thanksgiving and put the red berries in the centre of the table and washed Jane and Anne home from summer camp in the big tub and made them lamb chops for supper. I kept pictures of them all in my albums that I kept in a closet with Japanese woodblocks. And Jane was my child. But the nurse thinks I am her child. She sees only my large eyes in my face which is now small over my jaw which is now small. And she sees my eyes which said hold me, my hands which reached for their hands, my eyes which said stroke my white hair, which my tongue would never say, could not say, would not have said. And Katherine told me I would drop the baby but I did not. I have held Katherine, and now she is dead. Do I cast a light? Is my hair . . . white?

A STORY

This is a story about two women who love each other. The beginning of the story is not just one beginning but two. Two women were born. They were born and lived each for 28 years before they met, one wearing a beautiful pea-coat, the other in a white neck brace. Or rather, one writing poetry and reading it to everyone, the other writing poetry and folding it into a small square and putting it in her pocket. You could say that the one thought she loved the other more than the other loved her. Or rather that the other loved also a man and was not sure who she loved more, or rather who she wanted to be with. Or rather you could say that they loved each other equally, but one, or rather, both, did not believe the love was there. Or rather the one thought she was needed and so she served and believed that was why the other spoke of love. Or you could even say she never believed anyone loved her. And that might have been said about the other too, only she did know, because she felt happy at times, that there was love between the two. The question with her was more that she wanted all the love because she thought if the other gave away too much love in other places to other people there would not be enough left. And really, what she was sure she knew was that if the other ever got far enough away to love someone else she most certainly would prefer that other person, and then, she would go away. Well, anyway, in the midst of all this fear of the one and the indecision of the other, they became 29 and then they became 30 and they still lived in the same house and they still loved each other but they did not make love. That is they did not touch each other on the breasts or vagina but only slept near one another or curled up together or stroked their heads, or rubbed their backs, or held one another, or kissed goodbye and in the morning. These things they did but it was what they did not do that made the one upset. Upset and angry and hurt and all those feelings. And the other felt bad, bad for causing the hurt, and the other felt anyway that she was always causing hurt, just by existing, or by sitting down and putting her feet on the ottoman. For instance, the one who wore the beautiful pea-coat and stuffed her poems in her pocket and did not want to make love would always take care of the other. The other was sick for a long while. And for instance, the caring one would say, to give an example which is very exaggerated but shows the point, '*I am sorry that I cannot carry you up the stairs.*' And at first the other was very touched that the one would even want to carry her up the stairs but she said, '*First, I am too heavy for you, and second, I can walk up the stairs myself.'* And this went on, this very conversation, for a while. But gradually the conversation changed and it became like this, *'Really, I can't carry you up the stairs, I'm so tired.'* And then the other would say, *'I never asked you to.'* And finally the one who didn't ask began to believe she had asked and decided she had to prove that she had offered to carry the other up the stairs, or at least would if she could, only everyone knew she had a weak back. And there were other conversations of a different and of the same nature. And both women worked very hard to show that each was good herself, and each woman felt each herself that she herself was very selfish. But there was a truth apart from the feeling and that was that the woman with the pea-coat, though she did not carry the talkative poet up the stairs, did nearly everything else for her. And all the other could do was to say thank you or occasionally to loan the caring woman money. This she herself felt was very cheap since she knew there was no reason but luck that she had the money to loan or to give. But the caring woman felt guilty about the money. And in any case it was true that there is no comparison between money and caring. And the one who had been sick felt guilty. And so, she tried to give love. And this was only partly accepted, not in the sense of making love, but in the sense of belief. And in addition, the sick woman could not really accept the caring woman's care. She would at first pretend she did not need the care, and then if she asked for the care, did so in a tone of voice implying that the caring woman did not want to give care. You can see that nothing in this story is simple. You can see that but you must also begin to be suspecting the outcome. More and more, as the sickness and the caring went on, the two women felt selfish inside. Finally, they gave each other as much pain as they did love. And the one who wore the neck brace would say to the caring one, *'You should not feel guilty,'* and then later she would say, *'Last night I was sick and you did not know'*. And she would also say, *'I think you should not make love to me if you do not want to but I think you should make love to me.'* And she would also say, *'You should not always do what you should but do what you want.'* As you can see the one was very confused. And the other, for her part, would say, *'You should not be afraid that I will leave you because if you keep on acting afraid, I will leave you.'* And the other would also say, *'You are always acting so fair; you are always acting so self-righteous.'* But if the one became then unfair, or angry, or even nasty, the other would say, *'You'll be sorry,'* and she would walk out the door. This went on and on in between what the one still remembers as tenderness and love and joy until one night the conversation repeated itself again and the one with the folded-up poems left the house again. And she did not come back. And the truth is that she may never have come back because the truth is that she wanted to die. And by this, the other was frightened almost to death. And this then is the ending of one story about the two and also the beginning of two more stories, as only time will tell.

Like the Iris of an Eye

The earlier poems in this collection were first published as Dear Sky *in 1971 by The Shameless Hussy Press, and as* Let Them Be Said, *in 1974 by MaMa Press. Later they were published in the larger collection* Like the Iris of an Eye *by Harper & Row, New York, in 1976. This book is currently out of print.*

Love Should Grow Up Like a Wild Iris in the Fields

Love should grow up like a wild iris in the fields,
unexpected, after a terrible storm, opening a purple
mouth to the rain, with not a thought to the future,
ignorant of the grass and the graveyard of leaves
around, forgetting its own beginning. Love should
grow like a wild iris
but does not.
Love more often is to be found in kitchens at the dinner
hour,
tired out and hungry, lingers over tables in houses where
the walls record movements; while the cook is probably
angry,
and the ingredients of the meal are budgeted, while
a child cries feed me now and her mother not quite
hysterical says over and over, wait just a bit, just a bit,
love should grow up in the fields like a wild iris
but never does
really startle anyone, was to be expected, was to be
predicted, is almost absurd, goes on from day to day, not
quite
blindly, gets taken to the cleaners every fall, sings old

songs over and over, and falls on the same piece of rug
that
never gets tacked down, gives up, wants to hide, is not
brave, knows too much, is not like an
iris growing wild but more like
staring into space
in the street
not quite sure
which door it was, annoyed about the sidewalk being
slippery, trying all the doors, thinking
if love wished the world to be well, it would be well.
Love should
grow up like a wild iris, but doesn't, it comes from
the midst of everything else, sees like the iris
of an eye, when the light is right,
feels in blindness and when there is nothing else is
tender, blinks, and opens
face up to the skies.

Revolution

I would not have gotten in this boat with
you.
I would not
except
where else was there
at the dock's end
to go?
The water
was cold.

I would not have let you row the boat.
I could see
what kind of man you were.
I would not but
who was there to choose
between
you and me?

I would not have let you throw away the
oars.
I knew what would happen next,
except
what else was there to do,
struggle
in a boat with a leak
over cold water?

Is the Air Political Today?

Is the air political today?
The air, my thoughts,
is this a
political hour? did you
choose a political chair
to sit in; was
my logic political, were my
eyes, did they
show a political grief or
was it personal; would my political
self have been happy
when I was not; would they
have fought over me
struggling over the tongue; is my tongue
political when it rests still
between my teeth and I dream;
what was birth
the placenta that was pulled from me
was that political?
I cannot
shut myself up
anywhere; is that
a political feeling? Are you
more political than I, tonight,
or were you this morning and tell
me now
in which journal shall I write
that I miss my child

and want to hold
her, let her political
head rest between my
political breast and shoulder?

I Like to Think of Harriet Tubman

I like to think of Harriet Tubman.
Harriet Tubman who carried a revolver,
who had a scar on her head from a rock thrown
by a slave-master (because she
talked back), and who
had a ransom on her head
of thousands of dollars and who
was never caught, and who
had no use for the law
when the law was wrong,
who defied the law. I like
to think of her.
I like to think of her especially
when I think of the problem of
feeding children.

The legal answer
to the problem of feeding children
is ten free lunches every month,
being equal, in the child's real life,
to eating lunch every other day.
Monday but not Tuesday.
I like to think of the President
eating lunch Monday, but not
Tuesday.
And when I think of the President
and the law, and the problem of
feeding children, I like to
think of Harriet Tubman
and her revolver.

And then sometimes
I think of the President

and other men,
men who practise the law,
who revere the law,
who make the law,
who enforce the law,
who live behind
and operate through
and feed themselves
at the expense of
starving children
because of the law.

Men who sit in panelled offices
and think about vacations
and tell women
whose care it is
to feed children
not to be hysterical
not to be hysterical as in the word
hysterikos, the greek for
womb suffering,
not to suffer in their
wombs,
not to care,
not to bother the men
because they want to think
of other things
and do not want
to take the women seriously.
I want them
to take women seriously.

I want them to think about Harriet Tubman,
and remember,
remember she was beat by a white man
and she lived
and she lived to redress her grievances,
and she lived in swamps
and wore the clothes of a man
bringing hundreds of fugitives from
slavery, and was never caught,

and led an army,
and won a battle,
and defied the laws
because the laws were wrong, I want men
to take us seriously.
I am tired wanting them to think
about right and wrong.
I want them to fear.
I want them to feel fear now
as I have felt suffering in the womb, and
I want them
to know
that there is always a time
there is always a time to make right
what is wrong,
there is always a time
for retribution
and that time
is beginning.

In My Dream

I woke up
this morning in your arms
and drove directly
into the water; it was
storming a few days before
spring, I thought I would
drown.   Now,
sunlight fills my body,
swims behind my eyes.
I have travelled miles
in circles; I am still
in California, after months
in treacherous wet jungles,
after my ship went adrift,
several trains crashed in the night,
cars turned over.
I hitchèd and did not get a
ride for three weeks in the

Mojave desert, in the winter,
my daughter and I slept
curled together by the side of the road,
my thumb frozen west.
I am still in California
in a public park
but no one around me sees
that in my head
I am resting exhausted
on top of a mesa,
some mesa where the Navajo dwell,
artists of dryness,
doing paintings with sand. I
feel ancient, and each
flicker of my eye-
lids makes me young
again. Do these Navajos here
(I hear the sound of mothers
with children in the sand
surrounding me)
do they lie against one another
in this warmth, put their
faces into lovers' armpits,
lay their cheeks on bellies,
let the fluid of their bodies
flow together?
I have not loved in
so long, I imagine
I have never loved
the way these
Navajos in my mind
can love. This morning,
years ago,
when I woke up
in your arms, I was
in New England, had visited
the home of Emily Dickinson,
was travelling by coach
to Manhattan; the rain on
the leather roof steady,
the dark horse hooves

treading through rock
and mud, my mind sharp
and keen as the iris
in her eye, the poet
who said, the
soul is its own
lonely companion.
I have not seen you since you
left your marriage
leaving me in mine,
wondering what pain in you
drove you half wild
and to the East Coast.
I woke to rainfall and
your absence, sudden
as your being
which surprised me in
a dream.
(Now I hold the glittering
pieces of it
as sunlight dries the rain.)
I drove into the rain-
fall just to find you
again, as I had dreamed
standing among a party
of my friends.
I was shocked
you saw
I was going down
and touching me
my sorrow
rushed into you.
You had such wildness
when you left you nearly died
and that's what I wanted driving
on rain-wet curves.
We left marriage
and found ourselves
full of love; I thought
I would drown in it, now
sunlight

fills my body
in a park
where I walk
holding my daughter's hand,
she has played in the sand
and the grains on my skin
are turning hard and crystal
in the dark night of
dreams.

Archaeology of a Lost Woman: Fragments

i

A book stained with
years of use:
The Joy of Cooking.

The pieces
of a mixing bowl
taken apart
displayed
by her Granddaughter
as sculpture.

Her sweater, knitted
magenta wool.

Her hands, long
misshapen fingers spotted
brown.

The old needles
the old patterns.

He voice still saying,
'If my face is stern
it is because it has grown
to look that way
despite me.'

ii

A walk through a
museum, women
in photography, a
picture of
an ironing board, an
iron before a window,
a shadow cast in the
natural light.

iii

She remembers holding her hand,
her Grandmother's secret
knowledge,
the two boarding the trolley, the
yearly trip downtown,
the school clothes, the
joy that day, the
laughter between the two, the
promise of something sweet at
home, the old woman, her
promise.

She remembers longing
to walk
the light out there
beautiful
through the open door.

She remembers words
to her daughter, 'Hurry,
be
careful, don't
spill
over me.' She remembers

her Grandmother's voice
the hardness, then,
the weariness.

iv

Words in an old diary
Sunday, March 23, 1958

Home all day. Black clouds. Quite
dark at times. However I did laundry
so I could go out in the morning. Dried
in and out. Quite a breeze. Washed doll
clothes. Must make her a footstool.
Finally made Ernie's fudge. Fried the
chicken in the pan and was moist
and very good. Rest and after went
to sleep. Bed at 9:30. Read a bit.
. . .Awake for ages. Too tired to get
up or read. Just tossed and turned. . .

v

In the museum
photographs of women
their hands over their mouths,

women standing
side by side
not touching
the lassitude of
unloving
in them,

etching of a woman alone
called waiting,

woman and child
asleep in the railway station,

a face staring into the lens
'I am what I am
broken, you will
see that in time.'

a woman passed through
slavery, letting her eyes
blaze, 'My body
carries this pain

like an emblem.
I do not apologize.
I survive.'

vi

Child's memories
dolls cut
from cloth
new faces threaded
each year

candy distilled
to hardness
over the fire

an old drawing sent
through the mail,
'I love you
Mommy,'
Archaeology

the waters
of sleep we had
no time to swim

My cries at night
the ache in my knees
her old stockings
around my legs

my daughter's nightmare
my arms around her, my
face pleading, 'Don't
wake up again.'

Her tenderness, my desire to
please breaking like vases
along the line of
old faults,

the flower I gave her
she did not believe would bloom

ink spilled on the satin

bed covers, the furies
if you don't
welling inside her
stop crying
the darkness of my room
if you don't
stop

vii

waters of sleep
flowers blooming
my daughter brought forward
like a sweet

My Grandmother
floats in my dreams
we sleep
like sisters in
the peach-coloured room
where I slept
as a child, and in
my womb I feed
the Great Grandchild
she always wanted.

Archaeos, the
shards of
disbelief
the last words never
spoken how I
loved you old
complaining woman, the
pieces, the stairs
were slippery,
and she slipped,
broken one more
time,
pieces
her mixing bowl on my
the silver bell she saved for me

viii

Do you know
I ask her
calling through time
I write this
with your pen?

ix

Becky, my
daughter rocks
in my Great Grand
mother's chair, that
chair,
I tell her,
sat
in my Grandmother's house
in the peach-coloured room,
don't sit too hard
it's been
years.

x

Night, darkness, the healing
sleep, the vessel fused
once more,
one of us writes in her journal
A tiredness has left me
A heaviness
one of us whispers
O world is this what you were
and tenderness,
Grandmother
your tenderness sings
in my skin.

The Woman Who Swims in Her Tears

The woman who swims in her tears
the woman who dives down deep
                in her weeping, the
woman who floats downstream in
                her grieving, the
woman who lives in the depths of her
                    crying
                  of her aching
                  of her holding
                  herself
           with her own arms
           and rocking, the
woman who has no mother, the
woman who mothers,
the woman filled with love
who looks at herself
through a closed glass window
and wonders why she cannot touch.

The woman
who slept beside the body of one
other woman weeping,
the women who wept.
the women whose tears wet
      each other's hair
the woman who wrapped her legs
      around another woman's thigh
  and said I am afraid.
the woman who put her head
      in the
place between the shoulder and breast
  of the other woman and
  said, 'Am I wrong?'
the women who wept together
the women who pressed
        their faces together
      their hands together
      their eyes together
      their thighs together

who pressed into each other
who cried together
who cried
who cried out
who cried out joy
the women who
cried out joy
together.

A Woman Defending Herself
Examines Her Own Character Witness

QUESTION: Who am I?
ANSWER: You are a woman.
Q.   How did you come to meet me?
A.   I came to meet you through my own pain and suffering.
Q.   How long have you known me?
A.   I feel I have known you since my first conscious moment.
Q.   But how long really?
A.   Since my first conscious moment – for four years.
Q.   How old are you?
A.   Thirty-one years old.
Q.   Will you explain this to the court?
A.   I was not conscious until I met you through my own pain and
     suffering.
Q.   And this was four years ago?
A.   This was four years ago.
Q.   Why did it take you so long?
A.   I was told lies.
Q.   What kind of lies?
A.   Lies about you.
Q.   Who told you these lies?
A.   Everyone. Most only repeating the lies they were told.
Q.   And how did you find out the truth?
A.   I did not. I only stopped hearing lies.
Q.   No more lies were told?
A.   Oh no. The lies are still told, but I stopped hearing them.
Q.   Why?
A.   My own feelings became too loud.

Q.   You could not silence your own feelings any longer?
A.   That is correct.
Q.   What kind of woman am I?
A.   You are a woman I recognize.
Q.   How do you recognize me?
A.   You are a woman who is angry.
     You are a woman who is tired.
     You are a woman who receives letters from her children.
     You are a woman who was raped.
     You are a woman who speaks too loudly.
     You are a woman without a degree.
     You are a woman with short hair.
     You are a woman who takes her mother home from the hospital.
     You are a woman who reads books about other women.
     You are a woman whose light is on at four in the morning.
     You are a woman who wants more.
     You are a woman who stopped in her tracks.
     You are a woman who will not say please.
     You are a woman who has had enough.
     You are a woman clear in your rage.
     And they are afraid of you
     I know
     they are afraid of you.
Q.   This last must be stricken from the record as the witness does not
     know it for a fact.
A.   I know it for a fact that they are afraid of you.
Q.   How do you know?
A.   Because of the way they tell lies about you.
Q.   If you go on with this line you will be instructed to remain silent.
A.   And that is what they require of us.

Mother and Child

           Mother
           I write home
           I am alone and
           give me my
           body back.

(She drank
she drank and
did not feed me
I was the child at home.)

You have given me disease:
All
the old
areas of infection reopen themselves:
my breath
rasps,
my head
is an
argument,
my blood ebbs, you
and your damned Irish genes
did this to me.

I pretend
someone else
cares for me,
catches my
falling body,
cradles my
aching head,
cries when my fever rises
in alarm.

And meanwhile
mother
from my dying bed
I have
finished you, you are
not even a
spot upon the sheet,
you are gamma rayed
clean gone.

You are not

absent anymore
you
never were.

And your child
is the driven snow, she
is innocent of
all action, the
articulate say victim,
a word
she neither speaks nor
knows.

She is buried. She is only
bone, polished clean and white
as if with
agonized toil
a shrunken jeweller
crouched inside
her box
tumbling her body
by hand but
she was alone.

She was alone„but
her casket
was glass. And when she
cried she turned
her body
in shame
to the earth, and
turning and turning
wore her
body away.

Now
in my dreams
the mother who never was
finds the bones of her child
and says,
'How we have both suffered.'

Now the
child opens the
box which becomes
a mirror. She stares at her
bony self
and does not
look away.

Breviary

'Do not let them kill me before you speak to me
Touch me!
*   Behold me!'*

Meridel Le Sueur
from 'Behold Me! Touch Me!'

She is in a white dress
kneeling.
K is for kneeling
in the breviary and
W is for woman.
Women kneel,
small girls wear white dresses
for communion
for communion,
into the bread
the flesh,
the wine and the blood
and the women kneel
for our bread
for our blood.
Do not let them
and the woman
smiles out from her window
offering the picture-taker
a loaf of bread
Do not let them
kill me,
stroking the soft hair
on the head
of her

baby (but we saw the second
picture, the small buttocks
in a pool of blood)
before you speak to me
and the women in white dresses
speak softly to the saints
and the saints answer,
'love befits the man
and fear befits the woman.'
the words of the saints spelled
out in gold in the air
sung out by the voices
of small boys, high and light
and pure.
In the other picture one sees a woman crying,
a small old woman, holding on to a younger woman
who is also crying. And under the picture the
cameraman's words tell us that moments later
the daughter was raped and then killed.
The photographer could do nothing. The photographs were what he did. He was certain he would
be court-martialled or killed for taking them. He
could not stop the massacres. There was nothing
he could do.
Do not let them kill me
before you speak to me
touch me, behold me
And it might have been different if he had
been in his own country or this were not a
war because men act differently in a war.
For I am innocent
and she removed her blouse
she showed her white neck
she opened her empty palms
she kneeled
she wept
she carried a child
she squatted down
she cried
and left a child where she had been
and she whispered to her daughter, stand

she whispered to her daughter, run.
What he wanted or why he did it no one
especially knew. 'She's lucky to be alive,'
the police said. She has parts of knives still
in her and knife wounds in her heart, her lung,
her liver, her spleen and her throat. She fought
him off and she lived. She is well except for
some hoarseness. The doctor does not know if her
voice will return to normal.
And the young boys' voices sang out
Holy Mary
high and beautiful
Mother of God
with a red heart in her breast
and a red fruit in her mouth
and a slow movement of her thighs
the red tongue of a tiger lily
the red blood of birth
the cry of a child between her thighs
her thighs down hard
birthing the new voice
which is the end of the old voice
blood on the palms of her hands
miraculous and sudden
blood on the sheet that was white
she was in a white dress
kneeling
K is for kneeling
W is for woman
B is for bless, and bread and blood
at the hands of a man,
H is for heathen and healing,
R is for rape, M is for massacre,
W is for woman and the words of the saints,
P is for picture and pool of blood
and for purity and prayer, for prayer and S is for she,
she,
she is in a white dress
kneeling.

Two Thousand Years

1

There you are at the stove again
a woman too intelligent for absolute
paranoia, stirring the cereal
again, is there something that draws you
back and back to this
the light, the plant you must
water, the bacon, the eggs in the pan
you consider five years in this
place, two lunches made in the
ice box, your daughter with
one big tooth crowding the babies
makes blue snakes in the next room,
the cereal is poured in blue
bowls with blue rims,
you have chosen the colour
chosen your daughter
chosen the number on the house.

2

You say the
entire world can exist
in one imagination.
And you tell the story
of the sisters over
in your mind
how they longed for the city
how they died in the country
and that not in the city
but somewhere
behind them
not in the country
but behind them, was a shadow, a glimpse, a thought
lying under speech.

3

Always one step ahead of despair

I dreamed last night
the men made plans for the future
your husband and mine
with the correct explosions
underground, they said, we locate caves
and stay there while the holocaust
rages on the surface, then
according to the laws of probability
we will find our way out
in two thousand years.

4

No, I woke up screaming
I would rather die
in the fires.

5

And you wake
to a quick silence
like disaster, like the
moment the pot falling
seems to rest in air
before it
splits in two
and you wonder
is the fire
real?

6

You remind yourself how easily you forget
the mind thinking itself quick recites outlines
and leaves out all the textures,
invents a reason
and is irritated by the wrong details.
The body goes on defending itself
every movement, the boiling of water on
the stove, the pouring of salt in a shaker
a proof of theorems, when suddenly
I remember every moment.

7

Self-preservation in the making of breakfast.
Self-preservation in the cry on waking.
Self-preservation in reason.
Self-preservation in memory.
I remember every moment, I am shocked
at the daily loss.

Immersion 1976–82

This is a new book of poetry in the process of completion.

Three Love Poems for Kim Chernin

1

You suddenly like
Einstein in this picture the
power of his vision making his
body almost frail like
light shining through his ribs
only he smiles and his hand
touches his lips and he thinks
with enormous pleasure of all the
clutter of papers surrounding
his lucid joy and you
smiled turning your head quickly
back in the midst of one flash
of knowledge between us to
tell your daughter the time of
her birth and then that birth
played over the bones of your
cheeks, the turning of your
shoulders so quickly its power
making you instantly frail
you looked then smiling at me
hands on the wheel and changing
gears, laughing because you had
forgotten the money your mind
at the same time studying this

fact and all its intricate
being radiant between us your
daughter's intelligence measuring
stars and we vibrant with
meaning with where this car
is taking us.

2

Love for you sucks me like a
light-winged being or the petals of
a bloom floating back on a warm wind
into this house of my own language
where you would know me, where you might
find me should some thread of me uncoil
in you, should you want me,
but where I refuse to wait and refusing
drive through the force of my longing
for you, into myself, finding
a secret solitude and my own meanings
and I shudder with unfaithful joy even
in being here alone: how the world
swims in my eyes, now a clear and objective
presence, gleaming, as if I had not
seen the faces of things before,
nor light, and such
extraordinary music strains the walls –
I see even the cat dances, and almost
say, I have not *seen* this cat dance
before, when suddenly in the
kitchen, *Kim,* a voice rushes the sound
of your name into the air, and this
air, this solitary air fills
with tears to know you, thus.

3

The sweet soul is sexual, we say
lost in each other, what he called

the id is so much more and
no object in the universe travels faster
than the speed of light, we whisper,
love, this motion of light
does not change, I see it
in the saying of it to you,
I hear in your hearing
your hands find me saying
yes, how everything
I could die, fits together,
and the sweet soul
is so large, so large, and hold
me so that bone bursts upon bone
and this is the bone of your face
I say astonished and let me be
possessed by astonishment
of you, your being and the history
of your bright speech breaking in me
as light on every distant feeling
the story of how you came here
evokes to fullness in me, taste
and take into your mouth, love, this sweetness
your sweetness you made in me
we say, shuddering, delight.

Dear Skull

1

I keep placing my hands over
my face, the finger tips just
resting on the place where I feel
my eyebrows and the fine end
of a bone. My eyes are covered
with the blood of my hands, my
palms hold
my jaws. I do this at dinner
my daughter says
Are you alright
and by a common miracle

when I smile
she knows I am.

2

I ask her what she will do
after we eat. Sleep she
tells me. But I will clean
the deer skull, wash it.

3

You gave me this skull in the woods
told me to bring it clean
and tell the story I had told you
before, about how the deer had
come to me, and I said I would.

4

And I put this skull on an old
newspaper, pulled the lower part
of the jaws free, touched it first
carefully, as if it would fall apart
in my hands, the bone paper
thin, and then I saw I could
scrub, so brushed the surface with
steel and my fingers and more
and more this surface became
familiar to me.

5

I wanted to see the lines of it
what it would be if it had been
polished by the wind, the water
and my hands this agent making
the skull more itself.
Slowly I was not afraid at all
and my fingers went into the deepest
holes of this thing, not afraid
for myself or it, feeling
suddenly as if my cleaning this

small fragment of earth away
from the crevices inside was
like loving.

6

But it was when I touched the place
where the eyes were that I knew
this was the shell of the deer that had
lived here, this was this deer
and not this deer, her home and
now empty of her, but not
empty of her, I knew also, not
empty of her, as my hands
trembled.

7

And in that instant remembered you
had been in that body of
that deer dying, what
does it feel like to be a deer
dying, the death consumes
you like birth, you are
nowhere else but in the centre.

8

Remembering those gentle deer
that watched me as I wept,
or the deer that leapt as if
out of my mind, when I saw
speaking there in that green place
the authority of the heart,
and the deer of the woods where
my feet stood stared at me until
I whispered to her and cried
at her presence.

9

And when I cleaned the skull
I washed myself and sat

my body half out of the water
and put my hands again over
my face, my fingers edging the
bone over my eyes, and I thought
how good this feels and this
is a gesture you make.

10

Tell this story of the deer's skull
you asked gently and so I
came in my own time to put
these words carefully here
slowly listing each motion
on this thin paper
as fragile and as tough
as knowledge.

Forest

I wake feeling green grown over me
And the death of a friend in my dreams.
The dead one and I
float in the water.
Around her are all the flowers
I meant to give her,
as shame comes up a liquid
out of her mouth
and I hold her pleading
this is alright, oh
let yourself be comforted,
let yourself *be*.

I wake thick with memory and the paintings of trees.
The dead one, and the one who mourns her mother,
and the one whose distance I mourn, stay with me,
and this story, recently told: that one twin brother
breaks a knee, and the other breaks another bone,
and the one breaks his hand.

Because her mother had died,
we touched the edge of hands, blessed, we
gave her a green heart, a blue heart
to circle her throat, her bone, we
made a hole in the earth and ringed
a tree in her mother's name.

Because of distance, I wrote letters
forsaking my old friend, I imagined
both of us free.

This is what we saw happen:
Two boys made mirrors
of each other's bodies
fell apart like petals
then broke bones to show
the world something
had happened.

Waking I heard the painter
painting the trees
said
nothing is dead
not even a
corpse.

And I remembered myself
a small girl
who talked to her dog
whose tears streamed slowly down her cheeks
as she whispered into the curling fur
how she had a centre
a brown ache like the cave
in the trunk of a tree.

When I dream of the dead
I ask the air now as
silence waits in my ears
do the dead hear?

Because daily I long to

make a green arc back
across distance. I imagine
a pain beyond touching.

Painting the forest
the painter said
should you sit down
the great, dry, green sea
would sweep over and engulf you.

Awake now, I feel part
of the forest
sunken deep
in the green not
drowning not dead
but alive with the dead and
the distant a cave
in the centre filled with
weeping and singing the old cry
of longing, the old cry of loss
come home.

The Awful Mother

The whole weight of history bears down
on the awful mother's shoulders.
Hiroshima, the Holocaust, the Inquisition
each massacre of innocents
her own childhood
and the childhood of her mother
and the childhood of her child.
What can she do?
She remembers.
The child's drawing, the lost
mittens, the child
cold, the awful mother shouting
the child's story of shadows
in her room, the child waiting
the awful mother

waiting, and *her* mother
waiting, already asleep
and the awful mother
knowing too late
the howling of children
in cattle cars and fires.
The wind blows so hard
it is as if the earth had fallen
on its side.
But nobody wakes up.
Only the awful mother stirs stricken
with grief.

Our Mother

At the centre of the earth there is a mother.
If any of us who are her children choose to die
she feels a grief like a wound deeper
than any of us can imagine.
She puts her hands
to her face
like this:
her two palms open on her cheeks.
Put them there like she does
Her fingers cover her eyes.
She presses her hands into her eyes.
Do that.
She tries to howl.
Some of us have decided
this mother cannot hear all of us
in our desperate wishes.
Here, in this time,
our hearts have been cut
into small chambers
like ration cards
and we can no longer imagine every
morsel nor each tiny
thought at once, as
she still can.
This is normal,

she tries to tell us,
but we don't listen.
Sometimes someone has a faint memory
of all this, and she
suffers.
She is wrong to imagine
she suffers alone.
Do you think we are not all
hearing and speaking
at the same time?
Our mother is sombre.
She is thinking.
She puts her big ear
against the sky
to comfort herself.
Do this. She calls to us,
Do this.

Immersion

1

This is the beginning.
You are chilled to the bone.
How can one speak of it?
You have taken off your clothes and
walked into the wind.
How can this be told?
You have immersed yourself.

2

We sail up a brilliant coast.
Some of us will swim ashore.
The sharks are indifferent
but I am bleeding.
Not this close in,
I'm told, trust
this water.
A long swim and

hard, they say.
Black caves, red valley,
sand shore so vivid,
terror in my body,
I slip into the sea.

3

Joy comes loose
inside me.
I am maddened.
You stand under the waterfall.
In your element.
Now I know you.
The cave looms large behind us.
Such beauty has
ripped away all pretence,
all the normal.

4

Back on the boat
I am still alive.
Porpoises met us meaning
wonder. I was so
afraid,
there in the water.
I sank in fear.
I was fear.
I was immersed.

5

How water
on the skin
washes away and
awakens.

6

And who are you
sitting beside me
drawn into yourself

on the boat's bow?
You sleep beside me and can go
away into darkness can become
only a voice promising return.

.7

Every way that I turn
to the vast void of the sea
the high fingering cliffs
the emotional slap of waves
whether I am angry, holding
myself away from you, afraid,
whether I resist or resent
this or that object left
the complaint, the irritation shading
perfection, whether you jump to
conclusions, give orders, create
disorder, cause sleeplessness
I listen all morning for your footsteps
everywhere I turn
a question you answer over and over
opens out in me, everywhere

8

In my dreams I look
into the water, the deepest
water I've seen looks back and the
brightest with wonders
beneath the surface. Close to me
fish dazzle yellow white orange green
red large I cannot
resist them though
two sharks haunt the distance.
My heart pulls me down.
I will risk this.
I swim into what
is precious to me.

9

You are away from home.
I stare into fire.
The shape of the smoke is
exquisite.
Time is present.
When I say I
miss you, this is a feeling
in my body like pain.
Each day you come closer to home.
At the edge of this sorrow is
delight.

Voices

Voices was originally written in 1974 for the public radio. Since then it has been produced on TV (where it won an Emmy Award) and on the stage throughout the United States and Europe. In New York, it was directed off off Broadway by Estelle Parsons. The action of the play takes place in the mind, or on the stage. The five characters can be thought of as one character, and at the same time as five different people. They have never spoken to one another. The play has a structure like a musical fugue.

MAYA: I have had two children
forty-nine lovers
one marriage
two affairs,
and now you ask me
what am I going to do?
Good Lord!
A question like that
is inhumane.

KATE: What one does comes out of circumstance.
The question is, 'What is one.'
One goes on with courage.
One goes on with discipline.
I have my work.
God knows for me
the circumstances were fortunate.
I have no regrets.
No, I did not have children.
No, I was never married.
But I have had my friends and
lovers.

One cannot have everything in life,
only some things.

ERIN: But some things are necessary.
Some things are absolutely necessary.
Food,
Shelter,
Clothing,
and love, what about love?
No one is to blame really;
for me, there is no future.
Life has been too painful –
it is as simple as that,
as simple as circumstances.

ROSALINDE: Like walking in the rain!
Like walking in the rain!
Haven't you always
wanted to walk naked
in the rain,
or ride a horse in the
rain,
furiously
delivering the
essential
message so that
the revolution
can go on, riding
furiously
day and night without
sleep
the modern Joan of Arc
and she
performed this
heroic task, they will say
in her fifth month of
pregnancy!

GRACE: Oh yes,
but if only you could
manage not to lose your coats.

You are beautiful
every one of you,
but you'll have to remember
your own coats from now on.
I've been a mother too long.
You ask me about my
future, and I tell you
about my children.
There are four of them.
We had large families
in my day
and now
there will be grandchildren.
Do you know
when I was a girl
I wrote poetry and
wanted to be a lawyer?
If I told my children
they'd laugh.

MAYA: My name is Maya.
At nine o'clock in the morning
to have the children off to school
the house back together
beds made, myself dressed, myself
dressed, is a great
accomplishment.
After the children leave, it
takes me at least three minutes
to remember my name.
I was up past
midnight last night. Talking
about a lover.
I wrote him a letter
and then read it
to all my friends, over
the telephone.
The children woke up by themselves in the morning and while
they watched the television
I slept in a thousand dreams –

women played pianos and
carried candelabras,
a woman came and put her arms around my
waist. We listened to the
music, I wept.
When I turned to see who held me
the woman vanished.
And then?
At nine a.m. I take out my
notebooks. I play my
tapes and type them.
People's lives reel out
before me.
Stories of marriages,
divorces, jobs
lost, moves from city to
city, the children
don't speak to
the parents, the parents
have funerals for
the children.
And for me?
This is the year
of the dissertation,
the year Danny entered Kindergarten,
Rachel entered second grade, or
the
year of
the
Food Stamps,
the last year
of my grant from the Bank of America.
The Bank is becoming suspicious. 'Six
years', they ask me
whispering so they won't embarrass me
in front of all the savers,
'Isn't that time enough
for a doctor degree?'
That's enough time,
I answer,
for some boy

just old enough to drink
whose proud father
wants him to be the
first Professor with his
surname, but if
you spent two
years of graduate school
in divorce courts
and lawyers' offices,
and another two
typing other people's theses
and the rest of the
time   ,
falling in love. . .
my dissertation
is on the
Death of the
American Family.

KATE: My name is Kate.
One makes
Choices.
I don't mean though
that one should be narrow.
Within those choices the
full range.
I acted for years in movies
before I went on the
classical stage. It
always makes me
sad when someone says
'I'm too old.' The only
time
you are too old is
when you are dead, I
say.
Oh, I suppose
I wanted children once.
But what one
does one must
do well.

Even if it takes years
of study or
practice or
sacrifice.
For one scene in a movie
in which I played
an American spy
behind the Maginot line
I learned to parachute.
I
wanted the experience,if
I was
to play that role I
had to know
what it felt like
to fall from the sky
into a strange field in
a strange country
my head
reeling from the pull of
gravity
and the sheer beauty
of space
following
space
following space
in a quiet
descent that
lasts hours and only
seconds
at the same time.
That fall
changed my walk
for the next few weeks –
I was bruised,
but also athletic:
my body was sure of
itself, I had had
to train for weeks;
and if I
had been a mother

all that time
the needs of my children
would have pursued me and
only half my
spirit
would be in that
jump.

ERIN: My name is Erin and
if I jump
from a window
or a bridge or a
tall building in the
next day,
don't cry.
Think of me
as in ecstasy.
For the first moments in my life
I will be free.
It is myself,
I am fleeing.
Then death will
surround what is
left of me,
an inert soft form
in blankets of darkness.
I dream of it.

ROSALINDE: To dream of death?
Once I was
climbing a mountain with
some friends.
The rock above gave way
and there I was
stranded
holding on by
only one toe.
I waited while
the others helped them-
selves to the top, some
of them were crying.

I enjoyed the view,
a sheer drop
of half a mile
into a green rolling valley.
Can you imagine such a death?
They were in tears.
But I climbed over the
cliff in two steps,
grinning like Captain Jack.
For the rest of the day I was
giddy. And ever since then
I've wanted
to be a trapeze artist.
I tried to join the circus
when I was
twelve. They told me
to come back when I was
over eighteen. What a
put down.
But at eighteen
instead of the circus
I enrolled in
Art School. This was
the compromise we made
my parents and I
between the circus
and
teacher's college.
Actually I
wanted to go to
Vietnam
to fight,
with the NLF of
course. But the
war ended before I
could save
money for a plane
ticket.
Art School lasted
for two years.
For my last sculpture

I filled a child's swimming pool
with cherry jello
and immersed
myself nude with some marshmallows
all day until
we jelled.
Then I asked my friends to
eat around me.
The piece was called
'Virgin'.
I am called Rosalinde.

GRACE: They call me Grace.
Yesterday I went
to the grocery store.
I had filled up
the cart
and was half way through
the check stand
before I realized
I had shopped for the whole family.
The last child left
two years ago.
I don't know what
got into
me.
I was too embarrassed
to take things back
so I spent the week cooking
casseroles.
I feel like one of those
eternal motion machines
designed for an
obsolete task
that just keeps on
running.
I certainly don't want them
back either.
When the
last baby stopped getting
up at

night, I didn't stop.
I would get up at four
or sometimes even
three, every
morning and roam
the house.
There was something I
loved about the
house at that
hour, in the blue light,
the streets
absolutely still
though in the morning
I was so tired. It took me
almost four years to learn
to sleep all night
again.
And William never
understood. To him
if you are tired, you sleep.
I have never been able to
penetrate the
simplicity of his logic
which is
after all
the logic
of most of the world.

MAYA: I had a dream
I was in a swimming pool.
I was swimming back and forth
as fast as I could
because
while I was swimming
the lifeguard
was letting the water out
of the pool.
I swim to escape my
children,
my dissertation
my lovers or

lack of lovers.
Now I am in another
recovery period. Now
I look at
each new
affair, each new lover, and
question what
particular form of
disaster will be
revealed beneath this
latest ecstasy.
I have done studies.
I take notes on my own life
drawing graphs
adding and comparing statistics.
I come from a
stable
family unit:
Mother, Father
two sisters.
And I still
speak to them
all!
At least
over the telephone.
My mother
was married once
before.
That man
walked out on her
leaving her and
my oldest sister
alone in the midst of the
depression.
Her mother and father were
both dead.
As far as I know
they died of
poverty.
My Grandmother
I am told

worked the sewing machines
twelve hours a day
until my mother
was born and after she was
in school. My
Grandfather
worked the steel yards
and breathed in what
my Uncle Henry called
'bad air'. They
both died of
tuberculosis when my mother
was fifteen. She went to work
in the cannery, looked after
Henry and when he was
old enough to be alone
she went to school at night.
Her mother
on her death bed
between fits of violent coughing
made her promise
to get an education.
She never forgot my
Grandmother,
her picture
as a young woman
hangs
in my parents'
apartment.
She wears
a grey
cape. She had
large brown eyes,
timid
bright eyes.

My mother says
I have her eyes,
but without
the timidity.
My mother met my

father at City College
where they both
studied at
night, they both
joined a young
communist club and still
volumes from
the little Lenin
library line
their walls.
'Surplus Labour and Capital Profit'
'The Woman Question'
'What is to be Done?'
Of course
it was a woman
who first asked that
question, only she
asked in a
different tone, 'What
is to be
done?'

KATE: My father
had plans for me
from birth.
I was an only child and
hence
my mother's
daughter,
my father's son.
My father though
was stronger willed.
Ma Ma succeeded in getting me
into dresses for
a few years. And I did
come out
at a ridiculous party
where I drank too much
and fell into a fountain.
My mother insisted until
the day of her death

that I jumped.
Father had
decided I should be
a lawyer.
Since he couldn't get me
into Harvard,
he sent me to
the Sorbonne for a
general education – Well
that was the end of the
law because when I went to Paris
I saw
Isadora Duncan.
Isa
dor
a
Dun
can.
Isadora
Isadora
Isadora
Dun
can.

She was
better than
falling in
love.
I was only
seventeen, and she
in her thirties then
but she made me feel
as if up to that moment
I had been dying.
I wanted to move.
I wanted to stand up and take off
my clothes.
The Sorbonne saw less and
less of me.
I began to take classes
in the neighbourhood

of the *Ecole des
Beaux Arts*
dance
voice
weaving. I
met Isadora's
brother
and began to wear
sandals even in the cold
Paris rain.
I went to the same cafes
where Hemingway and Joyce
sat, Picabia,
Max Jacob,
and met people
who had known
everyone famous
intimately.
Everyone spoke of their
art; it was the
first I heard
of such devotion to
anything beside
religion and even that
in my New England
home was very
subdued . . . You
could not even
call it
a passion. On
Sundays
my father
read me portions
of Emerson.
I knew about
self-reliance
before I could
cross the street
alone.

ERIN: From birth

circumstance
has surrounded me
like an encroaching army.
I was six
when my parents
gave me a second birth.
They gave up
my life
to my mother's mother.
Mother had gone mad.
Of course
there were
weekends before the break
when my brother
my twin
and I
would beg around the
neighbourhood for food.
Mother would have
gone off. Maybe she
took a bus to the furthest destination
the deepest centre of the city
and someone
my father or my Grandfather
would find her wandering
hair uncombed
her face a
memorable bleached white
singing girl songs
or in a different phase of
her moon lunacy
picking an innocent
object on the street
(she was timid)
to accuse
letting loose
a diatribe of accusations,
'You think you can get away with
it this time like all
the others. Well you can't.
I've had enough. I'm

finished.'
My father was
a simple man, too
simple
for
sunrise
conversations with
stop signs
in the produce district.
'Who are you talking to
Rosie,
who are you talking to?'
he would plead,
softly,
shaking his head,
or he would
burst out at her
shaking her in a rage,
'Stop that
stop that
get a hold of
yourself.'
This of course
I did not know
when I was
six, nor did
Eric as we
did our own
wanderings,
we never
knew where she was
but only
the empty house
and our
empty stomachs
and a cold
clawing feeling of fear
as the sun cast long shadows
through the venetian
blinds and no sounds
came of keys

in the door
or plates descending
in the kitchen.
When our mother
was not mad
she was the perfect
mother. She made
cookies in the shapes
of lambs and hearts.
She let us keep cats
and grow a vegetable garden.
We had an
intricately
decorated
doll house, and wore
little outfits
she knit for us
to match.
But by my
sixth birth-
day
sanity never lasted
more than a
day and those
days were grim.
On that day
I hated the dress
she gave me
and vomited
her special dinner.
Mother was a beautiful
child and a
beautiful woman
they told me.
I was deposited
one evening
from the back seat
of my father's car
into my Grandmother's living
room. And Eric
was sent to

New Mexico
to live with my
father's mother
a strong
woman who grew
flowers
in the middle of
the desert, kept a goat
and slew her own chickens,
If he'd lived there
he would have been all right.
But soon he came
back to the
Irish side of the family
the respectable family
with our laced
tablecloths
our silver
sequestered like treasure in a
sideboard, to
our vacant numbed days
lying like flowered wallpaper
over our violent nights.

ROSALINDE: I dreamt I gave birth
to myself.
My body was huge
as I lay
in a silk-sheeted
bed in a geodesic
dome
in the forest.
Muir Woods!
All I saw was my own
belly button
distended and pink
sinking up and down
with the undulations of
my womb.
I kissed the skin
of my belly

to welcome the
new child. My father
held up a mirror
in a baroque silver frame
so I could see the child's hair
falling in black and curly
cascades
from between my thighs.
Then as
the hair
grew longer and longer to the floor
my father
grasped inside my
legs and
pulled out
a face.
What?
My face, an
infant me,
and as he pulled
and as I saw
the face
my body trembled
and opened and
the sky itself
seemed to pour
right through
my teeth
I felt so
sweet.
He slipped
the infant by
the head
out of me.
Her head was covered
with blood, and then
blood came from the skies
spattering over the glass
walls of our dome
and washing off
as clean as rain.

Then he put the child
down on the floor
and she herself
climbed up the bed
and sat on
top of me, already
prattling, telling me
the
funniest stories I've
ever heard,
if only I
could
remember them.

Actually
I have a mother and
father like everyone else.
They are concerned about me
send me money, plane
tickets and letters
and recipes for custard.
And once a year
I visit them
and usually bring a friend
whom they
dote over and at the same time
check out for lice.

My mother is a teacher,
a liberal democrat
and a sensible person
who always had her lesson plans,
her modern furniture
and her efficient grocery lists.
My father
is an
anaesthesiologist.
They spent
a year apart the year
my younger sister
graduated college

as if
the event were
scheduled and proper.
They announced
their separation to me
in funereal tones
almost offering in the
same breath to
send me to a therapist.
But I was delighted
and invited my
mother to join me
in my Women's Collective
which I lived in that
year,
before our group
suffered a polemical split
between the
Feminists and the
Socialists and the
bisexuals, straights and
gays and
that house
like my parents
separated.
Of course they were
back together
in a year.
And now they're like they always were:
the Bobbsey Twins of
domestic
peace.

GRACE: I stand here
and try to
remember myself as a
girl. Who was I
before I met William?
Before Andy
and
then Jessica and then

Kathy and then
Dan was born.
I was not very old.
I finished
a year and a half
of college,
a year and a half
reading
Shakespeare and learning
the names of English kings.
The war was
over on my eighteenth birthday.
For two years I had
danced with soldiers
and wrapped bandages
with my mother.
I dreamed of a wedding
like Katharine Hepburn in
the *Philadelphia Story*
which of course
like her
I would walk out of
for the attentions of
a man like Cary Grant.
But I was not
born into
the Philadelphia
élite, though
we were
respectable enough
our fortune
was not impressive,
and I was not
anywhere so
wild as
that heroine,
except in my
daydreams.
I kept poems in
a black and grey
diary in my desk–

as far as I know they
were dreadful but
all I
worked for was to be
an English teacher,
though earlier
in the war
I had wanted to be a lawyer.
I loved
Rosalind Russell in
shoulder pads rushing
about cities, her eyes
wide open, her tongue
jabbing,
arguing law cases, reporting
murder stories, and
even
being a mayor. Though
in that movie she
retired into marriage and that's
what I did
though I had
a lover first
and thought myself
old and jaded.
He had been
my Classics
professor;
he was,
of course,
married. We
dined in plush
restaurants
red walls around us
chandeliers above us.
We drove to the country
where we lay in fields
and he read me
poetry by Pindar
and mediaeval
lyrics,

Timor mortis
Conturbat me.
He taught me
to drink wine;
we ate a fish course
and a meat course.
He laughed at
everything I said
until I thought myself
a great wit.
He had a deep voice
greying hair
and dressed like the dethroned duke
of England.
Next to him
all the
younger men
with hair greased down
so that their ears stuck out
and worried looks
and voices on the edge of loudness
spattering out
their life plans
as if they were
declarations of state
seemed
idiots.
But then
I found myself one day
exactly
no where.
I had thought I was
pregnant and my professor
in one day
found a proper Doctor in New York
bought a plane ticket,
gave me $500 in cash
and said, 'Goodbye',
he could hurt me no longer.
In New York
I found I

wasn't
pregnant.
So I stayed.
I went to the Empire
State Building, the
Statue of Liberty, the
Metropolitan, Whitney
and Modern Museums.
I never went back to
the University,
and feared even
Philadelphia might be
too small.
When I wrote
my parents said
I must come home
or
go to work.
I was proud.
It's funny how often
women of my age
look back and say those
words, I
was
proud.

Thanksgiving

Thanksgiving *is a new play, completed in 1982. It tells the story of a childhood. In it, characters move freely from past to present, recalling the past, and playing themselves both as children and as adults.*

Three women are seated at a table. They are Martha, her sister Sarah and her mother Alice. The table is laid as if for a Thanksgiving meal, with a turkey, cranberry sauce, bread. Part of the table is in darkness. Obscured from the audience, four other people sit at the table. These are Martha and Sarah's father, Ralph; Alice's mother and father, Katherine and Franklin; and Katherine's sister, Aunt Agnes.

MARTHA: When I sit down
the child in me
shouts, 'Where's everybody else?'
We used to have a larger family.
This is my mother 'Alice',
my sister 'Sarah'.
We're the survivors.
Daddy, Grandma and Grandpa, my
mother's parents, Aunt Agnes,
my Grandmother's sister, Brewster,
my mother's second husband, they're
all dead.
But here. We remember them.
If I tell you the story of my
childhood, I must tell you
about all of us, the dead and
the living. And I want to
tell this story. That's what this
play is about: Thanksgiving.

Let's hold hands,
Ma Ma, Sarah,
touch, give thanks.
These moments make us shy.
My mother is embarrassed
and Sarah
grins like a child.

(They grasp each other's hands.)

ALICE: *(lowering her head)* I hope the turkey
isn't overdone
I wanted this
my two girls
to feed them
to have them
with me.

SARAH: *(her head lowered)*
I take your hands
Martha, Martha
Mother, we lived together
through a long tunnel
of grief, I take
your hands.

(After a moment of silence the lights come up slowly revealing the rest of the table, and the other dinner guests. At the same time Martha moves into darkness where she speaks but cannot be seen.)

MARTHA: I am not born.
I have become
only an idea
a wild hope in
someone else's
imagination.

KATHERINE: She must have another
child.
Angie would you have a biscuit?
Franklin, pass her the biscuits,
Sarah, don't eat that with
your fingers.
Alice, what do you teach

                that child?
                Sarah, sit up straight,
                Ralph, give Alice
                another child, this
                will
                make a bond
                grow between you.

ALICE: *(stroking Sarah's hair)*
                Sarah, don't eat with
                your fingers.
                Don't eat with your
                Sarah
                don't eat . . .
                Why shouldn't she eat with
                her fingers?
                She's *my* child.
                Sarah, keep eating with your
                fingers.

RALPH: Alice.

ALICE: Are you always going to do
                what *she* tells you to?
                Daddy? what do you think?

FRANKLIN: Listen to your mother, Alice.

KATHERINE: It's not as if
                you've been able to figure
                things out
                by yourselves.
                We shouldn't have let
                this happen. This
                marriage should have
                been annulled.
                But now that it's here
                it's time for you to
                grow up, Alice.
                You have a child here to
                think of.

ALICE: And what you think I need
                is another.

FRANKLIN: Last week I went
to bring her home from
Harry's Two O'Clock High
in the middle of the day.

RALPH: Maybe this would work
for us
Alice, maybe.

AUNT AGNES: Katherine
can't you let the
children see
their way themselves?
They have to learn
from life.

KATHERINE: You talk!
What children have you
raised. Cried over.
Years of worry and
work,
sewing, and meals
and schoolwork, and to see it all
come to this, Alice.

(She cries.)

FRANKLIN: Now see, now see,
Alice, what you're
doing to your mother.

(Sarah starts to cry.)

ALICE: *(Shouts)*
All right! All right!
(Silence.)

ALICE: *(quieter)*
All right.
I like babies.
You want a brother or
a sister
don't you?
(Sarah nods)

(sweetly)
All right. We'll
give you one.
would that be
nice? Would you
like that? Good.
(angry, turning first to Ralph, then to others)
Now, are you *all* satisfied?

MARTHA: *(still in darkness)*
This is
how I was conceived,
thought up,
Sarah remembered.
Sarah told me how I began.

SARAH: They said
they were going to
go apart
I heard them
they thought I couldn't
but I knew they were going away
from me, and
all that would
keep them together
would be
another baby, I
couldn't do it,
I couldn't keep them
but this
new baby, this new
baby would.

(Lights up on Martha. The light focuses on Sarah and Martha.)

SARAH: I asked for you to be born.
I wanted someone to talk to.
You'll understand me.
I'll tell you what you need to know.
They have some problems, our
mother, our father, but
we are so happy.
We are *very* happy together.

I asked for you.
Our mother leaves you alone,
but I want to sit here with you
to talk to you,
to protect you.
I heard a bad man was stealing children
but I won't let him
I'm here. I'll keep you
safe. I'll tell you
all I know.
And tell you how I feel.
Now I have someone who will
listen to me.
I worry.
Our mother needs us. She wouldn't
be happy
alone. We're happy
together. *Very* happy.
Our mother goes off sometimes.
When she comes back
she's not like our mother, she
cries and then she yells.
Don't think this is the way
she *really* is.
She goes away and comes back
different.
Before you were born
we were *happy* together.
And we are now.
We are *happy* now.
And I *love* you.
I *love* you.
You are a baby.
You are a baby.
I'm not a baby.
I wanted a sister.
So I could see a baby.
Touch a baby.
Have a baby for my own.
I asked for you. You give us sweetness
sweet baby

                        you make us happy
                        sweet baby.

(Lights up on all.)

KATHERINE: Why you want
                        to go out there
                        I don't know.
                        Daddy could have
                        bought that land
                        and we would
                        have been rich.
                        Did I tell you that?
                        Well, he didn't.
                        Did you Franklin?
                        I suppose. I suppose,
                        we can't do anything
                        about it, if
                        you insist.
                        I tried my best.
                        I certainly did.
                        You do with your lives what you
                        want, after all
                        they're your lives.
                        But I warn you
                        don't come back
                        tails between your legs
                        and ask Daddy and I
                        to pick up the pieces
                        after all I've done for you
                        and the way you've treated me.

ALICE: Our house,
                        our house,
                        mine, out
                        there
                        out there in the valley
                        miles away
                        my kitchen, Sarah,
                        and Martha and me, alone
                        all day and no one
                        watching.
                        Ralph, can you imagine

the garden
will be
mine, I can pick
whatever flower, *grow*
whatever, did you
know Daddy
there is an *orchard*
next to the house
filled with walnut trees
and a block away a big red barn
and the nicest people
live next door.
Ralph
said they'd help him
build our own patio
and it has a
den.
I've *always*
wanted a den.

RALPH: There is this empty space
what should I say
this all will be fine
I'll sit up straight.
I have strong arms.
I can build the patio easily.
I hauled ice for my father up steep stairs.
I can lift anything.
Build anything.
I can put out fires, climb high ladders,
at the station, they call me
a good Joe, they can see
I'm a good Joe, I can handle
Alice, Alice, Alice,
do you hear
do you want . . .
There is this empty space,
they want me to walk into, to be in
to occupy, they want me to say
something, what should I

SARAH: Daddy, can I bring my bike?

RALPH: There will be
                lots of place to ride
                egg.

MARTHA: Will I have to leave my school?
                Will I have to leave my school?
                My Grandma. My Grandma?

KATHERINE: My precious. Yes.
                My little girl.
                They're taking you, along.
                No more little steps on the stairs
                when the noon bell goes off at
                                    the factory.

SARAH: I'll take you for rides
                Martha, on my bike.
                You'll see.
                You'll like it.

KATHERINE: If you go on
                letting that child
                lift her sister up that way
                she'll hurt her back.

MARTHA: Sarah puts cards on her
                bicycle, clips them
                with a clothes pin
                to the spokes.
                I ride on the back.
                Then it makes a sound
                Ta da, Ta da, Ta da.
                This is Sarah.
                She's *my* sister.

KATHERINE: They say it's not good to put those cards
                on the spokes of the wheel.
                I worry.

MARTHA: Daddy where is Sarah?

RALPH: She's gone to the orchard.
                She and her friend are
                building a fire, they're
                going to cook potatoes.

MARTHA: I want to go.
            I'm going.

RALPH: Listen, Martha
            you've got to let Sarah
            have some time to
            herself.

MARTHA: No! I want to go too.

RALPH: She likes to be with her friends.
            You're younger.
            When you're older.

MARTHA: I hate you.
            My sister loves me.
            She *wants* me to be with her.
            She *does*.
            She *loves* me.
            She wants me to cook potatoes with her.
            I hate you.
            You're lying to me.
            She loves me.
            She's magic, my sister.
            She does wonderful things.
            Makes fires.
            Fried potatoes are my favourites.
            My favourites.

MARTHA: *(to audience)*
            She went looking later
            in the orchard
            for her sister
            and did not find her
            though she thought she'd
            been everywhere
            deep into the woods
            she was desolate.

SARAH: Come see, Martha, come see!

MARTHA: What! What! The kitten! The kitten!
            The kittens have been born.*(to audience)*
            She held up a kitten to show me

lifted it from the depths of our toy box.

SARAH: Look Martha
                  our toys are all bloody.

(Martha and Sarah look as if into a toy box.)

MARTHA: Oh look.
                  Sarah started to cut
                  the hair of the monkey
                  Grandpa gave us and then
                  she let me cut some too.
                  He looked nice with his crew cut
                  didn't he Sarah?

SARAH: Here Martha
                  use this.
                  It will make you
                  like plastic man.

MARTHA: It will make me
                  like plastic man!
                  I will have arms that can reach
                  across a room, or a whole country even
                  and legs that can run *anywhere*
                  they'll get so long, as long as I
                  want!

SARAH: *(to audience)*
                  I made it from
                  mercurochrome and catsup
                  ponds creme and mayonnaise
                  and toothpaste.
                  I didn't know she'd cry
                  when it didn't work.
                  We were just *playing*.

MARTHA: Damn you.
                  Damn you.
                  Let me in the door.
                  In the door.
                  My compass,
                  the one I sent away for.
                  I've *lost* it.

It's *lost*.
Open the door.
Open this door.
Open the door.

MARTHA: *(to audience)*
Momma came out and gave me a
slap and said I had to stay outside
and I cried until my eyes were red
and I was afraid the girl across the street would know.

MARTHA: Where's Mommy, Sarah
where's Mommy?

SARAH: She's just gone shopping.
She's probably at a friend's.

MARTHA: But it's too long.
It's too long.
It's *already dark* Sarah.

SARAH: She's just shopping or
at a friend's.

MARTHA: Sarah, where's Mommy.
where's Momma, Sarah.
I'm *hungry*. It's almost *bed* time,
Sarah.

SARAH: *(she mimes a telephone, picking up the receiver, and
surreptitiously putting her finger on the button)*
Hello. Hello can I speak to Mrs Lyon.
Hello. Mother this is Sarah. Oh.
We were just wondering where you were.

MARTHA: Let me talk to her!
Let me talk.

SARAH: No!
(she pulls the telephone away)

MARTHA: Why!? Why!?

SARAH: Yes, mother. We'll be good. Goodbye.

MARTHA: Why couldn't *I* talk to her?

SARAH: *(to audience)*
            I was the only one who knew.
            I caught them
            and it was our secret.
            Momma's and mine and
            I didn't tell Daddy.
            And I felt terrible not to
            tell him and I
            hated him.

ALICE: Your father was a good man
            but I
            I just
            it wasn't anything small
            I couldn't stand, I just
            couldn't stand to go to bed
            with him
            I wished
            it had been different, he was
            a good man.

MARTHA: *(cries)*
            Momma was crazy eyed and yelling
            and Daddy slapped her.
            I won't never go back there
            Never.
            And it gets dark.
            And I can't stay in the orchard.
            Sarah!

ALICE: You had better tell them
            Ralph.

RALPH: Tell them what?

ALICE: You and Katherine took it out of my
            control. You think I have no
            say anymore with my own girls.

KATHERINE: *(from the semi-darkness)*
            You must leave the care of the girls to me.
            Promise me that Ralph
            or else I can't help you.

SARAH: *(to audience)*
In the divorce
Grandma had to say
it was Daddy
that Daddy was the one
who went away to
someone else's house at night.
The courts wouldn't hear
if it was the mother.

KATHERINE: *(from the semi-darkness)*
She cannot take care of those children
           properly
that much is clear.

AUNT AGNES: *(from the semi-darkness)*
But the two girls will be
too much for you, Katherine,
give Sarah to me.

KATHERINE: *(from the semi-darkness)*
Yes, Ralph, I can only take Martha.

RALPH: Well, my Grandmother can take
Sarah.

SARAH: Yes, Daddy?

KATHERINE: *(from the semi-darkness)*
But Nanna won't live long
Ralph, *mind*, think of
that before you act.

SARAH: Daddy?

RALPH: I know they won't like it
but we have no choice.

ALICE: No choice! Why? Because it's
what my mother wants?

RALPH: Alice! Cut it out!

ALICE: The girls have to be told, Ralph,
are you thinking of not even
telling them?

RALPH: Alice, stop this.
            You're upsetting them.

ALICE: Upsetting them, why
            don't you think they'll be upset?

SARAH: Telling us what? What!

            (Martha starts to cry.)

SARAH: Tell me. Tell me, Momma!

ALICE: Sarah, you're going to go live with Nana.

RALPH: Alice!

ALICE: You make *me* tell them, Ralph,
            You make me tell them, I'll never
            forgive you this.

SARAH: Not with Grandma? Doesn't Grandma
            want us there?

RALPH: It's not that. She wants you both
            but she can't take care of you
            both. And Nana isn't
            that far away. We can visit often.

MARTHA: Visit? We'll visit Momma?

SARAH: We'll visit Momma, won't we?

RALPH: Visit each other, Sarah, Martha.

MARTHA: *(to audience, alone in light)*
            Just me with Grandma and Grandpa
            Just me
            What!
            Tell me! Tell me!
            And Daddy someplace else.
            And Momma someplace else.
            What? Tell me.
            And Sa Sa? Sarah?
            Sarah! Sarah!
            (partly as the adult, partly as the child)
            How can this be? she said. *How can
            this be*? It was like an explosion, a

bomb, one body, spreading all over,
arms on a tree, legs on that
hill over there.
(pause; listens)
You hear?
A child crying. Always crying.
God I wish
She would stop. She
lived through it all, after all,
No one died –
they saw each other at Summer camp
Christmas and Thanksgiving.

Matter: How We Know

This is the closing passage from *Woman and Nature.*

Because we know ourselves to be made from this earth. See this grass. The patches of silver and brown. Worn by the wind. The grass reflecting all that lives in the soil. The light. The grass needing the soil. With roots deep in the earth. And patches of silver. Like the patches of silver in our hair. Worn by time. This bird flying low over the grass. Over the tules. The cattails, sedges, rushes, reeds, over the marsh. Because we know ourselves to be made from this earth. Temporary as this grass. Wet as this mud. Our cells filled with water. Like the mud of this swamp. Heather growing here because of the damp. Sphagnum moss floating on the surface, on the water standing in these pools. Places where the river washes out. Where the earth was shaped by the flow of lava. Or by the slow movements of glaciers. Because we know ourselves to be made from this earth, and shaped like the earth, by what has gone before. The lives of our mothers. What she told me was her life. And what I saw in her hands. The calcium in the joints, the aching as she hemmed my dress. These clothes she made for me. *The pools overgrown by grass, reed, sedge, the marsh over time, becoming dry, over centuries, plankton disappearing, crustaceans gone, clams, worms, sponges, what we see now floating in these pools, fish, birds flying close to the waters. This bird with the scarlet shoulders. This bird with the yellow throat. And the beautiful song. The song like flutes. Like violoncellos in an orchestra. The orchestra in our mind. The symphony which we imagine. The music which was our idea. What we wanted to be. The lives of our grandmothers. What we imagined them to be.* She told me what she had wanted to be. What she had wanted to do. That she wanted to act on the stage. To write. She showed me the stories she wrote before she was married. Before I was born. *Why we*

*were born when we were, as we were, we imagined. We imagined what
she imagined then, what lay under the surface, this still water, the water
not running over rocks, lacking air, the bacteria, fungi, dwelling at the
bottom, without light, no green bodies, freeing no air, the scent of
marsh gas, this bog we might lose ourselves in, sink in, the treachery
here, our voices calling for help and no one listening, the silence, we
made from this earth, returning to earth, the mud covering us, we
giving ourselves up to this place, the fungi, bacteria, fish, everything
struggling for air in this place, beetles capturing air bubbles on the
surface of the pond, mosquitoes reaching with tubes to the surface of
the water, fish with gills on the outsides of their bodies, fish gulping air
at the surface, air captured in small hairs on the bodies of insects, stored
in spaces in the stems of plants, in pockets in the tissue of leaves,
everything in this place struggling for light, stems and leaves with thin
skins, leaves divided into greater surfaces, numerous pores, tall plants
in shallow water, open to the light; a jungle of growth in the shallow
water at the edge, interwoven stems, matted leaves, places for wrens to
hide, for rails, bitterns, for red-winged blackbirds to protect their nests.
Fish hiding in plants underwater, insects' and snails' eggs, pupa cases,
larvae and nymphs and crayfish. Sunlight pouring into plants, ingested
into the bodies of fish, into the red-winged blackbird, into the bacteria,
into the fungi, into the earth itself, because we know ourselves to be
made of this earth, because we know sunlight moves through us, water
moves through us, everything moves, everything changes, and the
daughters are returned to their mothers. She always comes back. Back
from the darkness. And the earth grows green again. So we were
moved to feel these things. The body of the animal buried in the ground
rotting feeds the seed. The sheaf of grain held up to us silently.* Her
dreams, I know, she said, live on in my body as I write these words.
*This proof. This testimony. This shape of possibility. What we
dreamed to be. What we laboured for. What we had burned desiring.
What always returns. What she is to me. What she is to me, we said, and
do not turn your head away, we told them, those who had tried to name
us, those who had tried to keep us apart, do not turn your head away
when we tell you this, we said,* how she was smaller than I then, *we try
to tell you,* what tenderness I then felt for her, *we said,* as if she were
my daughter, as if some part of myself I had thought lost forever were
returned to me, *we said,* and then held her fiercely, *and we then made
you listen, you turning your head away, you who tried to make us be
still, you dividing yourself from this night we were turning through, but
we made you listen, we said, do not pretend you do not hear what we*

say to each other, we say, when she was returned to me and I to her that I became small to her, that my face became soft against her flesh, that through that night she held me, as if part of herself had returned, like mother to daughter *because we know we are made of this earth, and we know these meanings reach you, we said, the least comment of the stare, we said, the barely perceptible moment of despair,* I told her, *the eloquence of arms, those threaded daily causes, the fundaments of sound, cradling the infant's head, these cries,* the crying I heard in her body, *the years we had known together,* I know these meanings reach you, *we said, and the stars and their light we hold in our hands, this light telling the birds where they are, the same light which guides these birds to this place, and the light through which we imagine ourselves in the bodies of these birds, flying with them, low over the grass, weaving our nests like hammocks from blade to blade, from reed to reed. We standing at the edge of the marsh. Not daring to move closer. Keeping our distance. Watching these birds through the glass. Careful not to frighten them off. As they arrive. First the males, jet black, with a flash of red at their shoulders, a startling red which darts out of their blackness as they spread their wings. First the males and then the females flying together in the winter, now joining the males. The females with yellow throats, their wings brown and black, and light around their eyes. Now all of them calling. Calling or singing. Liquid and pleasant. Like the violoncello. We imagine like the violoncello, the cello we have in our minds, the violin we have imagined, as we have imagined the prison, as we have made up boundaries, or decided what the fate of these birds should be, as we have invented poison, as we have invented the cage, now we stand at the edge of this marsh and do not go closer, allow them their distance, penetrate them only with our minds, only with our hearts, because though we can advance upon the blackbird, though we may cage her, though we may torture her with our will, with the boundaries we imagine, this bird will never be ours, he may die, this minute heart stop beating, the body go cold and hard, we may tear the wings apart and cut open the body and remove what we want to see, but still this blackbird will not be ours and we will have nothing. And even if we keep her alive. Train her to stay indoors. Clip her wings. Train her to sit on our fingers, though we feed her, and give her water, still this is not the blackbird we have captured, for the blackbird, which flies now over our heads, whose song reminds us of a flute, who migrates with the stars, who lives among reeds and rushes, threading a nest like a hammock, who lives in flocks, chattering in the grasses, this creature is free of our hands, we cannot control her, and for the creature we have tamed, the creature we keep in our house, we must make a new word. For we did not invent the blackbird, we say, we only invented her name. And we never invented ourselves, we admit.* And my grandmother's body is now part of the soil, she said. *Only now, we name ourselves. Only now, as we think of ourselves as passing, do we utter the syllables. Do we list all that we are. That we know in ourselves. We know ourselves to be made from this earth. We know this earth is made from our bodies. For we see ourselves. And we are nature. We are nature seeing nature. We are nature with a concept of nature. Nature weeping. Nature speaking of nature to nature. The red-winged blackbird flies in us, in our inner sight. We see the arc of her flight. We measure the ellipse. We predict its climax. We are amazed. We are moved. We fly. We watch her wings negotiate the wind, the substance of the air, its elements and the elements of those elements, and count those elements found in other beings, the sea urchin's sting, ink, this paper, our bones, the flesh of our tongues with which we make the sound 'blackbird', the ears with which we hear, the eye which travels the arc of her flight. And yet the blackbird does not fly in us but is somewhere else free of our minds, and now even free of our sight, flying in the path of her own will,* she wrote, the ink from her pen flowing on this paper, her words, she thought, having nothing to do with this bird, except, she thought, as she breathes in the air this bird flies through, except, she thought, as the grass needs the body of the bird to pass its seeds, as the earth needs the grass, as we are made from this earth, she said, and the sunlight in the grass enters the body of the bird, *enters us,* she wrote on this paper, and the sunlight is pouring into my eyes from your eyes. Your eyes. Your eyes. The sun is in your eyes. I have made you smile. Your lips part. The sunlight in your mouth. Have I made the sun come into your mouth? I put my mouth on yours. To cover that light. To breathe it in. My tongue inside your mouth, your lips on my tongue, my body filled with light, filled with light, with light, shuddering, you make me shudder, you make the movement of the earth come into me, you fill me, you fill me with sound, is that my voice crying out? The sunlight in you is making my breath sing, sing your name, your name to you, beautiful one. I could kiss your bones, put my teeth in you, white gleam, whiteness, I chew, beautiful one, I am in you, I am filled with light inside you, I have no boundary, the light has extinguished my skin, I am perished in light, light filling you, shining through you, carrying you out, through the roofs of our mouths, the sky, the clouds, bursting, raining, raining free, falling piece by piece, dispersed over this earth, into the soil, deep, deeper into you, into the least hair on the deepest root in this earth, into the green heart flowing, into the green leaves and they grow, they grow into a profusion, moss, fern, and they bloom, cosmos, and they bloom, cyclamen, in your ears, in your ears, calling their names, this sound from my throat echoing, my breath in your ears, your eyes, your eyes continuing to see, continuing, your eyes telling, telling the light, the light. And she wrote, when I let this bird fly to her own purpose, when this bird flies in the path of his own will, the light from this bird enters my body, and when I see the beautiful arc of her flight, I love this bird, when I see, the arc of her flight, I fly with her, enter her with my mind, leave myself, die for an instant, live in the body of this bird whom I cannot live without, as part of the body of the bird will enter my daughter's body, because I know I am made from this earth, as my mother's hands were made from this earth, as her dreams came from this earth and all that I know, I know in this earth, the body of the bird, this pen, this paper, these hands, this tongue speaking, all that I know speaks to me through this earth and I long to tell you, you who are earth too, and listen *as we speak to each other of what we know: the light is in us.*